VIOLENT INTIMACY

Tiantian Zheng is SUNY Distinguished Professor at State University of New York, Cortland, with a PhD in Anthropology from Yale University. She is the author and co-author of ten academic books, five edited journal issues, and over a hundred articles. She has received two national book awards and one "Outstanding Academic Title" by *Choice* (the 2010 Sara A. Whaley Book Prize and 2011 Research Publication Book Award). She has testified before Congress, UNAIDS, and the United Nations and has been a featured guest speaker on NPR, BBC, and NBC. She has delivered over a hundred invited talks at key universities worldwide.

VIOLENT INTIMACY

Family Harmony, State Stability, and Intimate Partner Violence in Post-Socialist China

Tiantian Zheng

BLOOMSBURY ACADEMIC
LONDON • NEW YORK • OXFORD • NEW DELHI • SYDNEY

BLOOMSBURY ACADEMIC
Bloomsbury Publishing Plc
50 Bedford Square, London, WC1B 3DP, UK
1385 Broadway, New York, NY 10018, USA
29 Earlsfort Terrace, Dublin 2, Ireland

BLOOMSBURY, BLOOMSBURY ACADEMIC and the Diana logo are trademarks of
Bloomsbury Publishing Plc

First published in Great Britain 2022

Copyright © Tiantian Zheng 2022

Tiantian Zheng has asserted her right under the Copyright, Designs and Patents Act, 1988, to be identified as Author of this work.

For legal purposes the Acknowledgments on pp. ix–x constitute an extension of this copyright page.

Part of Chapter 5 appeared previously in a journal: Tiantian Zheng, 2015, "Intimate Partner Violence, Women, and Resistance in Postsocialist China," *Wagadu, a Journal of Transnational Women's and Gender Studies* 13: 155–82.

Cover design by Adriana Brioso
Cover images © Tunaru Dorin and PM Images/Getty Images

All rights reserved. No part of this publication may be reproduced or transmitted in any form or by any means, electronic or mechanical, including photocopying, recording, or any information storage or retrieval system, without prior permission in writing from the publishers.

Bloomsbury Publishing Plc does not have any control over, or responsibility for, any third-party websites referred to or in this book. All internet addresses given in this book were correct at the time of going to press. The author and publisher regret any inconvenience caused if addresses have changed or sites have ceased to exist, but can accept no responsibility for any such changes.

A catalogue record for this book is available from the British Library.

Library of Congress Cataloging-in-Publication Data
Names: Zheng, Tiantian, author.
Title: Violent intimacy : family harmony, state stability, and intimate partner violence in post-socialist China / Tiantian Zheng. Description: London ; New York : Bloomsbury Academic, 2022. | Includes bibliographical references and index.
Identifiers: LCCN 2021052027 (print) | LCCN 2021052028 (ebook) |
ISBN 9781350263437 (hardback) | ISBN 9781350263420 (paperback) |
ISBN 9781350263444 (epub) | ISBN 9781350263451 (adobe pdf) | ISBN 9781350263468
Subjects: LCSH: Intimate partner violence–China. | Sex role–China. |
Women–China–Social conditions.
Classification: LCC HV6626.23.C6 Z434 2022 (print) | LCC HV6626.23.C6 (ebook) | DDC 362.82/920951–dc23/eng/20220304
LC record available at https://lccn.loc.gov/2021052027
LC ebook record available at https://lccn.loc.gov/2021052028

ISBN: HB: 978-1-3502-6343-7
PB: 978-1-3502-6342-0
ePDF: 978-1-3502-6345-1
eBook: 978-1-3502-6344-4

Typeset by Newgen KnowledgeWorks Pvt. Ltd., Chennai, India

To find out more about our authors and books visit www.bloomsbury.com and sign up for our newsletters.

I dedicate this book to all the women and activists who are fighting against intimate partner violence

CONTENTS

Acknowledgments	ix
INTRODUCTION	1
Chapter 1 A SOCIAL AND CULTURAL HISTORY OF INTIMATE PARTNER VIOLENCE IN CHINA	25
Chapter 2 WORTHY VERSUS UNWORTHY VICTIMS OF SEXUAL VIOLENCE IN POST-SOCIALIST CHINA	41
Chapter 3 THE CRIMINAL JUSTICE SYSTEM AND INTIMATE PARTNER VIOLENCE	51
Chapter 4 MALE PERCEPTIONS AND RATIONALIZATIONS OF INTIMATE PARTNER VIOLENCE IN POST-SOCIALIST CHINA	91
Chapter 5 EVERYDAY RESISTANCE OF WOMEN AGAINST INTIMATE PARTNER VIOLENCE	99
Chapter 6 ACTIVISM AND INTIMATE PARTNER VIOLENCE	121
Afterword	161
Notes	171
References	175
Index	203

ACKNOWLEDGMENTS

I would like to extend my sincere thanks to all the women, activists, judges, police, and government officials who have shared with me their experiences, thoughts, and feelings. Without their support and contribution, fieldwork for this book would have been impossible.

During the course of my research and writing over the years, I have accumulated a great deal of debt toward my professors, colleagues, and friends. I would like to thank my advisors at Yale, William W. Kelly, Deborah Davis, Helen Siu, and Harold W. Scheffler, for their generous mentorship and supportive encouragement of my professional development during my study at Yale and after I graduated, without which I would not be where I am today. Professor William Kelly has been consistently offering me generous professional help, including providing invaluable advice on a potential press for this book. I was blessed to benefit from these four eminent advisors who have always shown an immense amount of faith in me, and have offered their helpful professional advice. It is their generous mentorship, continuous inspiration, and precious advice that have shaped me into who I am today as an anthropologist and a scholar. I thank them for having taught me, supported me, and encouraged me more than they could realize, for which I am forever grateful.

I thank my professor, mentor, and friend Jack Wortman for being my constant intellectual and emotional support during the past years. Jack Wortman has consistently mentored me in every aspect of my life—emotional, professional, and academic. Whenever I need someone to talk to, he is always there. He not only listens to me patiently, but also provides me with words of wisdom on problems and issues in my life. Over the years I have relied on his advice to resolve professional and emotional issues. His wealth of knowledge and insights has helped me understand myself, my cultural roots, and my internal conflicts. I thank him for guiding me through life. Beside this, I thank him for being a tireless and generous advisor who not only has assisted me in correcting the language of this book but has also inspired and stimulated me intellectually. My debts to him and to all the above-mentioned professors can never be repaid.

My thanks also go to Niko Besnier, Marc Blecher, Susan Brownell, Susan Dewey, Susan Greenhalgh, William Jankowiak, Jing Jun, Ralph Litzinger, Wanning Sun, Vanessa Fong, and Mayfair Yang for their continuous inspirations, unwavering support, and encouraging, incisive, and constructive comments that have played a vital role in improving the quality of my work, including this book. I thank Marc Blecher, William Jankowiak, Susan Dewey, Gareth Fisher, Robin McNeal, and Yunxiang Yan for inviting me to their campuses to deliver book talks. I also thank Marc Blecher for keeping me updated with interesting and stimulating issues in China as well as for offering me kind and generous support and invaluable advice on a potential press for this book.

My special thanks also go to Lisa Goodrum and Brigitte Shull. Lisa Goodrum contacted me to commission a book for Zed books. Though she left Zed books later, she has kept in touch with me and provided generous support and helpful advice. Brigitte Shull, who was the editor of my previous book, *Ethnographies of Prostitution*, has also offered precious support and generous advice.

I also thank President Erik Bitterbaum, Provost Mark Prus, Dean Bruce Mattingly, as well as my dear and respected colleagues Herbert Haines, Robert Spitzer, Sharon Steadman, for their unwavering support and encouragements over the years. I express my gratitude to Dave Grass, who has not only supported me emotionally but has also filled my life with happiness and joy. His curiosity toward life and his role as a stimulating intellectual interlocutor has helped me better understand the culture in the United States.

I would like to extend my special gratitude to my editor, Olivia Dellow at Bloomsbury Publishing Plc, for her enthusiasm about my project, for her kind and generous support, for her ingenious suggestion of the book title, and for all the time and effort she has kindly and generously invested in guiding me through the book preparation, reviews of the manuscript, book contract, book cover, and production process.

INTRODUCTION

I met Xiao Mei when she was several months pregnant, hiding from her husband at a friend's place. She had been married to her former college classmate for six years. Her husband was pursuing a doctoral degree in science at a key national university. After Xiao Mei became pregnant, she quit her job at a foreign venture company.

Xiao Mei told me that, prior to their marriage, her husband inflicted violence on her several times. After each episode, he knelt down in front of her, crying and apologizing to her. She forgave him each time. One time, he pushed her onto the concrete floor, fracturing her left arm. She went to the hospital and got it treated. The doctor put a cast on her arm. At first, she wore a heavy coat to hide the cast because she was afraid people would mock her. Later she took the cast off long before it was due. Worried that her colleagues would ask her about it, she lied to the company that she had fallen on her own and broken her arm. She told me that it took quite a few months before she had any feeling in her arm. Her arm was so weak that she could not even hold her purse.

Xiao Mei said her husband was a male chauvinist (da nan zi zhuyi). She said:

> He has to dominate everything. I have to submit to him on all accounts. If I don't, he'll act upon his bad temper and make me submit. So I've been enduring and tolerating everything, holding everything within myself.

Since she was pregnant, Xiao Mei quit her job and has been relying on him completely. He has been verbally abusing her, demeaning her, cursing her, calling her a "useless thing" (meiyong de dongxi) who "amounts to nothing" (sha dou bu shi) and "cannot do anything right." He told her that, because she only holds a BA degree, she is inferior to him, since he holds a more advanced doctoral degree. He said to her:

> You're completely dependent on me. You can't make any money and you don't have a job. You're good for nothing. You must listen to me in everything. You must submit to me at all times.

One night, she handed him a letter addressed to him from the mailbox. Insisting that there should be two letters, he got really upset that she had lost one. She responded: "Why're you so upset? We can look for it together." Her words only enraged him even further. He started cursing her, saying that she was useless, did not know anything, and could not do anything right except ruin things.

She later found the other letter lying on the floor. She said to him, "Now that we've found it, there's no need to worry about it." He was still angry, yelling at her. She shut herself in a room.

After a while, he knocked at her door. Thinking that he must have calmed down by now, she opened the door. He came in, grabbed her hair, lifted her out of the chair she was sitting in, and pushed her onto the wall. Every time she tried to get up, he pushed her onto the wall and then onto the floor, again and again, incessantly.

Xiao Mei said that everything happened so fast and so suddenly that all she could remember was being pushed onto the floor and the wall over and over, every time when she tried to get up. After this violent episode, she found her left eye bleeding, her arm fractured, and her finger broken.

It was midnight. Xiao Mei cried. She said:

> I wanted to die right then and there. Life was meaningless to me. I've never felt happiness in this marriage.

Xiao Mei called the emergency number for the police. When the police came, her husband told the police that she had been violent toward him and that she threatened his life. He showed the police a red mark on his shoulder. Hearing that, Xiao Mei almost fainted. She could not believe how that was even possible. She told the police that she did fight back, because he was the one who started the fight and gave her a bleeding eye, a fractured arm, and a broken finger. Her husband insisted to the police that he had done nothing. The police said, "You know, a harmonious family leads to a prosperous society (jiahe wanshi xing). Both of you got physical and fought. It's difficult for us police to deal with this kind of spousal matter. All we can do is mediate. You two should apologize to each other. Next time when this happens again, don't fight back; just call the police."

Xiao Mei said to me, "It was useless to call the police. I felt hopeless."

After the police left, Xiao Mei went to the hospital to get her injuries treated. After she was discharged from the hospital, she hid in a friend's place for about ten days.

During this time her husband texted her that he did not care if she requested a divorce. She showed me his text that read as follows:

> Because I have an advanced degree, a better job, and a better financial situation, I'm going to win the child custody rights with no problem at all in court. You'll end up with nothing. So I'm going to just sit here and see what you'll do.

She told me:

> He's right. If we do get a divorce in court, the judge is going to give him the child custody right because his job and financial situation is better. I'll lose the child.

> Even in a miracle case where I did get child custody, no one will financially support me and the child, as I've lost my job. In China, no men want a woman with a child, so it's impossible for me to find another man after divorce ... If I sue him in court for intimate partner violence, his entire family will take revenge against mine—who knows what kind of violence they will inflict on my family?

Xiao Mei's words suggest the continuing historical influence in China of what was once a clan system where the clan, or the family, sought justice rather than relying on an impartial state authority.

During the ten days when she hid in her friend's place, her family and friends told her that, because she was pregnant with a baby, she should go back to her husband. They said that fights were inevitable in a marriage, and that, as a wife, she had to endure and tolerate it all. As she was telling me this, she turned on her phone and showed me the numerous text messages from her female friends.

One female friend wrote: "Don't act like a child. Be an adult and go back home to him. Conflicts are a natural part of marriage." A second female friend wrote: "Give him another chance. For the sake of your child, return home. Live with him with a peaceful mind." A third female friend wrote: "Give in once more. You have given in for so long already. You can give in once more."

Xiao Mei's brother told her that he used to beat his wife. After they had kids, he changed and treated his wife better. He told Xiao Mei that he thinks her husband will change too. Xiao Mei's sister used to advise her to divorce her husband, as Xiao Mei told her about his violent behavior. However, this time when Xiao Mei talked to her, because she was pregnant and would soon have a baby, her sister said she had nothing to say and that it would be best to keep the family together.

Xiao Mei said to me:

> Other than my family and close friends, I didn't talk to anyone else about this, because it's really humiliating. If I tell other people about it, people will think that I am the reason for the violence, and that there is something wrong with me.

Ten days later, Xiao Mei went back home to her husband.

After a month or so, we planned to meet for dinner at a restaurant. Xiao Mei arrived early. Her husband arrived late. With a glowing smile on his face, he looked full of life. During dinner, he talked about the financial pressure of supporting three people— Xiao Mei, the to-be-born baby, and himself, his excessive workload, and his advisor who claimed credit for his work and imposed unreasonable demands on him. Later, I asked about his parents. He said:

> My parents always fight. My dad always wins. My mom always keeps quiet in the end, leaving my dad the winner. In China, the husband is the pillar of the house (ding liang zhu). Women have to listen to men. It's always been like this. My mom used to make more money than my dad, but she still listened to my dad. Now that my dad earns more money, my mom has to listen to him in everything. My mom also does all the housework at home.

Xiao Mei followed this by saying:

> My mom also does all the housework. My dad has never touched the dishes at home. As I grew up, my mom worked all day from morning until night, and then had to cook dinner and do all the dishes afterwards. My dad just lay in bed watching TV.

I did not mention her husband's violence, as Xiao Mei had warned me not to prior to the dinner.

After dinner, Xiao Mei shared her thoughts about her husband:

> He's the kind of person who treats his friends and his parents very well, but not me. When his friends were sick, he was seriously concerned and worried, visiting them all the time. If his friend hit his wife, he would tell his friend that it was his fault and that he should not have done that. He's this kind of strange person who is different from what he appears to be. To outsiders, he always pretends that he treats me very well. He knows how to pretend, very well.

Xiao Mei told me that her husband wrote her a promissory note, but she just put it away without reading it. She said:

> I know that he'll never admit that he hit me. In the past, I talked back to him when he insulted me with denigrating comments, but now I don't care, and I don't say anything anymore. I know that somewhere down the road, he's going to lose his temper again and get angry with me, but I'm going to just swallow and endure everything. I'm not going to argue with him anymore. I'll just keep silent whenever he is upset. I have stopped caring about anything, but I feel that I harbor some kind of hatred inside of me.

Looking down at her arm, she added, "My injured arm and finger are still hurting."

An Ethnography of Intimate Partner Violence in Postsocialist China

This book is the first ethnography of women's lived experiences of, discussions about, and responses to, intimate partner violence in their daily lives in post-socialist China. It has been estimated that 35.7 percent of women in post-socialist China have suffered intimate partner violence, over 95 percent of which have been committed by men against women (Huang 2008; Zhang 2004). Based on my ethnographic research with women, men, government officials, judges, police, and feminist activists from 2014 to 2021, this book explores both women's negotiations with violence and men's rationalizations for their violence. Situating intimate partner violence within its historical, legal, political, and sociocultural context, this book argues that violence against women is enabled, perpetuated, and reinforced by the invisible structural violence—the violence inherent in the legal, political, and historical, sociocultural structure. In compliance with the state discourse of "family harmony," victims of intimate partner violence are often returned to their abusers in order to maintain family harmony, social stability, and state legitimacy, at the expense of women's safety and well-being.

This state discourse on harmony reveals the state's anxiety and concern about social polarization and class conflict in order to reassert the state legitimacy and appease potential social uprisings. The "harmony" discourse prompts various state institutions such as the police and the All China Women's Federation to prioritize mediation as the paramount strategy to resolve domestic violence. The emphasis on women's responsibility to ensure family harmony and maintain political stability encourages women to endure domestic violence and stay with their abusers. Women's agency is often met with the inaction of the police and the court to punish abusers as well as a hostile and intimidating social system that is intent on returning them to the violent environment. Through examining the ways in which women's lives are constrained by various forms of violence, hierarchy, and inequality, this book shows that violence against women is a structural issue that is historically produced and politically, economically, and culturally perpetuated. It is by no means an individual issue that can be simply resolved by remedying individual behaviors.

More specifically, this book addresses the following questions: How has intimate partner violence been perceived, treated, and resolved at different stages of history in China? What is the state discourse on family harmony and why do the police evoke this discourse to mediate between victims and abusers? Why is mediation the pervasive mechanism to handle intimate partner violence? What does the Anti-Domestic Violence Law entail, and how does the criminal justice system deal with intimate partner violence and violence-related divorce cases? What are men's perceptions and attitudes toward intimate partner violence? How do men rationalize intimate partner violence? What are the reasons for sexual violence, and how is sexual violence depicted by medical, legal, and popular discourses? How do women from various social strata resist intimate partner violence in their daily lives, and how is their agency constrained by the legal, political, and sociocultural structure? What kind of interventions have activists in NGOs engaged in to fight against intimate partner violence, and what kind of limitations are entailed?

Intimate Partner Violence in China's History

Intimate partner violence is defined as behaviors toward an intimate partner that results in physical, sexual, or psychological harm or suffering. Such behaviors include but are not limited to physical abuse, psychological torment, forced sexual intercourse, and other forms of controlling behaviors. Although intimate partner violence has existed throughout human history, it has only recently become one of the most paramount issues faced by all societies and regions probably because of the worldwide women's movement (see Parish et al. 2004; Tellez 2008; Lodhia 2010; Alcalde 2006; Yount and Li 2009; Koepping 2003). Global studies by the World Health Organization indicate that one-third of women worldwide have experienced intimate partner abuse and that perpetrators are almost exclusively men (WHO

2017). Despite its prevalence, intimate partner violence continues to be hidden and underreported. It was not addressed until the 1980s when the issue of violence against women was put forth as a human rights violation (Merry 2006a: 21, 2006b). Indeed, intimate partner violence happens in all countries and in all societies. This book focuses on physical and sexual violence between intimate partners in China.

In China, for thousands of years, the society was dominated by the Confucian ideology. The family, according to this ideology, is the cornerstone of society, the stability of which is pivotal in maintaining the stability of the country as a whole. The stability and harmony of the family, according to the Confucian ideology, is contingent upon a hierarchical relationship between the husband and the wife. The husband is regarded as the ultimate authority in family issues, including financial decisions. The wife is assigned the role of daughter, wife, and mother who are obedient to the father before marriage, to the husband after marriage, and to the son after widowhood. Such patriarchal ideology is so deeply entrenched in Chinese society that intimate partner violence was often times, and continues to be, concealed as a private family issue, and hence ignored (Zhang 2014; Xu et al. 2005).

Two important practices that grew out of the Confucian culture fueled violence against women. They were arranged exogamy and foot-binding. Arranged exogamy was the practice of marrying outside of the small insular unit of one's own community through an arranged marriage, providing the perfect environment for violence against women. For thousands of years when China was an overwhelmingly rural culture, young girls were married off to boys in other villages. The marriage was arranged by women who specialized in matchmaking, and the boys and girls being married had no voice. Typically, the girl was carried in a covered sedan chair to the wedding that was held in her fiancée's village, and she would probably never see her family again. After the wedding, she was under the authority of a man she had never met before and her mother-in-law. One can imagine the trauma of going from the insularity of her own family to the confines of a family she had never met. These mothers-in-laws had a reputation of brutality, always getting the most work possible from their new labor. Here she was a stranger with no one to advocate for her. At the mercy of the kindness of strangers, this marriage practice laid a fertile ground for violence against them.[1]

The practice of foot-binding, dating back to the ninth century, was itself violence against women. The tradition of foot-binding started among the upper classes, but soon spread across the country. Eventually all Han girls had their feet bound. Typically, this began when a girl was anywhere from four to seven years old. Mothers bent the toes under the sole of the feet and tied bandages to keep the feet from growing (Wang 2000). The toes eventually grew into the sole of the foot and the bones broke. This process often took several painful years to complete. It was estimated that 10 percent of the girls died of gangrene and other infections due to foot-binding (Stewart 2014: 423). If the process was a success, the girl would have a "golden lily," a foot four inches in length or less. If less successful, she might have a silver lily, a five-inch foot (Wang 2000). So powerful was this cultural practice that a girl with unbound feet or even a silver lily might not find a husband and therefore would be without resources to survive (Wang 2000).

The severe pain, infections, and possible death as a result of this violent practice against women was imposed upon young girls to enhance the sexual pleasure of men, give men power and control, and thwart women's mobility and possible adultery. The literature suggests a kind of supreme irony, that part of the pleasure derived from this violent practice against women involved pity for the vulnerable and dependent girl who had been rendered pitiful and dependent for the pleasures of the patriarchy (Wang 2000).

What ended this violent practice against women was not primarily communism, but the May Fourth (1919) and New Culture Movements (1915–23) during early twentieth century. Gender inequality and violence against women were addressed as part of a political agenda by the Chinese Communist Party during the 1930s, 1940s, and 1950s. The Chinese Communist Party emphasized gender equality as a means of harnessing women's labor to participate in the rebuilding of China. Unbound feet allowed full exploitation of women's labor. Following the establishment of Communist China, however, the issue of violence against women struggled to contend with traditional values that remained even after the revolution (Hester 2012). While Mao famously said that "women held up half of the sky," the practical problem was the resistance to gender equality within the Chinese family.

Women's Status in Post-Socialist China

Post-socialist China witnessed a decline in women's social status associated with the change in state policies that undermined women's well-being (Wang 2003; Zheng 2009a). Economic transition from a planned economy to a market economy in China has shrunk state sectors and downsized state-owned enterprises. To bring this economic transition into fruition necessitated large-scale layoffs and rising unemployment. State discourse called on women to return home, to be laid off first, and to sacrifice for the success of economic reform (Zheng 2009b). It is important to note that since the Covid-19 pandemic in 2020, 37 percent of professional women have quit their jobs and returned home as caretakers (Zhi 2021). Control of wealth correlates with power. The loss of female income has decreased the bargaining power of women within the family, increasing the risk of intimate partner violence at home.

Xiancai Wang, a national committee member of the Chinese People's Political Consultative Conference, made a national address, encouraging married female workers to give up their work posts and return home to "take care of their husbands in daily life and educate and raise the next generation" (xiangfu jiaozi) and "manage the housework" (caochi jiazheng) (Wang 2001). Wang's call dovetails with most recent political addresses by Chinese President Xi Jinping, who called upon women to play their primary role as "dutiful wives and virtuous mothers" in producing family harmony through "raising and educating the next generation, taking care of their husbands, and supporting the elderly" (Chen, Zhenkai 2020).

This state discourse on harmony reveals the state's anxiety and concern about social polarization and class conflict as a result of the unevenly developed market economy. Utilizing the discourse on harmony is a way to reassert the state legitimacy and appease potential social uprisings. The emphasis on women's responsibility to ensure family harmony and resolve political stability encourages women to endure domestic violence and stay with abusers in order to maintain family harmony and preserve family unity.

President Xi's political addresses underscored the inextricable links between family harmony and state stability and women's responsibility in ensuring family harmony. Court judges and government workers follow and uphold this principle in their daily practices that deem women's sacrifices as a virtue and make women bear the brunt of protecting and safeguarding family harmony at the expense of their well-being and health. Led by this principle, saving marriages to preserve family harmony has become the ultimate goal for government agencies such as the court and the Public Security Bureau. To accomplish this goal, mediation rather than conviction for justice has been the key method in handling cases related to intimate partner violence.

In singling out women's crucial and "distinctive" role simply because of their gender, political leaders' public addresses made women bear the brunt of maintaining family harmony, social harmony, and state stability, failure of which would deem the women irresponsible (see more on this in Chapter 2). In his speech, Xiancai Wang asserted that a division of labor based on gender differences marks social progress (Wang 2001). Women's contribution toward society, he contended, is to raise the next generation and handle housework at home (Wang 2001). Wang commented:

> Taking care of their husbands and raising and educating children is a social responsibility ... We should encourage female workers to give up their work posts, return home, and take care of their family members ... Why don't we ask men to return home? It is fine if men return home too, but, after all, it is not their strong suit ... The more economically developed a country is, the sharper gendered division of labor is. Many women, after giving birth, quit their jobs and return home to take care of the next generation. (Wang 2001)

Following this trend, in 2011, a new bill was proposed by Xiaomei Zhang, another national committee member of the Chinese People's Political Consultative Conference, to encourage some women to return home to be full-time housewives and to help maintain family harmony, social stability, and state stability (Guo 2011; Li 2011). She asserted that, as a result of women competing with men in the job market, women have become "masculine and gender-neutral," "lacking the gender consciousness of being a woman and a mother, and lacking the qualities that a woman should have" (Guo 2011).

She remarked: "Women's return to home is not an historical regression, but a wise decision for women to achieve a more profound emancipation" (Guo 2011). She contended that women's return to home can also "optimize social human resources, raise social productivity, and ease the social issue of unemployment" (Guo 2011). She commented on "leftover women," which often refers to unmarried professional women in their late twenties and thirties with an advanced degree:

Aging (daling), leftover women should adjust their value system. They should realize that women have the responsibility to give birth and continue the national descendants. If a woman chooses to be single, it is harmful for her physical and psychological health ... An important reason they have become leftover women is that they do not know what a woman should do as a woman. They have an erroneous consciousness. (Guo 2011)

It is ironic that these current political leaders of the Communist Party have returned to the Confucian point of view that reduces women to an inferior status as a daughter, a wife, and a mother. Mao Zedong, and the Communist Party during its most revolutionary phase, rejected Confucianism as a return to feudalism and insisted that women held up half of the sky and should be equal to men. While this may have been more rhetoric than reality, Mao Zedong and his revolutionary party members during the Communist era (1949–79) would never have made statements praising Confucian-inculcated women's roles and arguing for an inferior status for women. Further, it might be argued that, by relegating women to the home, half of the intellectual potential of the society has been lost. In spite of the Confucian-inspired bias against women, it is very clear that women are the intellectual equals of men. These women might, in fact, be the people who can cure currently incurable diseases, create new and better technologies, and, in other ways, help invent a better future.

The government's call for female workers to return home has intensified since the open two-child policy in 2015. For instance, the Beijing Civil Affairs Bureau that issues marriage certificates to couples hung up a poster in the office that read as follows:

It is a woman's biggest feat to be a good housewife and a good mother. Why sharpen your heads and spit out your blood to compete with men for resources and terrains? (Yang 2015)

Led by this governing principle, state and popular media advocate that women give up their jobs, take up the role of full-time housewives, and contribute to family harmony and social stability (Zhao 2017; Zhou 2016). Media articles contend that it is the Chinese tradition of thousands of years that women stay at home, taking care of husbands and raising and educating the next generation (xiangfu jiaozi) (see Zhou 2016). It was also reported that a survey conducted by the All China Women's Federation and Statistics Bureau showed that 62 percent of men and 55 percent of women believe that "men belong to the public, and women belong at home" (Zhou 2016). A media report from the *Chinese Youth Newspaper*, a popular national newspaper, cites the dean of the Social Work Department from a key university in Shanghai who said:

Men and women have biological differences. Women, due to their natural mothering nature, are more suitable to take care of children at home. Therefore, women should take up the responsibility of housework and raising children. Men should make money and support the family financially. (Zhao 2017)

This biologically determined, gender-biased state policy has trickled down to the nooks and crannies of society, including colleges and universities, the job market, and companies.

Many colleges and universities required higher grades and a smaller acceptance quota for female applicants than for male applicants[2] (Huang 2020). For the uniform nationwide college entrance exams, many universities required female applicants to secure twenty to a hundred points higher than male applicants (Huang 2020). The required acceptance quota for female applicants was also far smaller than that for male applicants. For instance, the Guangdong International Relations University required female applicants to secure twenty points higher than male applicants, and an acceptance quota of three female students as opposed to twelve male students (Sun 2012). The South China University of Technology required an acceptance quota of five female students as opposed to fifty male students (Sun 2012). The Beijing Foreign Language University only accepted male students in certain majors (Sun 2012). The Chinese University of Political Science and Law required female applicants to secure forty-four points higher than male applicants (Mo 2021). The Information Engineering University required female applicants to secure a hundred points higher than male applicants and an acceptance ratio of 2 percent women as opposed to 98 percent men (Huang 2020).

When asked about this gender-based difference in qualifications and quotas, one university responded:

> Because our school has a heavy workload that requires students to stay up late, women's biological qualities are not strong enough, making them less likely to complete the study. So we require a higher college entrance exam grade for women so that only those fit can enter our school. (Huang 2020)

In response to this gender discrimination, in 2012, some female students shaved their heads on the streets of Guangzhou to show resistance against the "unfair college admission policy based on gender difference" (Sun 2012). In 2014, a female student wrote a letter to China's President Xi Jinping, exposing the gender-differentiated criteria for acceptance into colleges and universities (Huang 2020). She asked President Xi to eliminate the gender discrimination in the college acceptance process (Huang 2020). Five female lawyers in Beijing also posted a declaration online, protesting gender discrimination in the college acceptance process (Huang 2020). However, despite the Ministry of Education's Stipulations on College Acceptance that strictly bans gender-based criteria and gender-based quota in the acceptance process (2013), the situation unfortunately still persists in 2021 (Mo 2021).

In the job market, even though the Chinese Labor Law forbids gender discrimination (1994), a 2009 survey by the Women's Legal Center of Beijing University showed that one in four female applicants was rejected due to her gender; one in five women mentioned that their companies would not hire women who were of the child-bearing age and/or had not given birth (Chen 2012). More than one-fifth of companies reduced salaries and reassigned job posts for women during and after their pregnancy (Chen 2012).

Such gender discrimination in the job market has become increasingly grave since the open two-child and three-child policy in 2015 and 2021, respectively. One of the underlying reasons is that employers do not want to pay in full, as required by China's Labor Law, for the women's maternity leave between 128 days and a year after giving birth (Zhi 2021). After the two-child policy was instituted in 2015, a new survey showed that more than 75 percent of companies hesitated and/or refrained from hiring women (Jie 2016). Some companies forced women to sign a contract, promising that they will "automatically resign upon pregnancy" (Yang 2021). Some outright fired women upon their pregnancy or forced them to resign by reassigning them to job posts that were dangerous for pregnant women (Yang 2021; Zhi 2021; Stauffer 2021). At the time of appointment, some companies added a conditional clause in the form of a signed agreement that the woman would not be pregnant within five years of taking up the job (Liu, Yan 2019). Some forced women to undergo pregnancy tests as a condition for their appointment (Ye 2020). Others made it clear that they would not hire the women if they planned on giving birth (Stauffer 2021).

After the three-child policy was instituted in 2021, the National Health and Family Planning Committee announced that 42.9 percent of female workers had their salary reduced by half after having given birth (Duo 2021). The 2021 Survey of Women in the Job Market also showed that, for the same job position, the salary of women who had given birth was 31.6 percent less than men who had kids (Luo 2021).

In addition to this flagrant gender difference in salaries for the same position, the job market has also been saturated by posts that "are only limited to men" or "prioritize men" (Zhi 2021). It was reported in the 2021 Survey of Women in the Job Market conducted by the All China Women's Federation, a state apparatus, that 55.8 percent of female applicants have been asked whether they are married and when they plan on having children (Yang 2021). In 2019, gender limitations were required in 35.03 percent of the national civil service job posts, which are the most coveted jobs in China with a high salary, stable position, and handsome benefits after retirement, medical care, and house assignments (Zhi 2021; Ya 2020).

Due to such gender-biased state policies, it is not surprising that 60 percent of the current unemployed population in China are women, and that job loss and feminization of poverty have increased women's vulnerability to intimate partner violence.

Intimate Partner Violence in Post-Socialist China

The Third World Women's Conference in Nairobi in 1985 attended by Chinese female intellectuals prompted a recognition of violence against women as a social problem (Xu et al. 2005; Zhang 2009a; Edwards 2009; Hester 2012). In post-socialist China, intimate partner violence has become an increasingly severe problem. Sun Xiaomei, a professor at the Chinese Women's College, commented that "domestic violence is a social phenomenon that crosses all social strata and is becoming more and more common. There is an urgent need for legislation" (Jiao cited in He and Ng 2013a). In 2010, the state-supported organization All China Women's Federation,[3] after receiving 52,000 petitions from women who suffered from domestic violence, declared that "domestic violence poses a severe threat to women's rights in China" (He and Ng 2013a). It was reported that over 95 percent of intimate partner violence in China was committed by men against women (Zhang 2004). Intimate partner violence in China has reportedly increased by 25.4 percent since the 1980s (Hou et al. 2011; Liu 2018). It has been estimated that 35.7 percent of women in post-socialist China suffer intimate partner violence (Huang 2008). The Domestic Violence Law was enacted in March 2016 after two decades of campaigns by Chinese feminist advocates. It is not clear whether there is an actual increase of violence or simply an increase in awareness and therefore an increase in reporting.

Whether there is an actual increase of violence or an increase in reporting, it is clear that it is a severe social problem. It is surprising that, to date, no ethnographic studies of intimate partner violence in post-socialist China have been conducted. Indeed, in general, there is a dearth of anthropological research on this topic. Anthropologists have avoided studying, sometimes even acknowledging, this issue for a long time. The disciplinary silence on this topic risks perpetuating violence against women. To explain this silence, some suggest that studying this distasteful aspect of a culture risks a moral judgment that violates the cultural relativist principle so central to the discipline of anthropology (Beske 2016). Others argue that "perhaps domestic violence is not exotic enough. Unlike foot-binding, unlike suttee, unlike cannibalism, we ourselves perform this ugliness, just like 'exotic cultures'" (McClusky 2001: 7).

The truth is intimate partner violence can be extremely difficult to study (Wies and Haldane 2015; Plesset 2006). The paucity of anthropological research on this topic probably results from the difficulties of researching the private, intimate sphere of people's everyday lives, as well as from the stigma and embarrassment surrounding this topic that inhibits discussion. First, it is almost impossible for anthropologists to engage in the classic methodology of participant observation to observe the entire process of violence and abuse at home. Second, many women consider it such an embarrassing, humiliating, and stigmatizing private affair that it can keep them from telling their stories.

The literature on intimate partner violence in China has focused on collected oral stories of women, training materials provided to doctors and law officers, legal aid, international influences and organizations, and surveys and questionnaires to couples to determine the relationship between intimate partner violence and individuals' educational background, childhood experiences, and marital happiness (Song and Xue 2003; Zhang and Liu 2004; Tao 2004; Guo 2003; Zhang 2009b).[4] These studies have attributed intimate partner violence to a plethora of individual factors such as age, education, socioeconomic status, marital conflicts, history of abuse in childhood, and alcohol and drug use. Attention only to individual characteristics, however, reduces this social problem to a private, family issue. An exclusive cultural approach in feminist writings also obscures the political factors and economic conditions that spawn gender inequality and intimate partner violence. This point will be further explored below. As shown below, this book employs a combined historical, sociocultural, and political economic approach to the study of intimate partner violence in China.

This book contributes to the literature by bringing to the forefront women's experiences of, negotiations about, and contestations against violence and men's rationalizations for their violence. It foregrounds the role of history, structural inequalities, and the cultural system of power hierarchy in situating and constructing intimate partner violence. Centering on men's and women's narratives about violence, this book connects intimate partner violence with invisible structural violence—the historical, cultural, political, economic, and legal context that gives rise to and perpetuates violence against women. Through examining the ways in which women's lives are constrained by various forms of violence, hierarchy, and inequality, this book shows that violence against women is a structural issue that is historically produced and politically, economically, and culturally perpetuated. It is by no means an individual issue that can be simply resolved by remedying individual behaviors (see also Wires and Haldane 2015).

Sociocultural Approach to Violence

Anthropologists have historically studied violence and conflict, especially ethnicity-based violence, intergroup violence, state-perpetrated violence, and class-based violence (Scheper-Hughes and Bourgois 2004; Bourgeois 2004; Scheper-Hughes 2004a; Scheper-Hughes 2004b; Gordon 2017; Rosaldo 2004; Hinton 2002; Goldstein 2004; Green 1994; Malkki 1995; Nordstrom and Robben 1995; Robben and Suarez-Orozco 2000; Schmidt and Schroeder 2001; Sluka 1999; Tishkov 2004). However, it was not until recently that anthropologists have slowly come to realize the importance of gender-based violence at home and have started researching this topic (Alcalde 2010; Plesset 2006; Beske 2016; Wires and Haldane 2015). As a result, most of the existing works on gender-based intimate partner violence is written by sociologists, psychologists, social workers, and public health officials.

Research on intimate partner violence has attributed this problem to individual factors. These factors include but are not limited to religious beliefs, health issues, psychological or mental problems, stress, intergenerational continuity of abuse, alcohol use, substance abuse, unemployment, ethnic identity, age, education level, and occupation (Abraham 2000; Andrews 2001; Babu and Kar 2010; Bancroft 2003; Coker 2001; Duke 2011; Jukes 1999; McGillivray and Comaskey 1999; Rivera 2001; Stephen 2005; Todhunter and Deaton 2010; Vest et al. 2002; Yoshihama 2002). For instance, sociologists Straus, Gelles, and Steinmetz (1980) offer a list of reasons for violence at home that include stress factors such as isolation, alcoholism, unemployment, the degree of intimacy, the decline of community, competition, individualism, and changes in women's status. Gelles (1979) points to eleven factors to explain violence at home, including the duration of time that family members spend together, the extent to which family members commit to each other, privacy, age and sex differences, ascribed roles, vulnerability to stress, and involuntary membership (e.g., between children and parents or between divorced parents). While these particular factors undoubtedly contribute to intimate partner violence, they are not unique to China and are not going to be the focus of this book.

While previous research has focused on individual factors, they ignore and dismiss the fact that the macro-level social and cultural hierarchy of power is reflected in the micro-level relationships between intimate partners. Therefore, to understand the complexities of intimate partner violence, I argue that we have to address and analyze this macro-level social and cultural structure. Recent works on gender-based violence have argued that cultural systems such as patriarchy, asymmetry of gender ideologies, warfare, colonialism, land disputes, and kinship structures can lead to gender-based violence (Adelman 2004; Bryant-Davis 2010; Burazeri et al. 2006; Copelon 1995; Dobash 1979; Gremillion 2005; Hamby 2000; Hammer and Maynard 1987; Hoff 1990; Jeganathan 1995; Jones 1994; Karmen 2003; Kerns 1992; Luttrell 1996; Martin 1999; Merry 2009; Morrissey 1998; Naved and Persson 2005; Nicarthy 1989; Pournaghash-Tehrani 2011; Schecher 1982; Scheper-Hughes and Bourgois 2004; Sokoloff with Pratt 2005; Volpp 2013). As Gilsenan contends, "the study of violence can tell us much about the ways in which groups and persons organize and imagine themselves, constitute relations of power and hierarchy, and create social identities and meanings" (2002: 99).

This book opposes the individual-factor approach and argues for a sociocultural and political economic framework to study intimate partner violence. Linking cultural ideologies with structural factors in China, this book connects the personal with the structural to explore the broader cultural context that informs intimate partner violence and structures women's lived experiences. It demonstrates the ways in which violence is supported and bolstered by cultural discourses and broader social structures in China that hold women responsible for maintaining family harmony and political stability at the expense of their health and well-being. This cultural discourse defines women's primary role as "dutiful wives and virtuous mothers" and defines women's virtue in terms of their sacrifice for family harmony and state legitimacy. This cultural discourse also defines violence as only those activities causing severe physical injuries such as broken bones. Rather than holding men responsible for their violence, men's violence is defined in this cultural discourse as instinctual, biological, and uncontrollable. For instance, it portrays men's sexual urges that result in violence toward women as natural and something that must be accepted in the marriage contract. This cultural discourse also distinguishes worthy victims of sexual violence versus unworthy victims, and blurs the boundary between sexual coercion and consensual sex between intimate partners. These gender-based discourses represent a biologically determined, unequal gender approach to governance in post-socialist China.

The definition of women's virtue in terms of their sacrifice for family harmony and state legitimacy shows the historical continuation and perseverance of exploitation of women as an instrument for the state and the family patriarch. As I will show in Chapter 1, prior to the May Fourth and New Culture Movements at the turn of the twentieth century, a woman was seen as a commodity, possessed first by her father and then by her husband. She was ready to sacrifice at any time for the family order. She was ready to take her own life to save her family— her father, husband, and sons (Ko 1992). It was imperative that she affirm the hierarchy in a patriarchal family at the cost of her body, her mind, and her life. The importance of the patriarchal state and the family required selfless women. Knowing her place as an expendable subordinate commodity was her duty as a woman and defined her virtue.

Since early Chinese history, it has been the pattern that daughters and wives willingly self-sacrificed in their dedication to their patriarchs. For instance, during the Jin Dynasty (265–316), a man named Fan Jian committed a capital crime. His daughter willingly agreed to serve as a camp sexual slave to redeem his life, which was typical of the expectations of a good daughter (Liu 1993: 282). Good women accepted and internalized the values of the patriarchal state. What was new in the Qing dynasty was how outspoken women had become in their support of the patriarch (Ko 1992). Women martyrs killed themselves for the survival of husbands or sons and hence perpetuated family lines. In one dramatic case involving a Hunan woman named Madam Li during the late Yuan period (mid-fourteenth century),

> when starvation drove soldiers to seize human beings as food, her husband was taken and was soon to be cooked. Madame Li told the soldiers that "my husband is so starved that he is only skin and bones. I have heard that women who are plump and of dark complexion have delicious flesh. I am willing to be cooked in place of my husband"; she was said to have "won condolences from far and near." (Ko 1992: 465–7)

"This story wallows in gore—in cannibalism and the craving for a woman's flesh as sacrifice—and served as a doleful model for the women martyrs" (Ko 1992: 476). In another case, a woman sold herself in the market and had her head severed on the meat table in exchange for several thousand strings of cash sent to her husband. In a spirit of self-sacrifice, women were willing to rend their flesh and sacrifice their body organs. For example, daughters sliced off their buttocks or cut out their livers to make medicinal soup for ailing parents (Yu 2012). Women warriors such as Mu Lan Hua willingly took their ailing father's place in the draft and fought in battles; eventually they returned to a domestic existence (Li 1994). Although this was the antithesis of an ideal femininity, they served the cult of filial piety, loyalty, and domesticity. They made themselves symbols of obedient and filial women who lived and died for the patriarchs of their family.

Filial piety and sacrifice for the patriarchs of the family were the universal creed. Hence female warriors' unwomanly behavior and physical dislocation from domestic quarters were condoned because its ultimate goal was to serve the patriarchs of the family. They sent a clear message to other women that "they were judged ultimately, not by what they did or where they were, but by the moral intent informing their behavior" (Ko 1992: 485). This moral intent epitomized filial piety for the patriarchs of the family. This cult of loyalty toward the patriarchs could not have been produced without these moral crusaders: "The degree to which women subscribed to the good woman cult bespoke its persuasiveness" (Ko 1992: 486). Instead of a fetter, they viewed it as a fulfillment of their womanhood. Thus the Confucian gender system was predicated upon the active support and promotion of educated women themselves (Ko 1992). They embraced the cult of filial piety toward the patriarchs and celebrated their moral role.

Knowing this history helps us understand not only why the current state discourse on family harmony holds women responsible for sacrificing themselves for the family and state stability at the expense of women's own health and well-being, but also why the judges, government officials, and police, including women officials, often did not fulfil their legal obligations to the women who suffer intimate partner violence, but rather embraced their loyalty to the historical, patriarchal system that still exerts a great deal of influence in China today. What we are witnessing is a potential paradigm shift in China where this traditional culture advocated in the current state discourse on family harmony clashes with feminist activists who represent a new paradigm growing out of modernism as represented by the New Culture Movement and the Maoist era.

Political Economy and Intimate Partner Violence

Through examining how cultural ideologies interact with political and economic factors to induce and maintain violence, this book reveals that intimate partner violence is a microcosm of the invisible social system of hierarchy and power. Rather than treating violence as a set of individual events, this book seeks to unravel "those entrenched processes of ordering the social world and making (or realizing) cultures that themselves are forms of violence" (Kleinman 2000: 239). It provides a holistic exploration of the political, economic, cultural, and historical constructions of intimate partner violence. In so doing, it makes visible the invisible, showing the intersection of forms of structural violence that shape violence against women.

Researchers define structural violence as state-sanctioned and everyday violence that is often invisible. It results from social inequalities, poverty, social exclusion, economic exploitation, economic restructuring, displacement, gender power hierarchies, sexual oppression, racism, and other forms of social injustice (Anglin 1998; Farmer 2004a; Galtung 1969; Kleinman 2000). "The concept of structural violence is intended to inform the study of the social machinery of oppression" (Farmer 2004a: 307). It is an indirect form of violence that is inherent in an unjust, oppressive social structure, taken for granted by the powerful. Various researchers have demonstrated how structural violence shapes social suffering (Farmer 1996). Paul Farmer (2004b), for instance, illustrates the ways in which political violence, poverty, and racism dictate individuals' life choices and lead to suffering. As an example, he (1992) shows how the USAID-funded construction of a hydroelectric dam caused the displacement of peasants and their subsequent poverty and suffering. Arthur Kleinman (2000) argues that the collusion between the blood product industry and the US government in the early 1990s led to HIV infections in an entire age cohort of hemophiliacs, their spouses, and their children. Scheper-Hughes (2004a) shows that the bureaucratic indifference to infant and child mortality in Northeast Brazil perpetuates social suffering.

This book unearths the invisible structural violence in China through a multilayered historical, political, and economic approach. It provides a chronological narrative of a history of intimate partner violence, women's experiences of and responses to violence, men's perceptions about and rationalizations of their violence against women, the history of the legal framework of violence against women, limitations and strengths of activism, and cultural discourses that inform women's experiences of, and reactions to, sexual violence in their daily lives. Each approach adds an indispensable piece to the puzzle in order to allow us to fully grasp the complexity of the issue, weaving the micro-level individual experiences into the macro-level historical, cultural, and political economic structure in China.

As the book shows, in post-socialist China, women in general are disadvantaged because they lack economic opportunities, suffer salary gaps, and face job and education discrimination. In addition, the deeply seated patriarchal history of China that viewed women as instruments persists and underlies the issue of intimate partner violence. Women are expected to fulfil their traditional gendered roles, which are illustrated in state discourses on family harmony and men's rationalization of their violence against women. Women's unequal access to legal, social, and economic resources exacerbates violence against them. As this book shows, government officials, local officials, and law enforcement officials in the judicial system often hold deeply embedded patriarchal ideas of male dominance and favor men. Women's futile attempts to seek help from state institutions such as police stations, the courts, community committees, and the All China's Women's Federation contribute to the perpetuation of violence against women. The institutional inaction and male-biased deliberations lead to the glaring discrepancy between the law and practice, curtailing women's ability to leave the violent relationships, and prolonging and reinforcing the violence against them.

As this book demonstrates, police and judges make judgments not based upon the law, but based upon their personal cultural biases. Indeed, they ignore the law in handling intimate partner violence cases. This acceptance of authoritarian leaders over the authority of law is deeply rooted in Chinese history. The role of laws in traditional Chinese society is quite different from the Western legal tradition. In the West, the Christian idea of original sin suggested that fallible humans cannot be trusted. Therefore, at least in the liberal tradition, the West emphasizes the rule of law over the capricious rule of humans. In China, during the reign of the first emperor, the "legalist" tradition consisted of harsh rules applied arbitrarily by a tyrant and his minions. This discredited concept of law was rejected when Confucians regained influence. Confucians, who believed in the perfectibility of an educated elite, trusted the judgment of these educated, and therefore, moral judges over the impersonal and discredited legal codes. From a Western perspective, this led to an abuse of the judicial system under both Republican (1911–48) and Communist rule (1949–78). For example, guarantees of freedom of speech meant nothing if, as was usually the case, Communist judges overruled this freedom.

As Chapter 3 demonstrates, the Chinese criminal justice system as well as the social system have failed women, because of the lack of social services before and after divorce. This deficiency of support is also worsened because of the criminal justice system's preference for male abusers in awarding child custody rights and possession divisions, an emphasis on mediation, low issuance of Written Warning Notes, high threshold for Personal Safety Protection Orders, low recognition rates of violence in divorce cases, and high rejection rates of violence-related divorce cases. Directed by the state-sanctioned principle of family harmony and state stability at the expense of women's suffering and sacrifice, mediation, rather than criminalization, is championed and practiced by police and court judges to mediate between couples to resolve "family conflicts," the term they use to refer to intimate partner violence. Family harmony is deemed pivotal and indispensable to state stability and social security. The state discourse on family harmony encourages women to endure intimate partner violence and maintain family harmony and social stability at the expense of their health and well-being. Criminalization is only applied to abusers who inflict heavy injuries such as mutilation and paralysis. In so doing, the criminal justice system has failed women and in turn, has perpetuated intimate partner violence.

As Chapter 5 reveals, while women exert their agency to escape violence and actively seek help, they are often met with legal inertia—the inaction of the police and the court to punish abusers' violations of personal safety orders, as well as a hostile and intimidating social system that is intent on returning them to the violent environment from which they have escaped. In compliance with the state discourse of "family harmony," victims of intimate partner violence are often returned to their abusers in order to maintain family harmony and social stability, at the expense of women's safety and well-being. The harmony discourse prompts various state institutions such as the police and the All China Women's Federation to prioritize mediation as the paramount strategy to resolve intimate partner violence.

As Chapter 2 shows, the cultural discourse of the worthy, pure victim versus the unworthy, seductive woman and the criminal handling of sexual violence also institutionalize privileges of men. As Chapter 4 shows, condemnation of women's harsh mouth or strong mouth (zui ying) as the root cause of violence against women blames victims and legitimizes male violence. These multiple levels of hierarchy, power, and inequity inherent in the structure of violence help maintain and intensify violence against women.

Regulatory and Disciplinary Control and Neoliberal Governance

Neoliberalism in China refers to the transition beginning in 1978 to a quasi-market economy. This creates entrepreneurs who are individually held responsible in a way that they have not been before. As this book shows, this has become a new rationale that holds women responsible for the violence perpetuated against them. As Chapter 4 shows, men in my research invoke traditional stereotypes of women such as "zui ying" (harsh mouth or strong mouth) and "you mao bing" (have maladies, be at fault) to rationalize their violence against women. Chapter 2 continues to show that cultural discourse blames seductive, provocative women for sexual violence against them and thus redefines sexual coercion as women's responsibility. These discourses represent a disciplinary and regulatory control over women's bodies and sexuality, subjugating women's mouths, bodies, and sexuality to scrutiny, control, and regulation.

In *The History of Sexuality* (1978), Foucault argues that the old sovereign power over death was supplanted by the new power over life in the seventeenth and eighteenth centuries. Foucault theorizes two new basic forms of power over life— anatomo-politics and biopolitics/biopower. Anatomo-politics centers on the human body as a machine that must be disciplined into docility, production, and control—"its disciplining, the optimization of its capabilities, the extortion of its forces, the parallel increase of its usefulness and its docility, its integration into systems of efficient and economic controls" (Foucault 1978: 139). Biopolitics (Foucault 1978: 139) focuses on controlling and regulating the population of the human species through "propagation, births and morality, the level of health, life expectancy and longevity" (ibid.). Foucault contends that the anatomic and biological technology of power constitutes the two poles of power over life.

In lieu of threatening the subjects into subjugation with the power of death exercised by the sovereign, an anatomo-politics singles out the individual body to keep it under surveillance and disciplinary procedures so that its value can be maximized and its docility can be increased (Foucault 1978: 139). The diverse techniques used to subjugate bodies and control populations include institutional examinations, economic observation, and evaluation of resources and inhabitants. Anatomo-politics and biopower are techniques of power "present at every level of the social body and utilized by very diverse institutions"[5] and act as "factors of segregation and social hiearchization, exerting their influence on the respective forces of both these movements, guaranteeing relations of domination and effects of hegemony" (Foucault 1978: 141). Such techniques of power "to qualify, measure, appraise, and hierarchize" result in a "normalizing society" that operates on social norms "at the expense of the juridical system of the law" (Foucault 1978: 144).

This book demonstrates that the discourses of "zui ying" (harsh mouth or strong mouth), "you mao bing" (have maladies, be at fault), and "unworthy, seductive women" not only embody the anatomo-politics and biopower to regulate, control, and discipline women's mouths, bodies, and sexuality, but also form gender norms to dictate normative gendered bodies and behaviors. Violence is blamed on women's harsh mouths, loose sexuality, and "physical and mental diseases" or "maladies" that make them fail in fulfilling proper gendered roles and behaviors. Because these women are perceived as having violated gender norms, they are deemed unworthy victims, not deserving legal and other institutional protections or sympathy.

In post-socialist China, the mechanism of neoliberal governance places the responsibility for change on the marginalized population of victims of violence, thus shedding the state's responsibility (see also Zheng 2015). Informed by the neoliberal governing ideology, individuals are expected to be self-regulating, self-monitoring, self-disciplining, prudent, and responsible "entrepreneurs of themselves," capable of changing themselves and avoiding behaviors that could potentially subject them to physical and sexual violence. As Chapter 2 shows, sexual coercion is redefined as women's responsibility, and women are advised to transform themselves in order to end physical and sexual violence against themselves. Such neoliberal governance and disciplinary mechanisms conceal and mask structural violence that shapes and perpetuates violence against women.

Fieldwork

This book is the first ethnographic research on women's lived experiences of, discussions about, and responses to intimate partner violence in their daily lives in post-socialist China. During my first fieldwork with rural migrant karaoke bar hostesses for *Red Lights* (2009), many informants of mine experienced intimate partner violence from their boyfriends. Twenty-year-old Tong, for instance, was regularly beaten, even in front of other people, by her boyfriend Yu, who was a wealthy, married businessman. Tong often grabbed his beer bottles to fight back. Yu told me,

> Tong asked for it [the beating] because she dared to fight back. I beat her all the time to make a good woman out of her. I told her that, if she dares to sleep with other men, I'll destroy her face. I asked her: "What can you do without a face, right?" I said: "You can't do anything without it."

Tong eventually left this abusive relationship. She was one example of many others who experienced intimate partner violence during my fieldwork. During my fieldwork in hostesses' rural hometowns, I learned that husbands' beating of wives was so common that it was considered a normal part of life. It also reminded me of the time when I pursued my MA degree in China; my close classmate Chao was beaten by her boyfriend who broke her nose. I accompanied her to the hospital to have it treated. She told me, "The moment he started beating me, I felt he was so masculine, was such a real man." Despite these thoughts, she bravely broke up with him.

These experiences, from my previous fieldwork and from what my close classmate went through, have awakened me to the gravity of the issue of intimate partner violence in China. As an anthropologist and a social scientist, I have always considered it my mission to expose, explore, and analyze social issues and how individuals on the ground are affected by, negotiate through, and contest against them in their daily lives. That ushered me into this fieldwork on intimate partner violence.

During the two-decade period since 1998, I have conducted fieldwork in the northeastern city of Dalian that have yielded three ethnographies, on rural migrant karaoke bar hostess, condom use and disease control in the sex industry, and same-sex attracted men in China, respectively. My two-decade fieldwork in Dalian has resulted in a large network of people whom I have known, interviewed, worked together. They have become my lifetime friends and were ready to introduce me to people who would be helpful for my future research.

After I decided on the research topic of intimate partner violence in 2014, I have interviewed around fifty men from all walks of life, from 2014 to 2021, in Dalian to learn about their perceptions of intimate partner violence and why, in their opinions, men inflict violence on their partners. In addition to these men, I have also interviewed government officials from the All China's Women's Federation, who, after learning that I was a researcher from the United States, told me that "there is zero domestic violence in China."

This highlights the problem of doing research in China, where even the institutions charged with protecting women as well as relevant academic disciplines such as sociology and anthropology are subordinate to the government's discourse on any given subject. This would be laughable if it were not so tragic in its consequences. It is unrealistic to believe that in any society, no matter how enlightened it is, there is no domestic violence. As shown in Chapter 6, domestic violence and feminism are sensitive topics that can potentially expose the "dark sides" of China, and therefore need to be silenced and extinguished.

With the help of the network of people in the city, I have interviewed not only some government officials, but also court judges, police, and feminist activists from various NGOs. Apart from the ethnographic research, I have also conducted research analysis of the media coverage including newspapers, magazines, and TV shows to understand the cultural milieu in which intimate partner violence occurs.

From 2014 to 2021, I have been conducting research via online chat groups organized by victims of intimate partner violence, through which I have formed close friendships with about fifty women. I have not only been in regular contact with them via email and telephone, but have also traveled to physically meet them for follow-up interviews and interactions in their daily lives.

I have been an active participant in these groups on a daily basis, with my identity and research purpose fully disseminated to the women in the groups. At the beginning of my research, I looked for chat rooms that specifically address the issue of intimate partner violence and joined five chat rooms out of twenty that I had surveyed. Each of the chat rooms has over two hundred (some have five hundred) participants who are in conversation with each other every day. The majority of these women are in the age range of twenty-five to forty, ranging from stay-at-home mothers and full-time wives to working women, which shows that intimate partner violence happens among all social strata in society. Some of these women use their phones to access these chat rooms, some use computers, and others use internet cafes.

Anthropologists have conducted "ethnography in virtual communities" (Constable 2003). As they contend, the internet and relevant electronic forms of communication provide a new kind of "imagined global community" that traverses local, national, and global boundaries (ibid.). In my research, women told me that they were not able to tell anyone about the violence they experienced at home due to the stigma and embarrassment surrounding the topic. In their desperate need to talk about their experiences and seek support, they searched online chat rooms and found these groups that center on the issue of intimate partner violence. In these chat rooms they exchanged their stories, comforted each other, received emotional support, and offered advice to each other. Women told me that these chat rooms provided a space wherein they were able to talk about their suffering, vent repressed agony and anguish, and receive others' supportive responses, a process that most resembles talk therapy sessions.

Outline of the Book

The introductory chapter casts my research in the broader context of gender politics and political economy that are inherent in intimate partner violence in post-socialist China. Through examining how cultural ideologies interact with political and economic factors to induce and perpetuate violence, this book reveals that intimate partner violence is a microcosm of the invisible social system of hierarchy and power. Rather than treating violence as a set of individual events, this book provides a holistic exploration of the political, economic, cultural, and historical constructions of intimate partner violence. In so doing, it makes visible the invisible, intersecting forms of structural violence that shape violence against women.

Chapter 1, "A Social and Cultural History of Intimate Partner Violence in China," chronicles the ways in which intimate partner violence against women has been viewed, dealt with, and responded to in different historical eras under different political regimes in China—the imperial era, the Republican era, the Maoist era, and the post-socialist era prior to the 2015 Anti-Domestic Violence Law. This chapter shows that women were used across stages of history to advance the interests of the nation-state. Prior to 1911, husbands and parents had the absolute power to discipline, beat, abuse, and/or kill their wives and daughters. Intellectuals during the Republican era heralded women's liberation and freedom from abuse in order to propose and fulfil their political agenda of nation building. The Maoist era advocated women's liberation and freedom from abuse in order to tap into the vast resource of women as a group to accomplish the goal of socialist construction and the building of a socialist nation. The post-socialist era upheld women's freedom from abuse yet advocated women's sacrifice to promote family harmony and state stability.

Chapter 2, "Worthy versus Unworthy Victims of Sexual Violence in Post-Socialist China," drawing on women's lived experiences of sexual violence and sexual coercion in their lives, uncovers the cultural system of power hierarchy that creates injustice and inequity. Women in my research who have experienced sexual coercion by their partners have chosen not to report it in court. In their minds, the damage and contamination to their bodies have been done. Publicizing their names with a public sex scandal can only intensify and expand the damage to their lives. Their sense of disgrace and shame runs so deep that they are afraid that publicizing it can invite condemnation and humiliation and ruin their social reputation. Tarnishing their moral status can undermine and jeopardize their family relationships, future romantic relationships, and professional jobs. Such fear perpetuates and reinforces public silence and social tolerance of this issue. Cultural discourse also blurs the boundary between sexual coercion and consensual sex in a relationship and dichotomizes the unworthy versus worthy victims of sexual violence. This worthy versus unworthy victim distinction embodies the cultural system of gender hierarchy and a politics of sexuality that polices and regulates women's bodies and sexuality.

Chapter 3, "The Criminal Justice System and Intimate Partner Violence," explores how the criminal justice system as well as the social system have failed women, because of the lack of social services before and after divorce. This is aggravated by the criminal justice system's preference toward abusers in awarding child custody rights and possession divisions, an emphasis on mediation, low issuance of Written Warning Notes, high threshold for Personal Safety Protection Orders, low recognition rates of violence in divorce cases, and high rejection rates of violence-related divorce cases. Directed by the state-sanctioned principle of family harmony and state stability at the expense of women's suffering and sacrifice, mediation, rather than criminalization, is championed and practiced by police and court judges to mediate between couples to resolve "family conflicts," the term they use to refer to intimate partner violence. Family harmony is deemed pivotal and indispensable to state stability and social security. Criminalization is only applied to abusers who inflict severe damages such as mutilation, paralysis, and broken bones. In so doing, the criminal justice system has failed women and has perpetuated intimate partner violence.

Outside of the criminal justice system, the lack of support from friends, families, and social services also compelled many women to either stay with, or return to, their abusive husbands after divorce for survival and livelihood. As shown in this chapter, friends, family members, co-workers, and community and neighbors of women witnessed the intimate partner violence, but not only did not report it, but also advised them to endure it, in some cases, resulting in them being beaten to death by their husbands.

Drawing on interviews of around fifty local men from all walks of life in Dalian and research analysis of media coverage including newspapers, magazines, and TV shows, Chapter 4, "Male Perceptions and Rationalizations of Intimate Partner Violence in Post-Socialist China," examines popular perceptions of male-perpetrated intimate partner violence and argues that intimate partner violence is inexorably linked to structural inequality where the discourse employed to explain violence is a regulatory, disciplinary mechanism to control and discipline women's mouths ("harsh mouths"), bodies, and behaviors. Violence against women, in this framework, is not a monolithic phenomenon but a complex structural problem of multiple forms of oppression and social hierarchy. Portraying men's sexual and physical aggression as biological, inevitable, and uncontrollable evinces a biologically determined, unequal gender approach to governance in post-socialist China. Biology-based politics leave male violence and male infidelity unchallenged and hold women responsible for self-regulation.

Chapter 5, "Everyday Resistance of Women against Intimate Partner Violence," analyzes and explores women's resistance against violence in post-socialist China. This chapter debunks assumptions that women who experience intimate partner violence passively and helplessly accept their abuse. Rather, as illustrated in this chapter, some women actively engage in a number of strategies and struggles to resist violence in their daily lives. Through foregrounding women's experiences from diverse social locations and giving them voice, this chapter demonstrates that their agency is constrained and hindered by structural inequalities such as economic, social, and legal limits. In the absence of legal protection and social support, whether they stay with or leave their violent husbands not only depends on the efficacy of their strategies and resistance, but also depends on other factors such as their children, their parents, their economic dependence, and their financial constraints.

Based on interviews with anti-domestic violence activists, Chapter 6, "Activism and Intimate Partner Violence," examines the efforts and endeavors that activists and nongovernment organizations in China have contributed to the cause. The nongovernment organizations and activists have made interventions at grassroots level to provide an alternative route to the institutional impediments that women face in their pursuit of justice. These interventions include counselling, sheltering, and assisting in court cases. However, in appropriating the state discourse of family harmony and social stability in their activist rhetoric, activists legitimized their activism as well as state power. Through strategically advocating to the state that their activism sought to maintain social harmony and social stability through dissolving and repressing domestic violence as a social conflict, they proclaimed themselves as an indispensable part and parcel of the state apparatus to maintain state order. In so doing, they risk losing their independent status, identity, and voice, while at the same time legitimizing and reinforcing state power.

The Afterword describes the current situation of intimate partner violence during the Covid-19 pandemic in China, summarizes the book's theoretical contributions, and provides an analysis of patriarchy in Western civilization vis-à-vis China.

Chapter 1

A SOCIAL AND CULTURAL HISTORY OF INTIMATE PARTNER VIOLENCE IN CHINA

Intimate partner violence has been identified as one of the most common forms of violence against women worldwide (Jeyaseelan 2004). It refers to violence, threats, or any acts committed by the husband toward the wife that causes the wife sexual, physical, or psychological suffering or harm (United Nations 2006). At least one woman in every three in the world has been beaten, coerced into sex, or abused in her lifetime (Ku 2011).

In China, although intimate partner violence has been stipulated as a crime in the law, it was, for a long time, dismissed as a private affair between the husband and wife (Gilmartin 1990; Honig and Hershatter 1988). This chapter traces the social issue of intimate partner violence from the imperial era prior to 1911 to the post-socialist era prior to the legislation of the 2015 Anti-Domestic Violence Law. In portraying a social and cultural history of intimate partner violence, which the Chinese call "wife-beating" (da laopo), this chapter examines the ways in which different political regimes at different stages of history in China perceive, treat, and resolve this social problem. Through pinpointing the structural factors of the dynamics between the nature of the political regimes and the subjugation of women, I argue that a scrutiny of the archival histories, media coverage, and scholarly works will highlight the nuances and complexities of the power relationships between women and the Chinese state at various stages of history.

Below I will scrutinize the issue of intimate partner violence, or wife-beating, through the different stages of history: the Imperial era (pre-1911), the Republican era (1911–48), the Communist era (1949–78), and the post-socialist era prior to the legislation of the 2015 Anti-Domestic Violence Law (1978–2015). I will draw some conclusions in the end.

The Imperial Era

"Wife-beating," or violence against women in the family, was rooted in the dominant patriarchal ideology during this time. The Confucian patriarchal order of patrilineality, patriarchy, and patrilocality dominated the family and society as a whole. Women were positioned at the bottom of the social structure, subject to polygamy, patrilineality, patrilocal residence systems, foot-binding, widow chastity, and commodification (e.g., bride price and dowry) (Ebrey 1990; Watson 1991). In this system where women were possessions of fathers, fathers-in-laws, husbands, and sons, women were excluded from social or familial status until they produced a son. In the marriage exchange of betrothal gifts and dowry, women became commodities and had no control over economic resources in the economic unit (Watson 1991). The only context in which they could exhibit a bit of agency was in the uterine family with their sons (Wolf 1972).

The law offered a woman almost no protection or power. A woman's husband and parents were recognized by law to possess the power and legal right to discipline her. A husband could beat, abuse, or kill his adulterous wife with impunity. A husband was also given the legal right to return the wife to her natal home, which was considered an ultimate social disgrace for her. Grounds for the return of the wife included but were not limited to failure to obey and serve his parents, failure to bear a son, jealousy, lasciviousness, and disease. A woman, however, had no such corresponding rights. The criminal code during the Ming and Qing dynasties stipulated that a wife who escaped a husband would be punished by being whipped a hundred times with bamboo strips and by being sold by the husband afterward. If she married another man afterward, she would be hanged (Tian and Tian 1999). Even the death of her husband was not sufficient to release her from the marriage. An ideal widowed woman, no matter how young she was, should remain chaste for the rest of her life.

Although the dominant cultural ideology of Confucianism did not incite or endorse violence against women or wife-beating, it did, however, provide a cultural and legal bedrock for the institutionalization of wife-beating in Chinese society. Therefore, the patriarchal, patrilineal, and patrilocal family system ensured a social structure wherein women were subordinate to men. Such a social, cultural, and legal context produced abusive cultural practices against women such as wife-beating.

The Republican Era (1911–48)

At the end of the nineteenth century when China was threatened by the imperialist powers, intellectuals pondered how to strengthen China. The May Fourth Movement (1919) and the New Culture Movement (1915–23) attributed the failure of the Revolution of 1911 to the oppression of women and the suppression of individualism in China's Confucian tradition. The movements called for the liberation of women and a complete reevaluation of the Chinese culture.

Reformers contended that women's independence and gender equality signified a modern nation. The theme of gender equality in Europe, America, and Japan dominated many journals and newspapers (Lin 1899). Newspaper articles at that time showed that many American, Japanese, and European women worked as professionals (Jiang 1930; Yong 1898; Fan 1902, 1905a, Fan 1905b; Fan 1906). Although women in these countries had not yet obtained the right to vote at that time, they were accorded greater rights and opportunities than women in China and, therefore, served as a model for the Chinese reformers. These writings compared independent and professional women in "modern nations" with the cloistered, crippled, and subservient women in China who did not work (Lin 1905).

The oppression of Chinese women, epitomized by foot-binding and other abuses by men, was seen as a crucial indicator of national weakness. The image of victimized women became a symbol of China as the Sick Man of East Asia, "raped and dominated by virile foreign powers" (Ko 1994: 2). The image of a chaste and domestic wife was transformed "from a symbol of a civilized, prosperous empire to a symbol of a backward and weak nation" (Brownell and Wasserstrom 2002: 89). Reformers attacked family patriarchy in the Confucian family structure as the greatest obstacle to individual freedom and national reform (Guan 2005; Chen 1979; Glosser 2002). They argued that such a Confucian family structure oppressed women and produced a passive and weak nation (Jing 1933).

The liberation of women became a prerequisite for national liberation and China's entry into the modern world (Grieder 1970; Peng 1995; Larson 1998, 2002; Siu 1990). The May Fourth Movement urged women to free themselves from the oppressive grip of family patriarchy. Intellectuals eschewed women's traditional virtues of domesticity and subservience, and launched a debate on "authentic" modern women as fundamental to national revival, modernization, and strengthening of the self (Edwards 2000; Ko 1994). They argued for strong educated women to be partners to their husbands.

During this period, while some "New Women" who received education from women's schools and women's colleges managed to escape abusive marriages and/or to practice lifelong celibacy, others found the struggle too difficult and ended their lives in suicide or death, such as in the case of Zhang Sijing (Xin, Hou, and Xi 2008; Wang 1979; Lei 2005;Zhang 2015; Jin 1928). Zhang, educated in Tianjing Women's University, was actively involved in the May Fourth Movement as an executive committee member of the Tianjin Female Society. After graduation, she entered an arranged marriage and was subsequently severely abused by her husband. She died of intolerable mental and physical abuse by her husband at the age of twenty-one (Li 2003; Xin, Hou, and Xi 2008).

Indeed, many women during this era suffered intimate partner abuse in arranged marriages, and only a few were successful in their resistance (Zhang 2007; Liu 1984; Tian and Tian 1999; Tan 2007). Women's responses to the common practice of domestic abuse varied from endurance to escape to murder to suicide and to filing for divorce (Tan 2007; Fan 1990). Some resisted through suicide or murder. According to some accounts, in 1929, women who committed suicide as a result of unbearable abuse by their husbands accounted for 57.46 percent of all suicide cases (Tan 2007; Fan 1990). It was reported that in 1946, this ratio was 45.07 percent and in 1948 it was 42.77 percent (Wang 2008). Also, news reports revealed that from May to September 1925, 40.6 percent of the criminals sentenced to death were women who had killed their abusive husbands in retaliation against their violence (Wang 1984).

Some filed for divorce, thanks to the first divorce law in Chinese history. It was reported that during this era, the husband's insufferable abuse was the major reason for women to file for divorce (Wang 2008; Tan 2007). In Guangxi, for instance, 62 percent of all divorce cases cited unbearable abuse by the husband as the reason for divorce (Wang 2008). In Shanghai, this ratio was 88.8 percent in 1946 (Guo 2000).

Indeed, the Republican era witnessed the first civil law that asserted freedom of divorce for the first time in Chinese history. The 1915 Civil Law stipulated that divorce be granted to a couple when both had agreed on a divorce. The law also stated that the party that was unable to endure the abuse and abandonment could file for divorce. The law required a six-month waiting period for a divorce after the time of the abuse (Civil Law Deliberation 1933a: 256). If the party approached the court after a lapse of six months post-abuse, the request would be rejected (ibid.).

It was estimated that almost half of the divorce cases throughout the country were filed by women who were taking advantage of their new rights (Ai 2006; Jia 2008; Yue 1994; Wang 2008).[1] Typical examples cited in legal cases during this era include the following: a husband who shackled his wife with iron chains and starved her (Tan 2007); a husband who locked up his wife and beat her body black-and-blue (Lu 1930); husbands who beat their wives with sticks, whips, clubs, or hoes multiple times a month, causing hemorrhages and severe physical injuries (Jiang 1929; Liu 1927; Tan 2007; Yang 1931). One husband beat his wife so severely over time that it caused five miscarriages, finally resulting in her bleeding to death (Wu 1921). Unable to endure these consistent beatings, abuse, and deprivation of food and clothes, many wives committed suicide (Tan 2007).

In spite of the New Culture Movement and the progressive ideas that it put forward, many courts were dominated by conservative males who refused divorce requests by women on the basis of insufficient evidence or the lapse of six months after the abuse (Chen 1917; He 2001). Court deliberations made a distinction between habitual abuse and ad hoc abuse that was triggered by anger, deeming only habitual abuse as acceptable proof for divorce (Civil Law Deliberation 1933: 207). In some cases, the court also demanded a post-abuse reconciliation note provided to the wife by the husband's father as evidence of the abuse (Tan 2007). It was evident that the court favored men in their deliberations of divorce cases (Ai 2006).

In some cities, 52.4 percent of the divorce cases filed by women were rejected because of one of the following reasons: the injuries were not severe enough, the abuse was beyond the designated period of six months, the abuse was determined to be accidental—from anger and frustration and did not qualify as "habitual abuse" (Li 2005; Tan 2007; Tang 1931; Wei 1928; Shen 1928; Zhuxiangshi 1936). When a woman, Wang, filed for divorce, the Supreme Court ruled that since the abuse took place more than six months ago, her case was rejected (Wang 1944). A woman, Li, filed for divorce and presented the medical proof of her physical injuries. The court rejected her request as this evidence of a one-time injury was insufficient to prove her husband's habitual abuse (Li 1932). A woman, Zhu, stated that her husband had beaten her three times within the past six months and numerous times before that (Wu 1927). After investigations, the court announced that since each beating resulted from a skirmish between the couple, it was "normal" and "not surprising at all" (ibid.). The court ruled that "couple fighting" happened in all families and therefore should not be labeled as an abuse (ibid.).

The role of laws in traditional Chinese society is quite different from the Western legal tradition. In the West, the Christian idea of original sin suggested that fallible humans cannot be trusted. Therefore, at least in the liberal tradition, the West emphasizes the rule of law over the capricious rule of humans. In China, during the reign of the first emperor, the "legalist" tradition consisted of harsh rules applied arbitrarily by a tyrant and his minions. This discredited concept of law was rejected when Confucians regained influence. Confucians, who believed in the perfectibility of an educated elite, trusted the judgment of these educated, and therefore, moral judges over the impersonal and discredited legal codes. From a Western perspective, this led to an abuse of the judicial system under both Republican (1911–48) and Communist rule (1949–78). For example, guarantees of freedom of speech meant nothing if, as was usually the case, Communist judges overruled this freedom.

While rejecting many women's divorce requests on the basis of intimate partner abuse, court judges also favored mediation in lieu of granting a divorce (Zhu 1927; Shen 1928; Lu 1930; Yang 1931; News 1933). After rejection, some women such as Lu filed for divorce a second time due to the insufferable, multiple beatings every month by her husband (Lu 1930). However, the court consistently recommended mediation and would not grant the divorce, simply because the husband was not willing to divorce (ibid.). Clearly, the continuing power of a Confucian interpretation of the law was still very much at work here.

Some court judges even encouraged the husband to abuse his wife. In Shandong Province, for instance, when a woman, Wang, requested a divorce, the court judge rejected the request, admonishing the husband: "I am sentencing your wife to you. If she is not obedient, you can beat her to death! I will protect you" (Zhang and Meng 1997). In another case, the judge handed a whip to the husband: "Take the whip. If she is not obedient, use this whip to beat her! If you beat her dead, you can carry her dead body to the court. I will buy her a casket for you" (ibid.).

Courts also often rejected women's request for the husband to return their dowries, citing the reason as either a lack of a detailed record of the dowries or the husband's inadequate financial situation (Wang 1944). Although the law stipulated that the husband should offer the wife living expenses after divorce (Civil Law 1931), in reality, only in situations where the husband proposed divorce could the wife receive living expenses (Ai 2006). The husband often times falsified his possession report so that he not only evaded the responsibility of alimony to his wife, but also had the court order his wife to offer him the alimony (Nanjing Law Administration 2000). In cases where the husband was ordered by the court to provide living expenses for his wife, he would dismiss the order afterward. As a result, the wife often received nothing or a minimal amount (Qi 1936). Many divorced women sued their ex-husbands in court on this issue, but few won such cases (Bieju 1937).

Regarding the issue of child custody, although Civil Law No. 1051 and No. 1055 stipulated that children younger than five years of age would be given to the mother for custody (Civil Law 1931), the court often times ordered the child to be returned to the father, especially in situations where the mother was remarried or the mother was not able to support her children due to their ex-husbands' failure to offer living expenses (Ai 2006). A woman named Gao was originally given the custody of her baby by the court, but when she remarried, her ex-husband filed a request to regain the custody of the baby. The court granted the request and ordered that custody be transferred from the mother to the father due to the mother's remarriage, which shows the court's prejudice against remarried women (Verdict 1930).

Although some female intellectuals involved in the May Fourth Movement were successful in resisting their husbands' abuse through escape or divorce, in general they found it extremely difficult to live a happy life post-divorce due to social prejudices against divorced women (Xin, Hou, and Xi 2008). These female intellectuals commented that divorced men were often able to remarry and enjoy a happy life, yet it was a different situation for divorced women. Due to the deeply entrenched social and cultural stigma attached to divorced women, very few men were willing to marry divorced women (Jiang 1936; Jiang 1934). For women who did remarry, they continued to face slander and disdain. Despite the fact that they no longer suffered physical abuse from their new husbands, their mental state continued to suffer due to social derision (ibid.).

Divorced women often found themselves not only socially and culturally ostracized and discriminated against, but also financially destitute (Ai 2006; Gao 1914; Zhang 1922; Li 2005). Unable to endure her husband's daily abuse, a female student named Pan Zhongqin divorced her husband. After divorce, she had to quit school due to financial straits. Unable to find a job, she had no alternative but to remarry just to survive (Luo 1996). Like Pan, many women, after divorcing their abusive husbands, had to marry another man or enter prostitution for a livelihood (Gao 1914).

Police archives in Beijing reported that many women had nowhere to go after divorce (Zhang 2008). In 1913, for instance, a woman named Wen went back to her ex-husband's house and refused to leave. When the police learned that she had nowhere to stay, they sent her to an almshouse (Wen 1913). In 1926, a divorced woman named Wu went to the police station requesting for a place to stay. She was also sent to an almshouse (Wu 1926). In such cases, the police sent the women to a rescue home where they would be at the mercy of any men who showed up to claim them.

Since it cost so little to take these women home as wives, some men took advantage of the situation. They took the women home and sold them afterward into prostitution for high profits. In 1918, for instance, a clothes shop owner named Song contributed 30 yuan to the almshouse in exchange for Wu, a woman who had escaped her abusive husband. After Song took Wu home, Song sold her into prostitution for a total profit of 300 yuan (Song 1918). According to the almshouse, there were so many cases like this that the court was unable to keep up and punish people appropriately (ibid.).

As we have seen, women's economic dependence upon men not only curtailed their ability to escape or divorce, but also forced them to return to men or enter prostitution after divorce for economic survival. Patrilineal tradition determined inheritance during the pre-Republican era, and the 1931 Civil Law stipulated that the husband would possess the right to manage the collective possessions of the couple, including the wife's previous possessions such as her dowry (Tian and Tian 1999: 56). At the end of the 1930s, a new Civil Law stipulated that spouses would inherit each other's possessions, and all children, whether married or unmarried, would enjoy equal inheritance rights. Although women were given an equal inheritance right by the new Civil Law, in practice, women were consistently denied the inheritance right. In Shanghai, for instance, parents often provided dowries for daughters in marriage, but left no inheritance for daughters in their wills. Indeed, intellectuals (Chen 1920; Gao 1984) wrote about the tragedy of a woman named Chao Li, whose parents were affluent. Upon her parents' death, all the possessions were inherited by her brothers, who mistreated and abused Li, leading to her premature death. Throughout the country, during this period, despite the new 1931 Civil Law, women rarely inherited possessions, and few women went to court to appeal for their inheritance rights (Guo 2000). Once again, we see the triumph of cultural traditions over newly propagated laws in China.

Debates about women's liberation during this era remained part of a new ideology that failed to address the practical problem confronting women who were battling a 2,500-year-old cultural tradition. The liberation of women was only a means to the end of the liberation of the nation. Chinese intellectuals observed what they believed to be the central characteristics of Western superiority in the liberation of women. The liberation of women was not important in and of itself. It was always seen as a necessary element of liberating China and the progressive development of China, subordinate to the nationalist agenda (Brownell 1999). Although the new law stipulated freedom to divorce and guaranteed inheritance rights, as we have seen, women were faced with obstacles that thwarted their struggle for freedom from intimate partner abuse and their claim to inheritance rights. As numerous studies have shown, providing education to women is one of the most important factors in determining the liberation of women. As discussed, during the Republican era, the judicial system made it very difficult for women to gain their legitimate rights. The fact that 90 percent of women were illiterate during that time made this challenge all the more difficult (Zhang, Lulu 2015). Women's lack of education caused a lack of economic independence. In addition, the entrenched gender inequality in society and favoritism toward men in court also made it difficult for women to rebel against intimate partner abuse.

The Maoist Era *(1949–78)*

After the Communist liberation in 1949, the Communist Party promulgated the 1950 Marriage Law to outlaw "feudal" elements, including male dominance, marriage at a young age, arranged marriages, concubinage, prohibitions on the remarriage of widows, and marriage based upon cash transactions (Zhang 2001). The 1950 Marriage Law gave women equality in marriage, the right to divorce, and inheritance rights. It also gave women prior claims to underage children in the event of divorce.

The Communist Party leader, Chairman Mao, believed that women's active participation in labor was indispensable to the success of rebuilding a devastated agricultural and industrial infrastructure. By advocating women's liberation, Mao involved the energy and enthusiasm of women in the construction of a socialist country and economy. In 1949, the first congress of the All China Women's Federation was founded. They became active in land reform, the reforming of marriage law campaigns, and the recruitment of women into political leadership roles.

The 1950 Marriage Law ushered in an unprecedented tide of divorce in China, with as high as 1.17 million divorce cases in 1953 (You 1957). While the Marriage Law was implemented by local leaders and women's associations, it had to confront the enduring traditional attitudes toward women and the cultural practice of abusing women. Indeed, as shown below, a large number of women nationwide who employed the Marriage Law to seek divorce and liberate themselves from their abusive husbands were tortured, murdered, or forced to commit suicide by their husbands.

Newspapers reported that every year from 1950 until 1953, over eighty thousand women died as a result of the Marriage Law (Zhong 1953). In 1951 alone, after the implementation of the Marriage Law, a shocking number of women who requested a divorce were killed or committed suicide due to the abuse perpetrated by their husbands: 10,000 in four southern provinces, 11,500 in East China, 1,245 in Shandong Province, 2,189 in Guangdong Province, 606 in thirty-nine counties in Hunan Province, 119 in nine counties in Subei, 212 in Huaiyang of Henan Province, and 120 in Hui'an County of Fujian Province (Zhang 2001; Lin 1953; Lv 1951; Tang 2010; Ren 1953). Due to their divorce requests, these women were often brutally tortured, frequently leading to their death. One husband, Bingsheng Zhao from Shanxi Province, for instance, responded to his wife's request for divorce by inserting a burning hot, red iron inside her vagina, causing her death (Chang 2013). A husband from Suiyuan Province, learning of his wife's wish to divorce, dug out her left eye and cut her legs off with an axe and a chaffcutter (Qing 2000). Other examples of violent acts against wives who proposed divorce included chaining, slitting throats, and beating with a hoe, typically resulting in death (Qing 2000; Ding 1953; Fu 1952; Xia 1952).

Some officials chose to ignore the husbands' abuse of women and not prosecute these crimes (Huang 2009: 12). They attributed their failure to enforce the Marriage Law to their fear of possible social unrest (ibid.). Unfortunately, the failure to prosecute these crimes often led to further murder of women and suicide (Hu 1950; Xu 1951; Guo 1951). Often these crimes were particularly horrific. In Shanxi Province, for instance, a husband used a burning fire rod to burn his wife to death, but law enforcement and government officials did nothing and let the husband go scot-free with no legal consequences (Li 2008). In Henan Province, there were three murder cases wherein the husbands killed their wives. Despite physical proof and oral testimony against the husbands, law enforcement officials delayed the cases by more than two years, eventually dismissing all of them (ibid.). Many other murder cases nationwide repeated this scenario, resulting in further torture and death (ibid.). For instance, within a short period of several months, sixty-four women in two counties in Anhui Province and fourteen women in Quwo County, Shanxi Province, were beaten to death or driven to commit suicide by their husbands (Hu 1950; Xu 1951).

Some officials not only repeatedly rejected or refused to process women's divorce requests despite proof of the husbands' abuses, but also forced the women to return to their abusive husbands, resulting in more torture, murder, and suicide of women throughout the country (Lv 1951; Chang 2013: 87; Ben 1953; Lin 1953). In Henan Province, for instance, Wang Yu's divorce request on the basis of her husband's abuse was rejected by the law enforcement officials in court, resulting in her murder by her husband upon her return home (Fan 1950). In Pingyuan Province, the district court denied a woman's divorce request and forced her to return home. Upon returning home, she was beaten to death by her husband (Li 2008).[2]

Some officials not only resisted the Marriage Law, but also actively joined in the abuse of those women who requested a divorce (Huang 2009; Yang 1952). These officials often organized a unique Maoist practice called the struggle session, which was typically used against landlords, to turn the community against women seeking divorce (An 1952). The struggle session used a group psychology typically associated with lynching to turn the community violently against the women. This resulted in severe beating or death through mob violence. In Tongnan County, Hubei Province, for instance, officials tied up a woman who requested a divorce in a public meeting and then proceeded to turn the mob against her, subjecting her to severe beatings and humiliation (Hu 1950). The following day she committed suicide (ibid.). Humiliation was often a part of the punishment meted out to women who requested a divorce. In Shaanxi Province, Hongqi Sheng was stripped by officials, hung naked on the ceiling, and beaten until she died (Ben 1953). This kind of humiliation was not uncommon. The power of traditional culture even influenced women's attitude toward this issue, who one might expect to be more sympathetic toward other women who were abused. For instance, a female chair of a women's association in Xiangyang County, Hubei Province, referred to an abused woman who had sought divorce as "shameless," forcing her to promise to never request divorce, to never return to her natal family within three years, and to never speak to the villagers of her natal family. This female chair also required that she ask for permission from her husband when she needed to urinate or empty her bowels. Punishment for her violation of any one of these four promises, she was told, would be drinking three bowls of human excrements while kneeling on a hay cutter and being struggled against in public meetings (Huang 2009: 13). As bizarre as these punishments seem, they fit in with the model of personal humiliation as a means of social control.

Officials' abuse of women and violation of the Marriage Law led to a widespread saying among women: "Women's lives are less worthwhile than evil landlords, whose execution even requires some sort of procedures" (He 1950: 1247–8). In other words, beating a woman to death did not require any kind of procedure nor did it lead to any kind of legal consequences (ibid.).

As noted above, officials attributed their failure to abide by the Marriage Law to the fear that raising women's status would lead to social unrest or social chaos. Indeed, the Marriage Law was called by many men as the "Divorce Law" or "Women's Law," a law to "struggle against men" (Chang 2013: 88; Xi 1953). In rural areas, many male peasants felt that they had helped the Communist Party win the revolution, only to lose both their wives and the bride-price that they had incurred as a debt. Many considered the banning of husbands' abuse of wives within the purview of the Marriage Law an intervention into family affairs (Li and Chen 2013). They felt offended by the fact that the Marriage Law raised women's status and put restrains on the husbands and mothers-in-law (Diao 1952). To prevent their wives from requesting a divorce, many husbands forbade their wives to go to meetings, schools, or group activities (Fu 1950; Fu 1952; Xi 1953).

Resistance to the Marriage Law's ban on bride-price or "marriage based on gifts or money" was also widespread. Deeply entrenched cultural values ritualized bride-price. Not offering a bride-price was considered a lack of the most basic respect toward the bride's parents. Many women's parents found it difficult to understand why, in Communist China, their hard work of raising the daughter was wasted as they were forced to give away their daughter for free to the groom's family. Many men also viewed free-choice marriage as a threat to their chance of finding a bride (Xi 1953).

As a result of the fierce resistance to the Marriage Law, the high divorce rate, the threat of social instability, and the risk of losing male supporters, the Communist Party gradually retreated from the principles of the Marriage Law and focused on other political campaigns such as cooperatives, to assuage the conflict over the traditional attitudes toward women (Tang 2010).

The level of the husbands' violence against wives who wished to divorce showed how deeply rooted and institutionalized traditional values were toward women's roles and status. The Marriage Law was intended to offer women freedom, equality, liberation, and protection, and raise women's social status. However, as shown in this section, many women who seized the opportunity provided by the law to pursue freedom from abuse ended up either committing suicide or being murdered by their husbands.

Indeed, traditional values and attitudes toward women surfaced again and again during the Maoist era. For instance, despite the socialist assault on the traditional roles of women and the unprecedented level of women's participation in rebuilding China, including in the heavy industry and farm production sectors, women were often burdened with continuation of their traditional duties such as housework and child care. Finally, during the Maoist era, although land was allotted to women, often times it remained in the control of the family or the male head.

Despite the fact that patriarchy was attacked and certain phenomenon such as polygamy was eradicated, women still shouldered the traditional familial responsibilities. Many deeply seated cultural practices such as bride-price and domestic abuse of women still persisted, as the Party continued loosening its implementation of the Marriage Law. Ultimately, Maoist China viewed women as a key political resource to appropriate for state building, thus subsuming women's issues under state needs and state interests (see Zheng 2009a).

The Post-Socialist Era Prior to the 2015 Anti-Domestic Violence Law (1978–2015)

In the early 1990s, some Chinese female intellectuals attended the Third World Women's Conference in Nairobi, where the issue of violence against women was raised as a social problem (Xu et al. 2005; Zhang 2009a; Edwards 2009; Hester 2012). The 4th World Women's Conference held in Beijing in 1995 also listed domestic violence as one of the most pressing issues in the world, prompting more intellectuals to acknowledge the problem and to work to improve and ameliorate the situation in China (ibid.).

In post-socialist China, intimate partner violence has become more and more severe. As noted before, over 95 percent of intimate partner violence in China was committed by men against women (Zhang 2004). If one can trust Chinese government's statistics, which are not always reliable, the rate of abuse was reported as having risen by 25.4 percent since the 1980s, and showed that in current China 35.7 percent of women endure intimate partner violence (Hou et al. 2011; Huang 2008). It was reported that 10 percent of all murders originated from intimate partner violence (Zhang 2014; He and Ng 2013). Anecdotal evidence seems to suggest that both previous and present statistics understate the amount of violence toward women.

Prior to the legislation of the 2015 Anti-Domestic Violence Law, when women went to the police with severe injuries from their husbands' physical violence, often times, all the police did was to ask the husbands to apologize and write promises not to resume violence (see also Xing 2013; Kai 2014). Written apologies and promissory notes were far from enough to curb intimate partner abuse and violence. In Hainan, for instance, due to police inaction, three women were tortured to death by their husbands (Xing 2013).

Kim Lee, the American wife of Yang Li, a prominent Chinese businessman of a popular chain of English-language schools, endured a number of beatings by her husband in 2011. When she sought help at a police station with fresh bruises on her face and body, the police told her to calm down and go home to her husband (Lee 2014). Upon returning home, Lee posted pictures of her injured forehead on Weibo, a popular social media platform, and filed for divorce. In 2013, she was granted divorce by a Beijing court, with custody of their three children, including child support, part of his assets as a compensation for her mental distress, along with a restraining order, the first one in China (Lou 2013).

Kim Lee received 1,141 letters from women who told her about their sufferings from intimate partner violence (Wang 2013). Lee stated that intimate partner violence in China is far more prevalent than what the number suggests, as a massive number of attacks are unreported (Lee 2014). Her own experience and the 1,141 women who wrote to her showed that the police and the legal system favored men against women (ibid.).

Police inaction, prior to the legislation of the 2015 Anti-Domestic Violence Law, often led to the last legal option of a divorce in the civil court. However, statistics showed that in China, only about 3 percent of all divorces filed on the basis of intimate partner violence were awarded (ibid.). The court's nonrecognition of intimate partner violence meant that the wife often times not only suffered financially, but also ran the risk of losing custody of the children, as the court would appoint the parent with the highest income as the appropriate caretaker. In the absence of safe houses (see Chapter 5), a woman often found that there was no place to go, after losing her home and child at the end of a long divorce battle.[3] Indeed, there was almost no support service for them even in the largest cities.

Abused women's rights, prior to the legislation of the 2015 Anti-Domestic Violence Law, were undermined in divorce cases via judicial mediation (also see Chapter 3; He and Ng 2013a, He and Ng 2013b). In situations where the judges knew that intimate partner violence was committed by the husband, the violence was often erased at the stage of judicial mediation (ibid.). In general, mediation was a standard procedure for the police and the All China Women's Federation to persuade the husband to apologize to the wife. It should be noted that the All China Women's Federation, in spite of its positive-sounding name, was largely supportive of the traditional patriarchal values. In Sichuan Province, for instance, in 2013, among the 896 cases of intimate partner violence, 800 cases were mediated by the police and by the All China Women's Federation through educating and criticizing the abuser, often resulting in more violence from the abuser toward the wife (Kai 2014).

The lack of legal justice, prior to the legislation of the 2015 Anti-Domestic Violence Law, forced women to rely on their own ways to retaliate against the violence perpetrated on them. The most extreme of these strategies was termed "reprisal violence" in Chinese legal cases, which means that the abused women responded violently against their abusive husbands (Sun 2013). Around 11.2 percent of all crimes committed by women involved "reprisal violence" against their abusers (ibid.). As reported by Chinese scholars and organizations, women's jails were filled with women who had injured or killed their abusive husbands as a means of seeking justice on their own terms (Tatlow 2013). In one jail in Anshan in Liaoning Province, for instance, these women comprised 60 percent of all the inmates; in another one in Fujian Province, the percentage is 80 (ibid.).

Prior to the legislation of the 2015 Anti-Domestic Violence Law, many husbands who had beaten or tortured their wives to death were found innocent due to alleged mental illness or were sentenced only to three to six years in prison, but a woman who fought back and killed the abuser was often times sentenced by the court to death or a lifetime in prison (Guo 2014; Guo 2012; Tatlow 2013; Kai 2014). In 2009, Dong Shanshan, a 26-year-old woman in Beijing, reported to the local police eight times about her abusive husband (Guo 2012). The police repeatedly disregarded her bruises and injuries as "family problems." In 2009, Dong filed for divorce for the intolerable abuse inflicted by her husband. Infuriated by her divorce request, her husband beat her to death. He received a sentence of six and a half years (ibid.).

Women who resisted and fought back received much more severe sentences. In a jail in Sichuan, 71 out of 121 female inmates were sentenced to the death penalty or to a lifetime in prison for killing or attacking their abusive husbands (Xing 2011). Around 80 percent of the female inmates were sentenced to the heaviest penalties for causing physical harm to or for murdering their abusers, whereas their male counterparts were sentenced to three to six years in jail or were given no penalty for murder (ibid.). Since Chinese law recognizes the right of self-defense, this is severe injustice toward women who did not initiate the violence but rather responded to the violence against them.

Since then a great stride has taken place in the area of law. On December 27, 2015, China's legislature passed the Anti-Domestic Violence Law, which was implemented on March 1, 2016 (see Chapter 3). Domestic violence is defined in the law as "physical, psychological and other harm inflicted by family members with beatings, restraint or forcible limits on physical liberty." It stipulates that victims should appeal to the All China Women's Federation or report the abuse to the Public Security Bureau. It also mandates that the Public Security Office should impose administrative and criminal punishment on perpetrators of severe domestic violence. In the case of perpetrators of less severe abuse, the law further states that the Public Security Office should draft a written warning to correct behaviors, with a copy of the warning given to the All China Women's Federation. It should be noted that in socialist China, the law itself is not socialized. One must pay for representation. Since many women in this situation do not have sufficient wealth, their representation in the initial trial is usually not adequate. The possibility of appealing a negative decision in a higher court is generally out of the question.

The law also establishes personal safety protection orders, stipulating that victims of domestic violence should be granted the restraining order by the People's Court upon request, within twenty-four hours in case of emergencies. If victims are not available to submit such a request due to threats, then relatives, the All China Women's Federation, residential committees, aid offices, and the Public Security Office can make such a request on their behalf. Personal safety protection orders can be canceled, changed, or extended prior to their expiration date. Personal safety protection orders include but are not limited to a ban on harassment by the abuser and contact with the applicant. Violation of the restraining order will be penalized according to the level of severity, from a fine of 1,000 yuan to fifteen days of imprisonment. This new law demands that criminal charges follow criminal conviction according to the Chinese Criminal Law (see Chapter 3 for details).

The Anti-Domestic Violence Law also stipulates a compulsory responsibility to report on domestic violence upon discovery or suspicion by staff members, organizations, and institutions such as schools, aid offices, and residential committees. If severe consequences occur as a result of non-reporting, members who are in charge of those institutions will be penalized.

On the one hand, the law represents a legal step forward in the issue of intimate partner violence. On the other hand, the country's only NGO that specialized in domestic violence—the Anti-Domestic Partner Violence Network (ADVN)/Beijing Fanbao—was forced to end their fourteen years of work and was dissolved on May 18, 2014[4] (see Chapter 6). On January 28, 2016, the first nonprofit legal aid organization in China—Beijing Zhongze Women's Legal Aid Organization (the former Beijing University Law School Women's Legal Research and Service Center) that worked for women victims of intimate partner violence—was also forced to close down by the Chinese government, citing its foreign sponsorship as the reason for such an action (see Chapter 6). The underlying contradiction makes one wonder if part of the reason that the government co-opted the movement to put forth this Anti-Domestic Violence Law was to appease the activist coalition before breaking it up. As shown, the only two nongovernment organizations that offered services to women victims of intimate partner violence in China were closed. The relationships between the criminal justice system and intimate partner violence after the legislation of the 2015 Anti-Domestic Violence Law will be explored in Chapter 3.

Conclusion

This chapter chronicles the ways in which intimate partner violence against women has been viewed, dealt with, and responded to in different historical eras under different political regimes in China.

Prior to 1911, although violence was generally disapproved by the Chinese Confucian classics in its teaching of harmony and personal self-restraint, husbands' violence against wives was, however, accepted and widely practiced. This was due to the inferior and subordinate status ascribed to women during this time. The criminal code recognized the absolute right and power of the husband and the parents to discipline, beat, abuse, and/or kill their wives and daughters.

It was not until 1911, during the Republican era, that violence against wives was combated against as an embodiment of the backwardness and weakness of the nation. The liberation of women was perceived as equivalent to the liberation of the nation and the progress of the nation into modernity. The Republican era promulgated the first civil law in Chinese history that granted freedom of divorce to women with certain conditions and established women's inheritance rights.

The Communist era passed a watershed law—the 1950 Marriage Law. It rendered illegal a host of cultural practices such as the abuse of women, catapulting an unprecedented number of divorce cases in China, mostly filed by women on the basis of intimate partner violence. Post-socialist China continued the progress in the realm of law and ratified the Anti-Domestic Violence Law in 2015, outlawing different types of domestic violence as a whole. The newly passed Anti-Domestic

Violence Law included provisions on many levels: prevention, education, and rehabilitation of abusers.

From the point of view of the law, the political regimes of the Republican era, the Communist era, and the post-socialist era have increasingly made greater and greater strides in protecting women's rights and ensuring gender equality in stipulating it illegal for the husband to impose violence on the wife. However, as shown in this chapter, across all three historical periods, government officials, local officials, and law enforcement officials in the judicial system held deeply embedded patriarchal ideas of male dominance and favored men. Their inaction and male-biased deliberations led to the glaring discrepancy between the law and its practice, perpetuating and reinforcing the cultural practice of violence against women.

Underlying these stages of history is the bias in favor of men in court in the dismissal of the husband's violence against the wife, heavy penalties against women who defended themselves, light or no charges against abusive husbands, official negligence, and, at times, the mistreatment of women due to their divorce requests. During the Republican era, the court's favor of men demonstrates not only the deeply seated male-dominated cultural ethic, but also the political regime's priority to safeguard social mores by not granting divorce requests "except for those with impeccable evidence" (Qiao 1922). Indeed, a social terror was believed to be generated from women filing for divorce, as this era saw a backlash of public media that turned from promoting women's freedom of divorce to challenging and condemning the "new, liberated women" for the high divorce rate (Wei 1933; Li 1936).

In post-socialist China prior to the legislation of the 2015 Anti-Domestic Violence Law, even in the court that participated in China's national pilot program for protecting women against domestic violence, concern over violence was sidestepped and superseded by the compulsory requirement of mediation over adjudication for the courts (He and Ng 2013a; 2013b). Judicial mediation as an institutional procedure ended up reinforcing gender hierarchy, perpetuating patriarchal norms and values, and compromising and damaging the interests of the women (ibid.). The lack of legal protection convinced women that their lives were worthless, forcing them into a desperate and extreme form of resistance by killing their abusers, ultimately at the price of their own lives. A critical issue to be remembered is the powerful influence of Confucianism in empowering judges to disregard the law and favor their own judgment, which was heavily influenced by traditional patriarchal culture. This powerful cultural influence continues today even in contemporary Chinese culture, much to the detriment of justice to women.

The overview of the social and cultural history of intimate partner violence reveals to us that violence should not be understood as individual, private problems devoid of the political and social context in which it occurs. Rather, we should articulate the nature of the dynamics between women and the political state, which is "crucial to understanding how gender works, how change occurs" (Scott 1986: 1067). As shown in this chapter, women were used across the stages of history to advance the interests of the nation-state. Intellectuals during the

Republican era heralded women's liberation and freedom from abuse in order to propose and fulfil their political agenda of nation building. The Maoist era advocated women's liberation and freedom from abuse in order to tap into the vast resource of women as a group to accomplish the goal of socialist construction and the building of a socialist nation (Zheng 2009a; Zheng 2012). Post-socialist China upheld women's freedom from abuse yet preferred mediation to promote social stability.

Women victimized by intimate partner violence are subject to harm and damage to their physical and mental well-being that varies from injury to long-term health issues such as chronic pain, physical disability, drug abuse, depression, unintended pregnancy, STIs, and HIV/AIDS (see also Bryant-Davis 2010). With the lack of legal and social aid in China, women victims of intimate partner violence continue to be in a perilous situation, and this warrants social, political, and economic attention.

Chapter 2

WORTHY VERSUS UNWORTHY VICTIMS OF SEXUAL VIOLENCE IN POST-SOCIALIST CHINA

I have been with my boyfriend for more than two months. Even though we had occasionally shared a bed together, we had never had sex. He had asked for sex and I had steadfastly refused him. I didn't want to have sex with him because he had so many shortcomings that I wasn't sure if we would have a future together. A few days ago, we had a huge fight. I felt so depressed that I got drunk. He found me and took me to his apartment. He started undressing me. I told him to stop what he was doing and that I was having my period. He didn't stop. I tried very hard to push his knees away from me, but his knees didn't move. It was so painful that I kept yelling "No" and that he was hurting me. He continued pushing himself in despite my plea. I was in tremendous agony. I bled so much. He said he loves me, and this is how he loves me. I took emergency contraceptive pills the next day. I told him that when I needed comfort the most, he took advantage of me to satisfy his own desire. I told him that he's a scoundrel and that we're over … I feel so ashamed of myself. I feel my pride humiliated and my life destroyed. I hate him. I can't tell anyone about this. I feel that even if I find a man that I like in the future, I won't have the courage to be with him, as I'm not worthy of him. I don't deserve being loved, and I don't deserve being proud. Now I can't stop showering every day, as I feel that I can't rinse myself clean no matter what I do. Maybe I deserve this. Now I just want to end my life, as I feel so dirty. I want to die, and I want him to live in guilt all his life. I want to die. I am in such despair. I don't want to live any more.

Women like Xiao Hui related such stories of sexual violence to me. Sexual violence or sexual assault is defined by the World Health Organization as sexual acts or attempts via violence or coercion, directed against a person's sexuality, regardless of the relationship with the victim (World's Health Organization 2002: 149). It encompasses a wide range of acts from verbal harassment to forced penetration, including rape, unwanted sexual advances or sexual harassment, and sexual abuse. It is regarded as a serious public health and human rights problem with both short- and long-term consequences on women's physical, mental, sexual, and reproductive health (ibid.).

In China, although sexual harassment was included in the "Law to Protect Women's Rights" in 2005, it provided no legal definition of, or punishment for, the act, only stipulating the nature of sexual harassment as a civil affair rather than a criminal violation (An 2005). It was reported that in China, from 2010 to 2017, out of an estimated 50 million court cases, only thirty-four involved sexual harassment, and only two of these were initiated by the victims of sexual harassment (Richardson 2018). Both cases were rejected by the court due to insufficient evidence (ibid.).

In China, the archetypical definition of sexual violence is forced penetration of a victim through violence or intimidation. Such a definition does not apply to women who are in a relationship with their assailant. In the law on rape, there is no such thing as marital rape. This legal definition generally absolves intimate partners—boyfriends and husbands—from the crime of sexual violence. Based on interviews with victims of sexual violence and a survey of medical, popular, and legal discourses as well as legal cases, this chapter investigates the underlying reasons for the perceived division between worthy versus unworthy victims of sexual violence, and uncovers the cultural system of gender power hierarchy that creates injustice and inequity.

Medical and Popular Discourses

A survey of contemporary Chinese medical textbooks reveals that women's sexuality is depicted as passive and receptive, needing to be awakened by men. Men's sexuality is portrayed as the opposite of women's sexuality—passionate, uncontrollable, dominant, aggressive, with unruly biological urges (Li 2007). One Chinese medical textbook states that "men's sexual desire is much stronger than women's. Before marriage, some men may have experiences of masturbation, and almost all men have experiences of nocturnal emission … A man can become sexually aroused in only one or two minutes. Upon stimulation, men are biologically pressured to desire immediate sexual intercourse. Ejaculation occurs within minutes" (ibid.: 56). Regarding women's sexuality, the book continues,

> except for certain individuals, women do not experience sex drive or masturbation. After marriage, their sex drive is much weaker than men's, and their sexual reaction is much slower than men's. Women's sexual pleasure must be awakened by men's sexual stimulations such as kissing, hugging, and touching sexual organs … A large number of women do not experience any sexual pleasures at the beginning of marriage, and some never do for life. Women pursue emotional satisfaction much more than sexual pleasure (ibid.: 57)

These biological differences between men and women are the overarching themes in Chinese medical textbooks, which accentuate that women's low sex drive must be awakened by men (Zhang, Bayi 2018). While these textbooks argue that the differences between men and women are biological, most scientists would argue that the differences are largely cultural rather than biological. The attitude expressed by these textbooks reflect the traditional concept of yin and yang in Chinese culture, where yin represents femininity and passivity, and yang represents masculinity and activity. It is noteworthy how powerful this traditional culture remains in China. Patriarchal societies in general intend to socialize women to repress their sexual desires, with the understanding that this approach is tied to women's respectability and acceptability in society. China is no exception when it comes to this general principle.

This medical discourse portrays men as "biologically pressured" to have uncontrollable sexual urges and to desire immediate sexual intercourse upon stimulation. Women's slow sexual reaction and weak sex drive, however, indicate that their sexual desire and sexual pleasure are only derived from sexual experiences with men. In portraying sex as male action and female reception, medical discourse attributes dominance and aggression to male sexuality. It is considered the responsibility of men to take charge of sexual relationships with women and to awaken their sexual desires. Since women are expected to refuse sex due to biological and cultural reasons, men may consider physical persuasion or a certain amount of physical force to be acceptable, appropriate, or even a necessary precursor to awaken women's sexual desires and fulfil their own sexual pursuits.

In other words, the word "seduction" is important in explaining the male role. Seduction is a necessary part of a complete sexual fulfillment for both men and women. The assumption that men should sexually overpower women with physical force or persuasion blurs the line between coercion and consent. At the same time, due to men's "uncontrollable sexual urges," women are held responsible for men's sexual behaviors. They are advised to refrain from possibly stimulating men, including not staying in the same room with a man, not going to remote areas with a man, and not acting provocatively or seductively in front of a man (Qing 2019). As such, medical discourse makes women bear the brunt of sexual violence, while at the same time obscuring the line between coerced and consensual sex.

Unworthy versus Worthy Victims of Sexual Violence

Popular discourse perceives sexual coercion between intimate partners as a result of men's passion. Xiao Hui, whose story was narrated at the beginning of this chapter, told me that after she posted her story on Weibo (Chinese version of twitter), she was flooded by commentaries that chastised her for her tempting behaviors. She said,

> People told me that I should not have been in the same bed with him, because a normal man cannot resist such temptations. It's like putting a dumpling next to a dog. Flies do not bite an uncracked egg, they said. They comment that a normal man thinks with the lower part of his body and cannot resist temptations. They said I was cruelly torturing him when I was in bed with him but refused sex. In their words, I asked for it because I tempted him. They also said that it was all

a pretense on my part, as I must have achieved orgasm, to which I responded that I achieved nothing but agony and utter humiliation. They insisted that in a relationship, an unworthy woman may appear to be traditional, but deep in her heart, she always desires to do dirty things with her man. They also claimed that posting such a "vulgar" story does nothing but destroy your own reputation.

Implicit in this criticism is the distinction between a natural woman who is less sexually inclined and an unnatural woman who is highly sexual, and therefore unworthy.

As seen in these public commentaries, women like Xiao Hui are condemned as unworthy victims who are responsible for men's coercive sexual aggression because they allow themselves to be in the same bed with men, tempting men into sex. This cultural logic, rather than focusing on male violence, blames women by dividing women into two types: worthy victims who deserve justice versus unworthy, seductive women who contribute to their own downfall.

Worthy victims are defined as pure virgins who have never had sexual experiences and have no sexual knowledge. Their purity causes them to resist male aggression, even if it costs them their lives. Worthy victims also report the incident to the police immediately. Unworthy temptresses are embodied by their seductive wardrobe, salacious demeanor, loose sexual morality, and provocative conduct such as tantalizing and flirtatious interactions with men. In the case of Xiao Hui, she was compared to "a cracked egg" that invited flies to assault her. Because she was engaged in the seductive behavior of being in the same bed with her boyfriend, she was deemed an unworthy temptress, responsible for sexual coercion that she had invited upon herself.

Public responses to Xiao Hui's experience evince the popular perception that sexual coercion between intimate partners results from men's natural sexual desire, inflamed by women's temptations and secretly desired by unworthy women's deep psyche. Implicit in this cultural logic is that women like Xiao Hui secretly desire sex, but are culturally pressured to appear chaste. Therefore, they are perceived as obligated to verbally resist sex and conceal their deeply seated sexual desire. Unworthy women's verbal resistance is thus seen as nothing but a ruse to tempt men into sex, which is what their heart wants but are culturally forbidden to demonstrate. Such a cultural perception of blurred divisions between consensual and coercive sex fundamentally casts doubts on unworthy women's refusal to engage in sex.

Sexual Assault and Women's Responsibilities

Women are expected to regulate and control men's passions through their own behaviors. Indeed, popular discourse advises women to avoid behaviors that will subject them to sexual assault or rape. Sexual assault is thus reconfigured as women's individual responsibilities, in an effort to produce self-regulating, self-governing, and crime-avoiding female citizens. In 2015, the Public Security Ministry in He Nan Province published a document entitled "Eight Types of Women that Are the

Easiest Targets for Sexual Assault" (Public Security Ministry 2015). The document singles out "unworthy" victims who wear clothes that expose skin, flirt with men, drink and smoke, take advantage of men financially, seek professional advancement or promotion through an ambiguous relationship with their superior, worship celebrities, enjoy dating men on the internet, and engage in sex work.

This official document emphasizes that "most female victims of sexual assault have failed to protect themselves adequately. Women must remember that flies do not bite an uncracked egg. There is no free lunch in the world. No free pies will drop from the sky. Therefore, the best way a woman can prevent sexual assault is to have self-esteem, self-respect, self-improvement, and self-reliance" (ibid.). The document provides a detailed account of the ways in which behaviors of these "unworthy" victims lead to sexual assault. For instance, women who wear skimpy clothes can arouse men who are not strong-willed into committing a sexual assault. The underlying logic is that if a woman is sexually assaulted, she must be responsible for it.

This official document redefines sexual assault as the responsibility of these eight types of women, who are calculating and manipulative. It is these "unworthy" victims who are identified as being responsible for sexual assault by men. Informed by such official and popular discourse, it is not a surprise that women like Xiao Hui are publicly accused of engaging in immoral behaviors that invite sexual assault.

Women are advised in popular discourse to never be alone in a room with a man, never drink alcohol with a man, wear modest clothing, and act in a demure and proper way, and so on (Yi 2018). A lesson learned by many women is that sexual assault happens to women who are perceived as seductive. Xiao Chen, for instance, told me her story:

> One day in Junior High, I was forced by a boy to kiss him. I had always been a modest girl and was afraid to tell my mother about this. However, she learned about it later from the teacher. When she returned home, she went crazy. She scratched my face so hard that my skin cracked, and I bled a great deal. She then took out the scissors and cut almost all my hair. She cursed me, calling me debased and shameless for flirting with boys at such a young age. The next day, she forced me to wear ugly clothes to school. None of my classmates even recognized me.

Xiao Chen said that, at a young age, she learned that the reason she was harassed was because she dressed up too much and that it was her fault. When she was a freshman in college, she was sexually assaulted. She did not tell anyone due to this entrenched idea. She was afraid that her mother would cut her hair and scratch her face again. She said what hurt her the most was not the incident but her mother's response. Women like Xiao Chen told me that they kept silent about sexual assault to avoid being accused of being temptresses. They believe that talking about it can only ruin their reputation. As one woman told me, "if you are sexually assaulted, you must be at fault. If my colleagues and friends knew about the incident, the damage and distress would be a thousand times greater than the incident itself."

A victim of sexual assault, a female university student at Beijing University, Yan Gao, faced public defamation as a seductive temptress. She committed suicide at the age of twenty-one due to public slander related to the assault upon her (Zhang, Wu 2018). In her freshman year, nineteen-year-old Yan was given special care by Professor Shen, a married man who offered her free rides from school to her home every week. One day she was asked by Professor Shen to deliver her assignment to his house. Yan told her best friend that at his house, "he attacked me like a hungry wolf." Professor Shen stripped all her clothes and sexually assaulted her. He attributed his sexual assault to his love for her, and continued this behavior after the first incident. At the same time, however, Shen had sexual intercourse with another student, through whom he spread the rumor that it was Yan who had initiated sex with him, throwing herself into his arms and seducing him. This rumor quickly spread across campus, rendering the victim of assault a public target of malicious slander. Tortured by his sexual assaults and his defamation of her as a salacious woman, Yan committed suicide. After her suicide, Professor Shen announced that it proved nothing except his charm and charisma. During the investigations, Shen admitted kissing, hugging, and having had sex with Yan (Lu, Yijie 2018). Beijing University labeled his behavior "unethical in the teaching profession" (weifan shide) but gave him nothing more than a disciplinary warning as a member of the Communist Party (ibid.). Since Yan's suicide, Shen has been appointed a full professor, department chair, PhD advisor, and Distinguished Changjiang Professor by various key universities in China (ibid.).

As a victim of sexual assault, Yan was shamed and her reputation tainted. As shown in this incident, it was the victim who was enveloped by vicious gossip and slander, not the assailant. The destruction of their reputation serves as an effective weapon, silencing women. Although Yan never reported Shen's sexual assaults to the university, as a victim, she still faced a smear campaign against her reputation, causing her to take her own life at the age of twenty-one.

Victims of sexual assault are subject to not only defamation, but also structural, institutional, and legal obstacles. The recent #metoo movement in China, led by female university students, encountered insurmountable structural opposition (see Chapter 6).[1] In 2015, five female university students were arrested, detained, and jailed by the police for planning to disseminate stickers about sexual harassment on public transportation to commemorate International Women's Day in Beijing, Guangzhou, and Hangzhou (Wang, Zheng 2015). Despite the crackdown, this incident marked the first planned resistance against sexual harassment in China. In 2017, a former victim of sexual assault, Leilei Zhang, was forced by the police to move out of Guangzhou and cease carrying an anti-sexual-harassment sign in public, an activity that was emulated by two hundred women from various cities in China (Severdia 2017). Under pressure from the police, Zhang moved out of Guangzhou and posted an online note, publicly announcing her retreat from anti-sexual-harassment activities (ibid.).

Universities also tend to dismiss reports filed by female university students against sexual assaults by male professors. In 2017, four female students and one female professor in Sun Yat-Sen University reported sexual assault and sexual harassment by Professor Peng Zhang from 2011 to 2017, including unwanted kissing and touching. In one incident, his sexual assault on a freshman in a lab after 10:30pm was caught on the surveillance video, which was undeniable proof. However, despite the videotaped evidence, Zhang only received a disciplinary warning as a member of the Communist Party. My interviews with professors at the school in 2019 revealed that university leaders, at a campus-wide faculty meeting, dealt with the situation by reassuring the accused professor "not to feel any pressure and not to shoulder any burden about this accusation, as the school will take care of it." I was told that the accusations had no impact on his work or his status at the university, and that he continues working without any interruption.

Legal Cases

In Chinese Criminal Law, rape is defined as coerced sexual penetration against women's will, by the use of violence, force, and threat (National People's Congress 2017). The penalty for rape is three to ten years in prison (ibid.). This Criminal Law does not recognize marital rape, as "in marriage, both parties have the duty to copulate with each other and have a sexual relationship" (ibid.). The 2016 Anti-Domestic Violence Law only lists mental and physical violence by family members, leaving out sexual violence (National People's Congress Standing Committee 2016).

The following two legal cases are examples where husbands were found innocent after inflicting sexual violence on their wives (Li 1998). In the first case of a strained marital relationship, due to the wife's refusal of sex, the husband asked two male colleagues to help him tie his wife to bed, strip her clothes, and force intercourse with her. The wife reported it to the police right afterward. In the second case, after a divorce agreement was reached in the Civil Affairs Department Office, the husband forced his wife to engage in sex; she drank poison and committed suicide right afterward. Because the final divorce paper was not in hand in the second case and marriage was still intact in the first case, the husbands were found innocent (ibid.). It was reported that many wives went to the police with severe physical injuries caused by their husbands' sexual violence, only to be sent home because it was considered a private affair (Jia 2018).

Criminal regulations often dismiss sexual violence in intimate relationships and tend to identify rape as forced sexual penetration by a stranger on a woman through violence or intimidation. This is further justified when the woman fights back, having sustained physical injuries, and then reports it to the police immediately afterward. Rape charges can be considered credible and convictable only with medical proof of penetration such as a broken hymen, injuries resulting from violence that has been resisted by the victim, unambiguous relationships with the perpetrator, and immediate reporting after the incident. Failure to prove one of these conditions can result in unsuccessful rape charges (Chen 2015). Many reports of rape were disregarded and dismissed by the police simply because of the ambiguous relationships between the victim and the perpetrator (Lin 2012). In 2015, for instance, a senior college student reported to the police that she was raped by a professor at his home (Chen 2015). Although she filed a report right after the incident and the professor admitted having had sexual intercourse with her, her rape charge was still revoked by the police. The professor was found innocent due to her nonresistance, her ambiguous relationships with the professor, as well as her medical exam that showed an unbroken hymen (ibid.).

In some situations, only the choice of death over dishonor was sufficient evidence to prove rape. In one instance in 2016, a stay-at-home wife was raped by her neighbor despite her physical resistance (Qu 2016). She reported the incident to the police, but her account was revoked due to lack of evidence. The woman went home and committed suicide the next day. Only after her suicide did the police trust her rape charge and arrest the assailant (ibid.). As indicated in this case, rape charges are only successful when women can prove their resistance or honor through self-inflicted death. To the police, lack of injuries on a woman's body indicates that the incident is a consensual encounter. It shows that the woman has not resisted it with her life, otherwise she would have sustained injuries on her body. The true meaning of rape, to the police, is embodied by a woman's willingness to sacrifice her life to protect her chastity and honor.

The Chinese Supreme Court's Legal Directive indicated in 1984 that "some women have consensual intercourse with men, but blackmail them with rape charges when their relationships turn bad. This situation should be treated as women's 'half pushing and half acquiescing (bantui banjiu), not rape'" (Chinese Supreme Court 1984). Even though this Directive became defunct in 2013, it continues exerting a paramount influence on current legal practices in China.

This Directive pinpoints unworthy victims as cunning, immoral, and manipulative, and blurs the lines between consent and coercion. The phrase "half pushing and half acquiescing" is drawn from a Chinese classic love story titled *Romance of the Western Chamber* (Wang 1998). "Half pushing and half acquiescing" means that unworthy women pretend to refuse but in fact have already agreed to it. It captures the popular construction of women's role as always resisting sex but in fact secretly desiring it in their heart, rendering an unworthy woman's verbal refusal irrelevant, untrustworthy, and discreditable. An unworthy woman's resistance is perceived as dishonest and perfunctory, not representing her true sexual desire. This kind of woman desires sex, but understands that her culture expects her to be modest. Therefore, she pretends to resist sex as a virtuous woman would, as in "half pushing," though her heart yields to her secret desire for sex, as in "half acquiescing." In other words, she does not resist hard enough.

The cultural logic underlying this phrase indicates that this kind of woman will never initiate sex or admit the desire for sex; so it is a man's responsibility to fulfil her true wish and dismiss her performative refusals. The appropriation of this phrase in the law not only deems "unworthy women" untrustworthy and unreliable, but also blurs the line between consent and coercion. As such, this Directive from the Chinese Supreme Court requires judges to ignore objective evidence, the fact that the woman has been forcibly raped, in favor of the judge's subjective judgment as to whether or not she has adequately resisted. As shown in Chapter 6, China has 150,000 lawyers in total, which is about 1 lawyer for 10,000 people on average. Currently 90 percent of the lawyers work for only 10 percent of the population. It is not difficult to imagine the formidable financial, institutional, and social bulwark that the vulnerable populations of women have to face.

Informed by this Directive, police first investigate a woman's moral character, reputation, lifestyle, behavior and attitude before and after the incident, the place and time of the incident, whether she is a virgin, whether she knows the perpetrator, whether she has socialized with him prior to the rape, and whether she continues contact with him (Lv 2009). A woman is determined to be an unworthy victim if she appears seductive, manipulative, acts provocatively, has an ambiguous relationship with the man, socializes or flirts with him prior to the incident, continues contact with him after the incident, or willingly follows him into the hotel (Hou 2019). In these cases, despite evidence from her physical resistance, it is considered acquiesced sex and her rape charge is dismissed (Wei, Quan 2019).

While a woman's sexual reputation and sexual modesty are scrutinized to determine her moral character, a man's character is drawn from nonsexual issues, such as his family background, career, education, and relationships with his spouse and children (Li 2018). In a legal case in 2018, for instance, a woman reported being raped by a man (ibid.). In court, the man was determined to be moral and nonviolent because he was a state employee with an advanced degree and a good family background. He also had a close relationship with his wife and a "polite and graceful daughter" (ibid.). Despite the evidence of scratches on the woman's hands and under her neck, she was found to have socialized with the man prior to the incident and was judged to be flirtatious, seductive, and provocative. As a result, her account was ruled not credible and unreliable. The man was found innocent (ibid.).

Conclusion

As shown in this chapter, victims of sexual assault face institutional, cultural, structural, and legal impediments. Legal cases as well as medical, legal, and popular discourses obscure the boundary between coercion and consent and dichotomize unworthy versus worthy victims of sexual violence. Medical and popular discourse depicts men's sexuality as unruly biological urges that are implicated in violence and difficult to control. This is considered an extenuating circumstance in favor of the man's action. Women's sexuality, however, is portrayed as passive with a low sex drive. Women's sexual pleasure is perceived to be awakened by men through physical or verbal persuasion. Unworthy women are described as secretly desiring sex but understanding that they are culturally obligated to resist. The legal discourse of "half pushing and half acquiescing" deems an unworthy woman's verbal refusal perfunctory, dishonest, and discreditable. Therefore, men may perceive a certain level of physical force or physical persuasion to be acceptable or even necessary to awaken women's sexual desire and fulfil their deeply seated, true wish. This cultural logic redefines sexual assault as a result of women's responsibility, as women are expected to shoulder the dual responsibility for their own as well as their partners' sexual behaviors. As shown in legal cases, it is women's sexuality that is under harsh moral scrutiny, whereas men's nonsexual matters are assessed and evaluated.

As demonstrated in this chapter, worthy victims are identified as pure, chaste women who are willing to redeem their honor through sacrificing their lives against assailants, with whom they have never socialized and have never had any ambiguous relationships. Unworthy victims are immoral, seductive, and provocative temptresses who are blamed for having invited their own downfall. They are suspected for not having behaved responsibly, acting transgressively or provocatively, and having acquiesced to sex. The fact that they are not virgins prior to the sexual assault can also invalidate their accusations. If they have socialized with their partners intimately prior to the assault, it is their moral character and sexual modesty that are questioned, challenged, and blamed.

Women in my research who have experienced sexual coercion by their partners have chosen not to report it in court. In their minds, the damage and contamination to their bodies have already been done. Publicizing their names with a public sex scandal can only intensify and expand the damage to their lives. From Yan Gao's suicide to those malicious public commentaries to Xiao Hui's account of her boyfriend's rape, publicizing it can only invite condemnation and humiliation and ruin their social reputation. A tarnished reputation can only undermine and jeopardize their family relationships, future romantic relationships, and professional jobs. Such fear perpetuates and reinforces public silence and social tolerance on this issue.

Historian Sharon Block contends (2006: 240), "In a society built around the central pillar of marriage, sex was crucial to the appearance of social order. Sexual relations used wrongly could profoundly threaten the very social structures that they were meant to confirm." Sexual power is inextricably connected with political, economic, and cultural power. As shown in this chapter, legal institutions, police forces, medical doctors, and popular discourse form a formidable bulwark against a woman's ability to report sexual violence. These structural forces work together to draw the distinction between worthy versus unworthy victims, normalize the aberrant practice of sexual coercion, conflate uncontrollable sexual desires with coercive sex, and blur the boundaries between violent and consensual sexual practices. They embody a violent structural system of gender inequality and a politics of sexuality that polices and regulates women's bodies and sexuality.

Chapter 3

THE CRIMINAL JUSTICE SYSTEM AND INTIMATE PARTNER VIOLENCE

Hong, a 27-year-old bank clerk living in Shenzhen, has been in an intimate relationship with her boyfriend—23-year-old Shi, who works in an internet company in the same city. One night in the middle of February 2020, at Shi's apartment, a verbal conflict broke out when Hong pleaded with Shi to not go out to drink with his friends during the pandemic. Enraged, Shi slapped her face, strangled her, and continuously banged her head against the wall, threatening to kill her. Hong said that she felt her head was being torn from her body from the incessant banging onto the wall.[1]

The next morning, she managed to escape from his apartment and took a taxi to the police station. After she reported the case, the policeman at the station replied, "He has such a good job—what you are doing will destroy him, you know. You should consider the fact that he's a man." Hong then asked if she could call home. The policeman spit out the chewing gum from his mouth and asked, "Are you serious for such a tiny incident? Is there even a need to call someone?" Hearing his words, Hong rose and walked out of the police station.

After Hong returned to her home district, she went to the local police station to report her case. She was told that since the incident happened in a different district, there was nothing they could do. After Hong cried and reported how poorly she was treated at that police station, the police told her to go to the emergency department of a hospital specially designated to receive those who are injured in intimate partner violence.

Hong followed their advice and visited the hospital. After medical examinations and tests, a medical report was issued to her, stating that she suffered multiple injuries to her body, including temporary loss of vision in her left eye, which was swollen and bleeding, and bruises on both her legs.

Hong went back to the police station with the medical report and her written testimonies. The same policeman received her. He first commented on her written testimonies: "This is useless." Then he read the medical report that confirmed her injuries. He subsequently summoned her boyfriend Shi to the police station and started the mediating process.

Hong recorded the mediating process with her cell phone. Below are excerpts from the transcript of the audiotape:

Police [to Hong]:	He is even younger than you?
Hong:	He threatened to beat me to death.
Police:	You actually believed his words when he was drunk?! You actually were afraid?!
Hong:	[no response]
Police:	Early in your relationship, you realized that he was impulsive, yet you still continued to go with him? You waited until he beat you up before you thought of leaving? Why didn't you leave earlier?
Hong:	Even though we quarreled before, he didn't ... [interrupted]
Police:	When did the two of you quarrel?
Hong:	One evening ... [interrupted]
Police:	Did the two of you quarrel during these past two to three days?
Hong:	Yes, we did. The property manager ... [interrupted]
Police:	The two of you quarreled, yet you didn't think of leaving?
Hong:	At this point, the property manager came.
Police:	[raising his voice] If the two of you quarreled, how come you didn't think of leaving?
Hong:	I didn't realize that it could get so serious.
Police:	[raising his voice] Stop saying "I didn't realize." OK? At that time, what were you doing?
Hong:	I ... [interrupted]
Police:	How could you go to his place after knowing him for such a short period of time?
Hong:	He invited me to his place to eat. So I went, but afterward, I stayed for a few days.
Police:	When you were there, you never thought of leaving? You didn't leave just because he didn't want you to leave?
Hong:	I didn't think about it. I didn't ... [interrupted]
Police:	[raising his voice] Stop saying that you didn't think! You two are partners, even if you later break up, you two are still tied to each other, isn't that right? All you're trying to do is to destroy him, to kill him!
Hong:	All I want is to use the law to hold him accountable. If the law cannot protect me, who else can?
Police [to Shi]:	She didn't think this way before, but now she wants you dead.
Hong:	No, I don't. I just want to use the law to hold him accountable.
Police:	Yes, that's what I meant.
Hong:	He didn't beat only me. He beat his previous girlfriends too. I think it's important that he learns a lesson. Yes, I want to teach him a lesson.

Police: You mean that you want him detained, even imprisoned, right? Do you really want to go this far? Eh? Is this really necessary? [raising his voice] Are you sure this is really necessary? Eh? Are you listening? Let me ask you: Did he kill you? Did he mutilate you, right? Tell me what you want to do.
Hong: I don't want to destroy him.
Police: But what you're asking will destroy him!
Hong: He did this, so he should be held responsible.[2]

Throughout the mediating process, Hong was harshly interrogated and interrupted, making it difficult for her to even utter a complete sentence. Hong said, "I was scolded and berated by the police," who held her responsible for the violence inflicted upon her. Feeling helpless, Hong decided to post her experience online, which in turn sparked a social uproar. Hong said that, under media pressure, the Shenzhen Public Security Bureau later posted online that her boyfriend Shi had been detained for five days and fined 200RMB ($33). They added that the police mediator would receive an additional training to deal with intimate partner violence (Wang, Xiaoyi 2020).

This chapter contextualizes the ways in which the Chinese criminal justice system deals with intimate partner violence within the state discourse of family harmony and state stability. Based on interviews with victims of intimate partner violence, police, lawyers, and court judges in China, this chapter examines progress as well as issues and problems implicit in the current criminal justice system when handling intimate partner violence cases. An exploration of women's experiences and the ways in which the 2016 Anti-Domestic Violence Law has been implemented reveals the legal challenges as well as difficulties that victims face in order to win court cases involving intimate partner violence. In a nutshell, this chapter provides an overview of the legal structure that shapes women's experiences of court cases involving intimate partner violence.

Family Harmony and State Stability in the State Discourse

Since 2015, in numerous political addresses, President Xi Jinping has consistently emphasized the pivotal role of family harmony in maintaining state stability, social harmony, and the progress of the Chinese nation (Chen, Zhenkai 2020; Qu 2020; Zhan 2020). In his multiple public addresses, he has discussed the paramount importance of family harmony as a formidable bulwark to combat nationwide rampant corruption and social instability (ibid.). To quote his words, "With family harmony comes social stability. With family harmony comes social harmony. History and reality tell us that the fate of family is inexorably linked with the fate of our nation and state."

Confucius would agree with Xi on this point. He considered loyalty to the family even more important than loyalty to the Emperor, and an important building block in maintaining harmony within the state. Xi rationalized that family is a microcosm of society and the state:

> Family is the smallest state. The state is tens of thousands of families. Chinese culture has historically respected the ideology of the "commensurability of family and state." We need to connect the fate of "small family" with the fate of "big family." Only when the "cell" of family is good [harmonious], can society be good [harmonious], can the state be good [harmonious], and can our nation be good [harmonious]. When the family is bad [not harmonious], society is damaged, corruption is rampant, and our children and grandchildren are destroyed. (Yang 2018)

In the excerpt above, Xi Jinping evoked the Chinese ideology of "family-state" in ancient times, when family, clan, and country shared a common structural feature based on blood relationships—"commensurability of family and state" (jiaguo tonggou). Since the Communist Party established the People's Republic of China in 1949, this ideology was elevated into one "family-state" (jiaguo yiti), signifying the integration of family and state. In his speech above, Xi explained the inextricable link between "small family" and "big family," emphasizing that the state is a big family. This big family, of course, is led by the Communist Party. Its stability, legitimacy, and fate, according to Xi, hinged upon family harmony.

To ensure family-state harmony, in his multiple public addresses, Xi specifically called upon women to play their primary role in producing family harmony through educating the next generation and supporting the elderly. The following is an excerpt from one of his talks:

> We need to let women play their primary and distinctive role in family and social life. More specifically, we should let women play their role in developing Chinese family virtues and family harmony. Chinese people have always praised dutiful wives and virtuous mothers [xianqi liangmu], who not only take care of their husbands in daily life, but also educate and raise kids [xiangfu jiaozi], manage the household industriously and diligently [qinjian chijia], and assist their husbands in their careers. This is a significant component of the Chinese superior traditional culture. We need to emphasize the significant role women play in family and society because it is critical to family harmony, social harmony, and the well-being of the next generation. (Chen, Zhenkai 2020)

In singling out women's crucial and "distinctive" role simply because of their gender, Xi's public addresses made women bear the brunt of maintaining family harmony, social harmony, and state stability, failure of which would hold the women irresponsible. In his speeches, Xi frequently invoked the "superior Chinese culture" that emphasizes women's function as "dutiful wives and virtuous mothers" (xianqi liangmu) who "not only take care of their husbands in daily life, but also educate and raise kids (xiangfu jiaozi), manage the household industriously and diligently, and assist their husbands in their careers (qinjian chijia)." In his other talks, Xi also declared women's paramount responsibility in "promoting nationalist sentiments among family members," and "developing family harmony, neighborly solidarity, well-being of the next generation, and support of the elderly" (Chen, Zhenkai 2020). Xi emphasized that "women of the new era should take up their responsibilities for society and family" (ibid.). His public addresses to the country reinforced the gender-specific role of women and held women, not men, responsible for promoting social stability, state legitimacy, and the progress of the nation.

It is ironic that the current leader of the Communist Party has returned to the Confucian point of view about family and the state. Mao Zedong and the Communist Party during its most revolutionary phase rejected Confucianism as a return to feudalism and insisted that women held up half of the sky and should be equal to men. While this may have been more rhetoric than reality, Mao Zedong would never have made a statement implicitly praising Confucianism and arguing for an inferior status for women.

Led by this ideological tenet of women's responsibility in maintaining family harmony to ensure political stability, institutions such as the Public Security Bureau and courts tend to practice informal mediation as the primary resolution for cases of intimate partner violence at the expense of women's suffering, as shown in the vignette at the beginning of this chapter. A court judge said to me in an interview, "Family is the cell of society. The more harmonious a family is, the more stable society is. Our goal is to safeguard and restore family stability through mediation as an important method to resolve family conflicts."

Indeed, court judges and government workers were lauded for preserving family harmony and saving couples from divorce requests involving intimate partner violence. In 2017, a woman named Dong Fang in Chengdu was beaten by her husband so severely that she lost hearing in her left ear and became deaf (Rui 2020). After successfully acquiring a Personal Protection Order from the court, she sued for a divorce in court, but was rejected. Judge Zhang Yanbin said, "This kind of physical conflict between couples is not domestic violence" (ibid.). He was praised for following the Chinese popular idiom: "Rather demolish ten temples than destroy one marriage" (ningchaibaizuomiao, buhuiyizhuanghun), which underscores that destroying a marriage is worse than dismantling ten temples.

In 2016, when a wife in Hangzhou sued for divorce in a court due to her husband's physical abuse, the judge was exalted for spending three hours mediating between them and successfully "moving the husband with his sincerity" (Yi 2016). The abuser was reported to have "accept[ed] his [the judge's] advice and promised to modify his behavior and not to beat his wife anymore" (ibid.). In 2017, a woman in Guangxi sued for a divorce because her abusive husband not only beat her over a long period of time, but also threatened her life by putting a knife to her neck in front of their child (Xi 2017). The court judge rejected her case and was praised for "having saved a marriage" (ibid.). The judge contended that physical abuse had to meet the yardstick of both frequency and long-term to be defined as domestic violence. The judge ascertained that this case only met the long-term criterion, but not the frequency requirement. In 2017, when a woman in Nanning sued for a divorce in court due to her husband's numerous physical beatings, the judge denied her request, which was broadcast and applauded across the country as "an accomplishment of the court" (Wang 2017). News reports extolled the court for delivering "a prescription for marital happiness," which advised the couple to maintain "a cool head" during conflicts, not to "leap to discussions of divorce."

News reports also recommended that couples utilize communications, self-reflection, joint outings, and mutual recollections of happy times in the past to alleviate the tensions between them (ibid.).

As shown, following President Xi's political addresses that underscored the inextricable links between family harmony and state stability and women's responsibility in ensuring family harmony, court judges and government workers uphold this principle in their daily practices that deem women's sacrifices as a virtue and make women bear the brunt of protecting and safeguarding family harmony at the expense of their well-being and health. Led by this principle, saving marriages to preserve family harmony has become the ultimate goal for government agencies such as the court and the Public Security Bureau.

To accomplish this goal, mediation rather than conviction for justice has been the key method in handling cases related to intimate partner violence. In 2016, a government worker Xiong Ling at the Wuchang marriage registration office was applauded and awarded with the "Gold Medal of Matchmaker" on national TV and was covered in newspapers for "saving more than 500 marriages" through utilizing lies such as her printer broke down or the internet stopped working to send back couples who came for a divorce certificate (Ru 2016). Xiong said on the TV news, "The first character in the word 'marriage' contains 11 stokes and the second 9, symbolizing a forever lifetime (yishengyishi, tianchangdijiu) [these two numbers share the same pronunciation as the Chinese character "forever"]. Rather demolish ten temples than destroy one marriage (ningchaibaizuomiao, buhuiyizhuanghun)." As shown, this same idiom was invoked by Xiong as well as other government workers to safeguard family harmony as the cornerstone of social harmony, despite their dereliction of duties. According to the Chinese Marriage Law, government workers at marriage registration offices should register and issue a divorce certificate to couples who are willing to divorce and have agreed upon terms (Civil Affairs Department 2003). Xiong, however, neglected this duty by lying to the couples.

A new "People's Republic of China Civil Law" that requires a "30-day divorce cooling period" was implemented on January 1, 2021, to reduce the accelerating divorce rate in China since 2003 (Chen, Liyan 2020). It was reported that in 2019, the Chinese divorce rate was 3.3 out of 1,000 couples, higher than the US divorce rate of 2.9 out of 1,000 couples (Tang 2021). This rising nationwide divorce rate was considered "a signifier of social instability" that could lead to "even greater social instability" (Zhao, Jiandong 2019). To deter couples from divorce, "a 30-day divorce cooling-off period" and more procedures were included in the People's Republic of China Civil Law on May 28, 2020 in the Third Session of the 13th National People's Congress (Rui 2020).

The Chinese Marriage Law stipulates two routes to divorce. The first one is to receive a divorce certificate at a marriage registration office when the couple agrees on the divorce as well as the terms of the divorce. The second one is to sue for a divorce in court if one party refuses to divorce. The newly implemented People's Republic of China Civil Law added more procedures to these two routes to prolong the process and discourage couples from seeking a divorce, including the added procedures of application, handling, cooling-off period, investigation, and registration of divorce. After a couple meet at the marriage registration office for a divorce, they are required to go back home and wait for thirty more days before coming back to the same office again to apply for a divorce. If they fail to meet again at the office at the end of the thirty-day period, their absence is regarded as a withdrawal of their case. Some scholars argue that the added delay could potentially provide time for one party to transfer personal bank accounts elsewhere, leaving the vulnerable party nothing (ibid.).

This state discourse on harmony reveals the state's anxiety and concern about social polarization and class conflict as a result of the unevenly developed market economy. Utilizing the discourse on harmony is a way to reassert the state legitimacy and appease potential social uprisings. The emphasis on women's responsibility to ensure family harmony and resolve political stability encourages women to endure domestic violence and stay with their abusers in order to maintain family harmony and preserve family unity. As shown below, the harmony discourse prompts various state institutions such as the police and the All China Women's Federation[3] to prioritize mediation as the paramount strategy to resolve intimate partner violence.

Anti-Domestic Violence Law, Chinese Criminal Law of Abuse, and Chinese Criminal Law of Intentional Harm for Strangers

While the 2016 Anti-Domestic Violence Law is a civil law for misdemeanor assaults, the Chinese Criminal Law Regarding Abuse of Family Members, in Clause 1 of Article 260 of the Chinese Criminal Law (2020), is applied to "severe" abuse perpetrated by a family member, including "beating, freezing, starving, torturing, mutilating, refusing medical treatments, and forbidding mobility." The Chinese Criminal Law of Abuse stipulates that "only severe abuse constitute a crime. General abuses in light cases such as beating and cursing once or twice, occasional starving, occasional mobility-forbidding do not constitute a crime." The Criminal Law of Abuse (2020) further identifies four criteria to warrant a crime: duration, frequency, means, and consequence. The Criminal Law of Abuse states the following: First, short-term abuse is not considered a crime. Long-term abuse with a duration ranging from months to years is a crime. Second, a frequency of beating a wife ten times a month after she has just given birth to a child is a crime. Third, slapping the face and pulling them by their ear are not a crime. Using a burning hot iron-rod to burn a wife's vagina and breasts is a crime. Fourth, causing death, paralysis, bodily mutilation, such as the loss of limbs, and abetment to suicide are a crime.

The Chinese Criminal Law of Abuse stipulates that the penalty for "severe" abuse of family members, such as body mutilation as noted above, is "less than 2 years of imprisonment or detention (of 1 to 6 months), or restriction of mobility" (Chinese Criminal Law 2020). The penalty for causing death of family members is two to seven years of imprisonment (ibid.).

Much heavier sentences apply to cases where a stranger, not a family member, inflicts "intentional physical harm" on other strangers. The 234th stipulation in the Chinese Criminal Law states that causing physical harm to others constitutes the Crime of Intentional Harm (Chinese Criminal Law 2020). In defining the Crime of Intentional Harm, the Chinese Criminal Law stipulates that this crime "does not apply to general punching, kicking, beating, pushing, and pulling that does not cause physical harm" (ibid.). The Crime of Intentional Harm states that physical harm is required to meet the degree that "is more severe than light injuries." That is to say, the physical harm must induce "heavy" and "light injuries," defined in the section below, in order for it to be considered a crime (ibid.).

The 95th stipulation of the Chinese Criminal Law (2020) states that "heavy injuries" refer to bodily mutilation, paralysis, loss of hearing, loss of vision, loss of body organs, and life-endangering injuries. "Light injuries," according to the Chinese Criteria for Assessing the Extent of Bodily Injuries (2014), include scalp laceration of more than 40 cm, skull fracture, broken ribs, facial laceration of more than 6 cm, hearing impediment, burning over 20 percent of the body, spine fracture, ruptures of stomach, or gallbladder, or spleen, hip fracture, and penetrating injuries to the eyeballs.

In further explaining "light injuries," the Crime of Intentional Harm in the Chinese Criminal Law stipulates that "if an actor intends to cause light injuries but fails to cause light injuries, it does not constitute a crime" (Chinese Criminal Law 2020). This suggests that someone bullying another person for whatever reasons is acceptable so long as it does not produce severe damages such as broken bones.

The 234th stipulation in the Chinese Criminal Law states that the penalty for committing the Crime of Intentional Harm is less than three years of imprisonment. The penalty for causing "heavy injuries" such as bodily mutilation and paralysis is three to ten years of imprisonment. The penalty for causing death or using cruel means to cause severe paralysis is over ten years of imprisonment, or a lifetime sentence, or a death sentence (Chinese Criminal Law 2020).

"Minor injuries," defined as injuries such as broken bones, fall under the purview of the civil law rather than the criminal law. The Anti-Domestic Violence Law, as a civil law, states that causing "minor injuries" will be punished by imposing a fine or an administrative detainment of less than fifteen days. "Minor injuries," according to the Chinese Criteria for Assessing the Extent of Bodily Injuries (2014), include miscarriage, eye socket fracture, rib fracture, scalp laceration of more than 10 cm, facial burning area of more than 20 cm, body burning area of more than 40 cm, traumatic perforation of the tympanic, finger or wrist fracture, nose fracture, and foot fracture.

It is worth noting that "minor injuries" listed in the Chinese Criteria for Assessing the Extent of Bodily Injuries can induce severe harm to victims. However, as noted in the Chinese Criminal Law of Abuse, unless abusers commit long-term violence resulting in extreme injuries such as bodily mutilation, it is hard to impose criminal charges on them.

It is stipulated in the Anti-Domestic Violence Law that unless victims initiate the pursuit of administrative detention, detention cannot be implemented by the police. However, as shown in the vignette at the beginning of the chapter, even when the victim actively demanded administrative detention of the abuser, the police still ignored her request and forced her into mediation without holding the abuser accountable. Indeed, in failing to criminalize intimate partner violence, the Anti-Domestic Violence Law accords the police full discretion to utilize what they perceive as the appropriate means to respond to victims' calls for help.

As shown in the Chinese Criminal Law, causing the death of a family member leads to two to seven years of imprisonment. The punishment for causing "heavy injuries" such as bodily mutilation of a family member is less than two years of imprisonment, detention (of one to six months), or restriction of mobility. However, the punishment for causing a stranger's death is over ten years of imprisonment, or a lifetime sentence, or even a death sentence. Causing "heavy injuries" such as bodily mutilation of a stranger leads to three to ten years of imprisonment. Causing "minor injuries" of a family member that include broken bones is punished with civil measures such as a fine or an administrative detention of less than fifteen days. Due to this inequity in the law that applies much more severe sentences in cases involving strangers than cases involving family members, as we will see later in this chapter, light sentences between six months to six years were given to abusers who had brutally beaten their wives to death, but heavy sentences ranging between more than ten years in prison and a death sentence were given to wives who had killed their abusers in self-defense. The gender inequity implicit in this legal structure fails to provide victims with the necessary legal recourse to rectify the violence and seek justice. It also violates the Chinese Constitution that guarantees equal protection under the law.

Written Warning Notes and the Personal Safety Protection Order

The Anti-Domestic Violence Law was applauded by scholars in China for introducing new intervention procedures such as Written Warning Notes to educate and reprimand abusers, Personal Safety Protection Orders to safeguard victims, which was effective for fifteen days with a maximal period of six months, and a mandate of "compulsory reporting" of cases by institutions such as schools, hospitals, and residential committees (Li 2020). Written Warning Notes and Personal Safety Protection Orders represent two monumental accomplishments achieved through two decades of efforts by women's nongovernment organizations since the Beijing 1995 World Women's Conference. The 20th stipulation of the Anti-Domestic Violence Law states that "People's Court can recognize a legal case as domestic violence from the police record, Written Warning Notes, Personal Safety Protection Orders, and medical reports of injuries" (Anti-Domestic Violence Law 2015). This stipulation demonstrates that both Written Warning Notes and Personal Safety Protection Orders can be utilized in court as legal evidence to prove intimate partner violence in both civil affairs and criminal affairs (Wei 2017).

The 3rd stipulation in the Anti-Domestic Violence Law states, "In compliance with the Chinese characteristics, to safeguard family harmony, this system of the Written Warning Notes and Personal Safety Protection Orders represents a transitional measure from education and mediation to administrative punishment" (Anti-Domestic Violence Law 2015). The goal of this system, as emphasized, is to "prevent violence," through giving the perpetrator education, criticism, and a warning (ibid.). It is also stipulated that this system does not carry any legal force or produce any legal outcome (ibid.). Because they are civil measures intended to deter intimate partner violence, they impose no criminal penalties on the abusers who violate the Written Warning Notes or the Personal Safety Protection Orders (Jiang 2016). Hence, these two measures are insufficient to stop intimate partner violence.

Written Warning Notes

It was reported in 2017 that only 77 cases (0.85 percent) were issued the Written Warning Notes by the police, among the 8,989 nationwide victims who called the police seeking help against the violence (Wei 2017). The 16th stipulation of the Anti-Domestic Violence Law states, "In light cases of domestic violence that do not warrant the detainment penalty, the Public Security Bureau educates and criticizes [the perpetrator], or issues a Written Warning Note" (Anti-Domestic Violence Law 2015). As per this stipulation, oral criticisms and education should come first and foremost. A Written Warning Note is the last option, but is not the responsibility of the Public Security Bureau.

Hua, a woman that I interviewed in 2018, told me that her multiple calls to the police about her husband's violence had never resulted in a police-issued Written Warning note, but only in mediation. She said to me:

> I've studied the Anti-Domestic Violence Law and learned about the Written Warning Note, since I've been suffering long-term violence by my husband. The last time when I called and the police mediated again, I asked him directly, "Why don't you issue the Written Warning Note?" I didn't expect that my question would enrage him. He became really angry: "Are you my supervisor directing me on how I should do my job?" I was intimidated by his anger and didn't say anything afterward.

While Hua ceased her demand for the Written Warning Note due to her fear of the policeman's rage, another woman Xiao Jun told me in 2018 that she had to fight for the police to issue a Written Warning Note for her husband's violent behavior. Her husband was a supervisor at a company with an advanced degree. Xiao Jun told me that her husband beat her so severely that she was sent to the hospital emergency room. However, after her neighbors called the police, the latter chose mediation to reduce their workload and did not consider it their responsibility to issue a Written Warning note, despite the fact that the latter can constitute legal evidence in future court proceedings. The policeman's choice of mediation is in compliance with the 16th stipulation of the Anti-Domestic Violence Law, which states that a Written Warning note is an option that can be used after exploring mediation that consists of criticism and education of the perpetrator. It took Xiao Jun's threat to sue him in court to finally compel him to issue the Written Warning Note.

Once the Written Warning Note is issued by the police, it is copied and sent to victims, abusers, residential committees, All China Women's Federation, and police stations, which will be recognized as evidence in legal cases involved with intimate partner violence (Anti-Domestic Violence Law 2015). The 17th stipulation of the Anti-Domestic Violence Law states that the residential committee and Public Security Bureau are obligated to engage in follow-up measures including visiting victims and supervising abusers, in order to ensure that violence is no longer perpetrated. However, this kind of partner participation and involvement of the agencies is often not implemented in practice (Xue 2016). Xiao Jun told me that neither of these agencies visited her for a follow-up check.

In 2019, a woman named Dong was beaten to death by her husband Wei in Nanjing, demonstrating the useless function of the Written Warning Notes (Mei 2020). In 2018, Dong sued in court for a divorce due to her husband's long-term violence, but her request was rejected by the court. Afterward, she called the police six times seeking help against her husband's persistent violence. Two times out of six, her husband was summoned to the police station and was issued the Written Warning Notes. However, those two Warning Notes were far from enough to stop his violence. In June 2019, he beat Dong causing a concussion and bone fractures. In September 2019, he beat Dong to death, and also beat her mother unconscious (ibid.).

The Anti-Domestic Violence Law fails to specify the kinds of consequences resulting from violations of these stipulations. Nor does it specify how the police should get involved or the due process of police intervention. In practice, as shown in the vignette at the beginning of this chapter, the Anti-Domestic Violence Law is not implemented in a way that holds abusers accountable and ensures protection of victims. The underlying reasons include the law's ambiguous wordings, police's ignorance of the law, the lack of legal consequences of the failure to implement the law, as well as the entrenched structural gender inequality.

The Anti-Domestic Violence Law is vague in its stipulations about the Written Warning Notes that police are supposed to issue to abusers. Indeed, the Anti-Domestic Violence Law provides no detailed information on the layout, style, and content of the Warning Notes. Nor does it stipulate legal consequences for the abusers who continue the abuse after being issued the Written Warning Notes by the police (Liu, Yongting 2019). Without stipulating that Written Warning Notes should include abuser's identity, a statement of the violence committed, or the kinds of legal consequences upon violation of the warning, the Anti-Domestic Violence Law leaves Written Warning Notes as a mere gentle intervention without any real punishment.

Many police are ignorant of the Anti-Domestic Violence Law. In 2019, during an Anti-Domestic Violence Law training at the Hunan Police College, out of

167 police directors from different police stations in Hunan Province, less than 10 percent had even heard about the Anti-Domestic Violence Law. This 10 percent knew about the law not from their police training, but from the internet and news (Nan 2019). As a result, over 90 percent of the police had no knowledge about the content of the law, the Written Warning Note that they should issue to abusers, or the Personal Safety Protection Order issued by the court.[4] This lack of knowledge robbed victims of the opportunity to receive a copy of the Written Warning Note, which could later be used as an important piece of evidence to prove the violence in court. It also left abusers at large, allowing them to later violate the Personal Safety Protection Order issued by the court.

Though the 32nd stipulation of the Anti-Domestic Violence Law dictates that, in domestic violence cases, police should assist the court in the application and implementation of Personal Safety Protection Orders for victims, in practice, police mediation, rather than assistance, is practiced, as shown in the vignette at the beginning of this chapter (Wu 2020).

Personal Safety Protection Order

The Supreme Court announced that from 2013 to 2018, a total of 2,154 Personal Safety Protection Orders were issued nationwide, which means that less than 1 Personal Safety Protection Order was issued by each court out of more than 3,000 courts in China (Hu 2018). In Shanghai, for instance, with a population of 24 million people, less than 40 Personal Safety Protection Orders were issued annually, while the police received about 7,700 calls annually for emergency help with intimate partner violence (Feng 2020a). As mentioned above, both Written Warning Notes and Personal Safety Protection Orders are civil strategies meant to deter intimate partner violence, violation of both poses no criminal penalties, but criticisms or, in more severe cases, less than a 1,000RMB ($142) fine (a fine of 500RMB/$71 is more common), or less than fifteen days of administrative detention (Anti-Domestic Violence Law 2015). The Anti-Domestic Violence Law also stipulates that it is the court, not the police, that is responsible for the enforcement of the law. However, the law fails to specify the kind of implementation in practice and the role of the police in assisting the court in the implementation.

In practice, violation of the Personal Safety Protection Order often cost abusers a fine of around 500RMB ($71) or an administrative detainment of around seven days. In 2016, Ye, in Zhejiang Province, applied for the Protection Order as well as a divorce due to the long-term violence inflicted by her husband (Long 2016). The court issued her the Personal Safety Protection Order, but denied her divorce request. Several months later, she went back to the court reapplying for a divorce due to her husband's violation of the Protection Order with continued physical assaults, threats, and harassment. She was issued the Protection Order the second time. After the second Protection Order, her husband persisted with his harassment and threats. Ye appealed to the court for help. After investigations, the court confirmed his incessant violations of the Protection Order and fined him 500RMB ($71), a small amount of money considering the extent of violence inflicted upon her (ibid.).

In another case, in 2017, Jiang received a Personal Safety Protection Order due to her husband's long-term violence that induced light injuries, which, as we have seen in its definition earlier in this chapter, are far from light (e.g., scalp laceration of more than 40 cm, skull fracture, broken ribs, facial laceration of more than 6 cm, hearing impediment, burning over 20 percent of the body, spine fracture, ruptures of stomach, or gallbladder, or spleen, hip fracture, and penetrating injuries to the eyeballs) (Wei, Meng 2019). The order did not stop his violence. In 2019, in Zhuhai City, her husband chased her around the house with a cleaver. With the help of the landlord, Jiang, who was pregnant, jumped out of the window and called the police. Two months later, Yan received the second Protection Order that banned him from abusing, threatening, harassing, or tracking Jiang. However, the second order also did not stop his violence. Even after the issuance of the second order, he continued assaulting her. She called the police the first time he violated the order. Upon the police's arrival, he was criticized and expressed his remorse. The second time he violated the order, assaulting her in public, he was stopped by passersby. Despite the issuance of the order, Yan continued assaulting and harassing her, for which he was criticized the first time and then administratively detained for seven days the second time (ibid.).

Persistent violations of the Personal Safety Protection Order in these cases demonstrate that the courts lack the resources to adequately enforce the law and curb intimate partner violence. Indeed, after the promulgation of the law, legal experts in China, recognizing the inadequacy of the court's enforcement of the law, suggested that the police be responsible for the legal implementation (Liu 2020).

A woman Xiao Chen, whom I interviewed in my research, said to me, "What's the point of getting the Personal Safety Protection Order? Even if I get it, I still won't be protected by the police. He's going to beat me more." My research suggested that women like Xiao Chen harbored a tremendous amount of fear and were afraid that pursuit of the Personal Safety Protection Order would invite retribution from their husbands. Others who did apply and get the Protection Order told me that they received more beatings and even death threats after their husbands were released from the seven-day detainment or fined for their continuous violations of the Protection Order. Mei, for instance, after she hired a lawyer who helped her get the Protection Order, received threats from her husband to kill her or her child. Mei felt helpless without the assistance of the police. She said:

> I consulted with my lawyer, who told me that the court deals with violations of the Personal Safety Protection Order. I was told that he [her husband] will be given a fine or an administrative detainment of a week for the violation. The problem, though, is that he'll likely kill me or our child after he pays the fine or is released in a week. I worry about the safety of our child, so there's really nothing I can do but to go back to him.

Mei eventually made the painful decision to return to her abusive husband for the safety of their child. Another woman, Hui, who was pregnant was able to receive the Protection Order, but was ordered by the court to move out of her husband's apartment since the ownership of the apartment was under her husband's name. Hui said to me:

> I was about to give birth in a couple of months, but the court ordered me to move out. I didn't have a job and wasn't financially independent. So I had to move to my parents' apartment.

Even though Hui did receive the Protection Order, the court disregarded her financial situation and ordered her to move out of the apartment, which was in direct violation of the Anti-Domestic Violence Law that maintained that victims should be allowed to stay at their current residence (Anti-Domestic Violence Law 2015).

Since the Anti-Domestic Violence Law fails to define intimate partner violence as a crime unless it causes heavy injuries such as mutilation and paralysis, as a civil offence, domestic violence is not a crime, and therefore does not deter future violence.

As mentioned above, according to the Supreme court, from 2013 to 2018, a total of 2,154 Personal Safety Protection Orders were issued nationwide, which means that less than 1 Personal Safety Protection Order was issued by each court out of more than 3,000 courts in China (Hu 2018). A document promulgated by China's People's Court system maintained that courts should apply strict criteria to the eligibility of Personal Safety Protection Orders because it "directly interferes with family relationships" (Chu, Lun 2016). The document cited a legal case in Chongqing where a wife applied for the Protection Order after a "physical conflict" with her husband, but the court rejected her request. The document states:

> Issuing Personal Safety Protection Orders should have strict criteria. This legal care for victims should not become a means for legally spoiling victims [ni'ai]. Personal Safety Protection Orders are not meant to install a barricade against family relationships ... After all, Personal Safety Protection Orders are issued by the [authoritarian and powerful] court, which can be difficult for ordinary people [the abusers] to accept [This suggests the historically deep antipathy toward women in the Chinese society]. [Applying for and being issued Personal Safety Protection Orders] will eventually affect family relationships, building a formidable gulf between family members, which is by no means the original intent of the system of Personal Safety Protection Orders.
>
> Applicants should be careful utilizing the Personal Safety Protection Order. Family relationships, different from general social relationships, are tied together with blood, which involves family ethics. In long-term marriages, it is inevitable that couples quarrel and even engage in physical conflict over mundane affairs. This should be distinguished from domestic violence [which, as we have seen above, is defined as a crime only when heavy injuries are inflicted], otherwise court interferences can worsen spousal relationships and result in the opposite effect.

> Also, the 28th stipulation of the Anti-Domestic Violence Law requires that the People's Court make a decision within seventy-two hours after receiving the application, which requires judges to visit multiple places, request testimonies at different localities, and investigate the applicants' eligibility within such a short time period. All these court resources are wasted in the end because, in reality, very few applicants merit the eligibility.
>
> Judges should exercise common sense, flexibility, and life experience in assessing and determining whether an applicant has encountered domestic violence or faces danger … In a nutshell, whether to issue Personal Safety Protection Orders or not should be guided by strict criteria. Applicants should prioritize family relationships … Courts should not only be strict, but also utilize multifaceted conflict-resolving mechanisms to restore the wounded family relationships. (Chu, Lun 2016)

Clearly, the cohesion of the family is more important in this Chinese legal document than the safety of women, echoing the state-sanctioned call for women's sacrifice for family harmony and state stability. Directed by this document that calls for strict criteria for the eligibility of applicants, a differentiation of "physical conflict" from domestic violence, and the use of "common sense," "life experience," "flexibility," and a prioritization of family relationships in legal decisions, court judges either advised applicants not to apply for the Protection Order or rejected the application, citing reasons such as the lack of physical injuries suffered by the applicant (Lin 2021). In 2018, I interviewed a woman named Ying during my research, who had applied to the court for the Personal Safety Protection Order against her husband's violence, but her plea was rejected for "lack of evidence." Ying told me,

> I don't really know where I can get help. I went to the All China Women's Federation [for help], but their officials told me to be gentle, nice, and kind to my husband to avoid the violence. They told me that I should be there for my husband as his wife until death. They said applying for the Personal Safety Protection Order can only disrupt harmony and the stability of the family. They mediated between us. I thought my husband would keep his promise of not beating me again, but I was wrong. I now live in fear every day, but it's useless to go to the court or the All China Women's Federation again for help.

Like Ying, other women too had their applications for the Protection Order rejected due to "insufficient evidence." As the women told me, it was difficult for them to prove that their injuries were inflicted by their husbands, especially when their husbands denied it. The required 72-hour window for the court to investigate the evidence and issue a verdict also makes it more likely for court judges to disapprove their applications on grounds of "insufficient evidence." On top of that, as Ying discussed above, the All China Women's Federation discouraged and stopped her from applying for the Protection Order and asked her to accept their mediation, which ultimately was unable to terminate her husband's violence.

My interviews with court judges showed a high threshold and a high demand for evidence in order to approve an application for the Personal Safety Protection Order. One judge said to me in a 2019 interview:

> We don't issue the Personal Safety Protection Order unless it's a dire situation. In general, we don't see the need for the Personal Safety Protection Order in these conditions: if the applicant doesn't live with the defendant, if the applicant sustains no severe injuries or mutilations that are directly caused by the defendant, if the frequency of the violence is low, if the violence is not recent, or if the defendant accuses the applicant of extramarital affairs, faulty conduct, or other family conflicts. Since we are required by law to complete our investigation within seventy-two hours, it is critical that applicants submit all the materials, including medical records to prove that their severe injuries or mutilations are directly caused by the defendant, together with police records and records from the All China Women's Federation and the residential committee. We generally avoid issuing the Personal Safety Protection Order to a victim during a divorce lawsuit, as that will define the divorce case as a violence-related case and, in turn, make the case much more complicated.

As shown, court judges have followed the document promulgated by China's People's Court system and applied stringent guidelines to the eligibility of recipients of the Personal Safety Protection Order. The judge stressed the contributing factors including the short window of seventy-two hours and the lack of a workforce that is able to engage in the intense investigation, verification, and interviews with all parties including the applicant, defendant, the All China Women's Federation, the residential committee, and the police. He later discussed cases where he was unable to locate one of these key parties such as the defendant, which eventually delayed the process and made it impossible for him to confirm the case within the short 72-hour window. He had no alternative but to reject these applications at the end of the 72-hour window. The judge also expressed his true opinions about the Personal Safety Protection Order; that is, he did not believe in the efficacy of Personal Safety Protection Orders in curbing the violence. Indeed, as shown earlier, abusers continued to harass, beat, and abuse their victims despite the Personal Safety Protection Orders issued against them, for which they only received minor fines and one-week administrative detentions. The judge's belief that the Personal Safety Protection Order is a futile attempt may also account for the high rejection rate of applications.

A lawyer from a Beijing nongovernment organization reported a legal case in 2018 (Xia 2020). In this case, both the victim and her abusive husband were medical doctors with PhD degrees. They had a school-aged daughter and a newborn toddler. In 2018, her husband strangled her until she lost consciousness. He then grabbed her collar and banged her head on the concrete floor, resulting in physical injuries and the paralysis of her arms. She was hospitalized afterward. A Beijing nongovernment lawyer and the staff members offered help to apply for a Personal Safety Protection Order from the City Court, which was one of the few courts that had issued Protection Orders to victims before. However, when the lawyer and staff members handed in the application, the court asked them to take the documents back. Only after prolonged negotiations did the court finally accept the documents. The victim, who was still hospitalized, was unable to appear in court. Her abusive husband admitted his domestic violence in front of the judge, telling the judge that he is OK with the judge issuing the Personal Safety Protection Order (ibid.).

However, when the lawyer and staff members presented the medical reports and injury pictures to the judge, the judge merely glanced through the documents before throwing them onto the table, asking "Is this it?" She then commended the perpetrator for his good attitude, proclaiming that she could not issue the Personal Safety Protection Order because the extent of the injuries was not clear from the medical reports. This was in direct violation of the Anti-Domestic Law that stipulates that the Personal Safety Protection Order should be issued upon "threats" of domestic violence, not only in cases where severe physical injuries have been inflicted (Anti-Domestic Violence 2015). The perpetrator had already admitted domestic violence in court, which should have met the requirements to issue the Personal Safety Protection Order (Xia 2020).

However, when the lawyer and staff members insisted on their request for the Protection Order, the judge responded: "Only one beating, and you demand the Protection Order? What do you think the Court is?" After learning this, the victim removed the IV from her arms, left the hospital, and went to the court the next morning for the prearranged 9 am meeting with the court judge. However, the judge did not show up for the meeting. So they went to the local All China Women's Federation and requested help. After several hours, court clerks came to see them, saying,

> We've already criticized your husband, and he has promised not to beat you again. He's got a very good attitude. Harmony and stability are more important, you know. A family needs to be whole and complete. (ibid.)

Afterward no one else showed up until late afternoon, when a court clerk arrived with the court verdict of "rejection." Seeing the verdict, the victim burst into tears. The lawyer and staff members continued to negotiate with the court clerk. In the end, the court clerk brought the perpetrator over and mediated between them. Eventually the victim went home with the perpetrator (ibid.).

Compulsory Reporting

The 23rd stipulation of the Anti-Domestic Violence law states that victims' relatives, police in the Public Security Bureau, All China Women's Federation, and victims' residential committee should not only exercise "compulsory reporting," but also act as victims' proxy to apply to the court for the Personal Safety Protection Order, due to abusers' potential threat to victims. However, in reality, only 1.46 percent of requests were applied by a proxy, among the nationwide 1,172 Personal Safety Protection Order issued from March 2018 to February 2020 (Wu 2020). Many cases of abuse revealed that family members, neighbors, employers, and co-workers watched the violence playing out in silence and failed to report the violence that they had witnessed. For instance, in the 2019 case where a middle-school teacher, Xiaoling Zhao, in Guangzhou City was beaten to death by her abusive husband, she had reported his violent behavior to his employer, residential committee, All China Women's Federation, and the police at the Public Security Bureau, but no one helped, resulting in her being beaten to death by her abuser.

In 2019, a woman named Yongfen Wang in Hubei Province attempted suicide several times due to decades of violence inflicted by her husband, but her parents, brother, sister-in-law, and neighbors who witnessed the violence not only did not report it, but also advised her to continue tolerating the violence for the sake of her kids. She called the police on many occasions, but the police told her that they could not do anything because it was a family affair and her husband had denied the violence (Wei, Shengyao 2019). In 2016, a female doctor and owner of a medical clinic in Chongqing, Sichuan, Xiaoyan Zhang, was beaten and poisoned to death by her husband (Yong 2016). Prior to her death, her family members, co-workers, staff members, community, and neighbors watched multiple times as her husband beat her severely, but no one intervened or reported the multiple occurrences of violence (ibid.).

Other cases of violence-induced death also demonstrated the failure of bystanders in meeting the requirement of "compulsory reporting" or offering help. In a 2019 case in Shandong, teachers, schools, relatives, family members, court mediators, police, and lawyers were all aware of the severe violence a wife and her daughter had suffered, but no one reported or interfered in the matter, leading to the sixteen-year-old daughter being beaten to death by her father (Bei 2019). In another 2019 case in Hunan Province, the residential committee, the All China Women's Federation, the Public Security Bureau, the employers of both the abusers and the victim, and the family members were all cognizant of the violence, but no one offered any help, resulting in the victim being beaten to death by the abuser (Chen 2019). In a 2016 case in Inner Mongolia, dozens of family members and relatives of the wife were aware of the violence perpetrated by the husband. Not only did no one interfere, but also they advised her to continuously endure the violence. She was later beaten to death by her husband (Wang, Yongqin 2016).

Although the All China Women's Federation is a state-operated organization that was established in 1949 to safeguard women's rights, together with other parties, many local organizations not only failed to report cases, but also refrained from providing support for victims (Wu 2020). An official at a local All China Women's Federation told me in an interview in 2018, "We would rather demolish 10 temples than destroy 1 marriage (ningchaibaizuomiao, buhuiyizhuanghun). Mediation is our priority. As long as the husband promises to change his behavior, everything is fine." In many cases, officials at the All China Women's Federation even blame victims and uphold the patriarchal ideology of gender inequality. In my conversations with many victims, they told me that when they sought help from the local All China Women's Federation, they were told to resolve the issue by either changing themselves or seeking help elsewhere. One woman from a city in Liaoning Province said to me:

> I went to the local Women's Federation seeking help against my husband's physical beating. After I explained the situation to the female officer, she said to me, "You need to search for the root cause [for the violence]. Is it because he has extramarital affairs? Is it because you are not gentle enough? Is it because you are not virtuous [xianhui] enough? You need to start with yourself and make some adjustments to yourself in the hope of winning back your husband's heart. Your child is the nexus that links the two of you, so you should increase family time and travel together. Since he may not agree on couple activities, it is important for you to create opportunities to be with him. To sustain your relationships with each other, you need to be nicer to him and make some adjustments to yourself. You can also seek help from the residential committee, his employer, his friends, and his siblings who can advise him against violence.

Such a victim-blaming attitude from the All China Women's Federation deterred victims from seeking help. Though the Anti-Domestic Violence Law requires that police should help victims seek refuge in a safe house (see Chapter 5 about safe houses), in reality, many police are either ignorant about this or have no idea how to implement this introductory procedure due to the murky language in the Anti-Domestic Violence Law (Nan 2019).[5]

Light Sentences for Abusers, Death Sentence for Victims Using Self-Defense

It was recorded that an average of more than one death per day resulted from intimate partner violence from March 2016 to October 2017 (Xia 2020). To be more exact, within these 600 days, 637 deaths occurred due to intimate partner violence. In general, women who killed their abusers in self-defense were given a heavy sentence of ten years in prison or even a death sentence, but much lighter sentences were given to abusers who perpetrated violence against them. It was reported by the Beijing Fanbao organization that, between 2009 and 2012, across the country, 64 percent of the cases where women killed their abusers in defense were sentenced to a heavy penalty of over ten years in prison or even a death sentence (Feng 2013). Other studies also showed that a heavy sentence of over ten years in prison for killing their abusers in defense was given to 80 percent of the imprisoned women in Sichuan Province, 60 percent of the imprisoned women in Anshan City, Liaoning Province, and 80 percent of the imprisoned women in Fuzhou City, Fujian Province (Xiao 2021).[6]

In one example in Sichuan Province, Yan Li's husband, after their marriage in 2009, beat her several times every month, slapping her face, kicking her, using a knife to cut her, using cigarettes to burn her face, her breasts, and her vagina, hitting her head onto the wall, locking her outdoors in the freezing night, and using the chair to beat her (Zhou 2015). After each beating, he forced Li to engage in sex, while using cigarettes to burn her body parts. He did this even on the night after Li had a painful, long abortion procedure. He also committed sexual violence upon his stepdaughter (Li's daughter with the first husband) multiple times right in front of Li. As a result of years of abuse by her husband, Li suffered physical injuries, psychological trauma, and numerous gynecological diseases. In front of neighbors, Li's husband often kicked her face until her face was swollen, black-and-blue, and even bleeding. In one beating, he chopped off one of her fingers, causing her to permanently lose a finger. She sought help from the residential committee, the local All China Women's Federation, and the police, as well as the court, but to no avail. When she called the police, they hung up as soon as they learned that it was an issue between a married couple. In 2010, her husband hit her feet with the handle of a rifle, breaking off one of her toenails, and threatened to kill her. She resisted and killed her husband. In 2011, she was sentenced to immediate execution. Li appealed, but her appeal was rejected by the Sichuan Provincial Supreme Court. However, after this legal case received a tremendous amount of attention from the media, nongovernment organizations (NGOs), and 130 scholars and lawyers from both home and abroad, in 2015, Li's case went through another trial in court. With the help of several bona fide lawyers from the Beijing Qianqian Lawyer's Office, the verdict at the new trial was revised to a death sentence with a temporary reprieve (Ma 2015). Li's case was celebrated as one of the ten most influential court cases in 2015 by a number of organizations and media outlets.

In general, as shown below, light sentences of six months to six years in prison were given to abusers for beating their wives to death. In 2016, Huang in Chongqing City was sentenced to six months in prison after killing his wife by beating and poisoning her (Yong 2016).[7] In 2020, Zhang in Shandong Province was sentenced to two years and two months in prison for beating his 23-year-old wife to death (Liu 2021). In 2020, Wang Xiaoyang in Henan Province was sentenced to three years in prison for killing his three-year-old daughter with the intention of forcing his wife to return home (Cai 2020). In 2014, Shi in Anqing City was sentenced to four years in prison for beating his wife to death (Wang 2014).

In 2010, Wang was sentenced to six years and six months in prison for beating his 26-year-old wife Dong Shanshan to death. In 2014, Wang was released early from prison and went on to marry a 23-year-old woman, who had no idea that Wang had previously beaten his wife to death. In July 2014, she called the Beijing Legal Consultation hotline for help against the severe violence inflicted by her husband Wang, who beat her numerous times, threatened to kill her entire family, and broke four of her ribs in a single beating (Wu 2020). The light sentence Wang received for beating his first wife to death no doubt contributed to his continued violent behavior toward his new wife.

Much lighter sentences were given to abusers who caused victims severe injuries but not death. For instance, in December 2019, a man in Shenzhen City was detained for five days for beating his partner who sustained injuries, with the entire beating videotaped by a surveillance camera in the building (Huang, Youkai 2019). In March 2020, Luo in Sichuan Province was detained for seven days for beating his wife over a period of sixteen years. An episode of his beating was videotaped at home (Du 2020). In December 2019, Guang in Chongqing City was detained for twenty days for beating his girlfriend for more than half a year, rendering her unable to walk for an entire month. The last beating episode was fully videotaped by the surveillance camera inside an elevator (Wang, Ning 2019).[8] In December 2020, Liu in Hunan Province was sentenced to one year and two months in prison for knifing his ex-girlfriend over twenty times, causing over twenty injuries throughout her body (Zhou 2020). In 2019, Chen in Chengdu City was sentenced to one and a half years in prison for beating his wife and breaking her spleen—which was surgically removed afterward (Xia 2019). In 2016, Liu in Liaoning Province was sentenced to three years in prison for beating his girlfriend into a vegetative state (Ni 2019).

Such light sentences indubitably not only emboldened perpetration of more violence, but also intimidated individuals from offering help to victims. A woman I interviewed during my research told me that her abusive husband warned her, "If you dare to divorce me, I'll beat you to death just as Wang did to Dong Shanshan [in the well-known legal case in China]. After six years in jail, I'll come out and kill your entire family." She finally managed to escape home and was offered help by a female friend who took her in. However, after her friend learned about Wang's legal case from online news reports, she got so terrified that she asked her to leave. She told her that she dare not take her in at her place because of the light sentence meted out to a man for killing his wife.

Although the 2nd stipulation of the Anti-Domestic Violence Law defines domestic violence as "physical beating, tying up with ropes, mutilating, forcefully limiting physical freedom of family members," from 2014 to 2016, only 3.96 percent of 94,571 violence-related cases were recognized by courts as domestic violence (Wei 2017; Wu 2017). A court judge told me in an interview,

> In general, local courts have a very strict definition of domestic violence [*Jiabao*]. Some applicants in the legal cases use promissory notes or regret letters from alleged perpetrators to prove domestic violence. However, promissory notes only convey the wish not to beat his wife anymore. They cannot serve as proof of the time, frequency, or degree of the beating. Even in a case where an abuser admits to beating his wife in court, it still does not provide proof of the time, frequency, or degree of his wife-beating. That actually was often times seen as an expression of his remorse working in his favor. Many times, court judges set the frequency of beating and degree of harm as the yardsticks to determine whether a case can be recognized as domestic violence.

As shown, in handling domestic violence-related legal cases, court judges tend to rely on their own interpretations of the definition of domestic violence. While the law does not specify the time, frequency, and degree of beating as the criteria to define a case as domestic violence, court judges are inclined to interpret the law in their own disparate ways while issuing their verdicts on domestic violence-related cases. As a result, 96.04 percent of domestic violence-related legal cases from

2014 to 2016 were denied (Wei 2017; Wu 2017). It was reported that the court rulings tended to perceive long-term violence as well as severe physical injuries as sufficient evidence to constitute domestic violence (Zhuo 2017).

Mediation

Mediation is an indispensable measure ubiquitously and extensively utilized by court judges, Departments of Justice, Public Security Bureaus, All China Women's Federations, and residential committees in violence-related cases, including in violence-related divorce, application of Personal Protection Orders, and cases of severe violence where both civil and penal laws dictate administrative and punitive actions. According to the Anti-Domestic Violence Law, mediation should be performed by multiple organizations including employers, Women's Federations, and village and residential committees to "prevent and reduce domestic violence" (Anti-Domestic Violence Law 2015). Informed by the Anti-Domestic Violence Law, the courts and the Public Security Bureau implement mediation as a prerequisite legal procedure in violence-related cases. As shown in the vignette at the beginning of this section, court judges and police often ignore or overlook violence and resort to mediation as the pervasive method of resolution. It was reported that in China, in general, victims typically experienced thirty-five incidents of violence before calling the police, but their pleas mostly result in useless mediation (Qian 2015). Mediation through an oral education of abusers, instead of punitive actions against them, reflects the paramount principle of maintaining family harmony and state stability at the expense of women's well-being, which perpetuates violence and women's suffering.

From 2016 to 2020, the National Public Security Bureau reported having mediated 8.25 million "family conflicts" (Li 2020). Often times, victims were threatened by their abusers before they called the police. After victims risked their lives to call the police, however, the result was that either the police refused to come or did nothing but mediate. In my interview with police officers in a Northeastern region in China, a police officer told me, "The reality is, if a policeman doesn't do anything, s/he won't be penalized. However, if s/he does do something, it can lead to other issues and problems. So why would a policeman do something about it?" He noted that, in general, police are reluctant to get involved in such "family affairs" except in cases of severe injuries or death. Another police officer told me that due to their worry about impinging on the relationships between couples, they would generally mediate and treat it as a "family conflict" without issuing a police report.

Indeed, the Anti-Domestic Violence Law stipulates that "in light cases of domestic violence that do not warrant the detainment penalty, the Public Security Bureau educates and criticizes [the abuser], or issues a Warning Note" (Anti-Domestic Violence Law 2015). As stipulated by the Anti-Domestic Violence law, it is not the responsibility of the Public Security Bureau to issue a Warning Note in such cases. Rather, how to handle these cases is at the full discretion of the police, which is why, as they told me, they tend to do no more than mediate. A woman, Hong, whom I interviewed, told me that she called the police multiple times about her husband's violence, but it was handled via mediation each time. The last time she was beaten by him was at a hospital in 2016. His entire abuse was caught on the surveillance camera, but when a policeman came, all he did was, once again, mediate and ask her husband to write a note promising that he would not beat her again.

In 2019, a woman named Lingling Yang in Hubei Province was beaten by her husband and sustained injuries that required eight stitches in her right ear (Wei, Furong 2019). Yang called the police and demanded that her husband be detained. The policeman who came rejected her request, asking: "Where can you find couples that don't fight?" The policeman's response exacerbated her husband's violence, who mocked her for calling the police and told her that she should never even bother with the useless police-call anymore (ibid.).

In 2016, a woman named Zhang Xiaoyun in Chongqing City, who suffered long-term violence by her husband, called the police after one beating that caused injuries in her legs, which prevented her from going to the bathroom (Sun 2017). On the phone, the police asked, "Is he still beating you now?" She responded that his beating just ended. The police then hung up after telling her, "Then there's nothing we can do." Emboldened by police inaction, in 2016, after she refused to return home with him, he bit her nose off and ate it. As seen, police noninterference inflamed and escalated his violence, imposing a heavy toll on her physically, psychologically, and financially. She eventually approached the staff of a Beijing nongovernment organization of Gender Development, who helped her obtain a free nose reconstruction surgery at a Shanghai cosmetic surgery hospital (ibid.).

During my research, I found Xiao Hong's story below as representative of this kind of police mediation in violence-related cases. Xiao Hong and her husband worked at two different local companies in Hebei Province. Her husband had physically abused her earlier, but each time when she called the police, nothing came from it. In 2019, due to an argument, her husband kicked her in the stomach, strangled her, and continuously kicked her. She responded by fighting back and by calling the police. She told me:

> When I called the police and reported the violence, the policeman who answered the phone said, "I'm busy. Don't call for such trivial things [jimaosuanpi de xiaoshi]!" I said, "To you, it's trivial things, but to me, it's not. If two guys fight on the street, you police have to be there, right? I was beaten up. Shouldn't you be here? Do you want to wait until I am beaten to death by him and then come?" He finally responded, "OK." Over half an hour later, he came over and asked what happened. I described how my husband beat me up. He asked me if I beat him too. I said, "He was beating me up, so of course I had to resist and fight back!" He then asked my husband, who admitted that he did beat me quite severely this time. He asked my husband to stand up and apologize to me. Then he said, "It's difficult for us police to deal with such spousal matters. All we can do is mediate. If it gets too severe, you two can separate. If you insist on further procedures,

then both of you need to come with me to the police station as both of you have beaten the other person." I finally said, "What if he beats me again in the future?" He said, "Don't fight back. Just call the police." His words made me feel deflated, helpless, and powerless.

Xiao Hong did not know that, to the police, her fighting back translated as her having physically assaulted her husband, which complicated the matter and scared her from going to the police station in pursuit of further procedures against her husband. She said:

> Every time when we had an argument, he beat me up. I always fought back to protect myself. I wanted him to get a taste of being bullied and beaten [changchang beidabeiqifu de ziwei]. I know that it's wrong for me to fight violence with violence [yibaozhibao], but how can I just do nothing when he beats me up, as the police told me to?

Ultimately, police mediation made both her and her husband feel at fault, thereby leaving her abuser uncharged and her "deflated, helpless, and powerless."

Other women that I have interviewed during my research recounted numerous experiences of police mediation that not only failed to resolve anything, but also intensified the violence. One woman named Ling told me in 2017:

> Last time when my husband beat me, I told him that I'd call the police. He responded, "Don't you use the police to scare me. Police only come over to mediate—you think the police are on your side? Keep dreaming! Go ahead and call the police. You'll see if they really care about you!" I called the police. A policeman came over and said, "You two need to be nice to each other and not fight. You can discuss things nicely. A harmonious family leads to a prosperous society [jiahe wanshixing], you know." I asked the police to detain him. He said, "There's no severe consequence, so I can't take him away. Even if I did, I'd have to release him. We have to mediate." He then left. My husband said, "See, you called the police—do the police care about you? You dared to use the police to get me, uh?" Then he beat me more severely.

As shown, calling the police has become synonymous with calling for police mediation, which has not only failed to deter or stop the violence that women like Ling and Xiao Hong suffer but has also exacerbated the violence. Ling told me that when she sought help from officials from the Women's Federation, they, too, failed to offer any help. Xiao Hong also told me about her experience with the police concerning her husband's violence:

> Calling the police doesn't make any difference. After the police came, what you encountered was helplessness. Our legal system is such that it can't give you what you need. Before I called for the police, my husband gave me his cell phone and said twice that he was waiting for the police. The police came and asked me if

I had ever thought of the consequence of calling the police for such a matter, to which I didn't know how to respond. The policeman told him that it's not right to beat people. He criticized and attempted to educate [him], and then left, leaving me no evidence that I could use for future divorce.

Such police mediation, however, often led to further violence and suffering. Without police protection, the victim had to endure the threat of being killed or their child being killed if she dared to escape. As we have seen from one of the previously mentioned cases, the sixteen-year-old daughter was killed by her father in Shandong. It would seem that the threat of death is more likely if the child is a girl. Lin from Hunan called the police multiples times due to the long-term violence inflicted by her husband (Peng 2020). Each time the police mediation only exacerbated the violence. In 2019, she was beaten so severely that she sustained multiple injuries, including comminuted bone fracture, head injuries, facial tissue wounds, and multiple soft tissue injuries throughout her body. She went to the police station with detailed medical reports of the injuries she sustained and asked the police to file a police report about it. The police rejected her request, claiming that the case showed "no criminal activity, thus not constituting a crime." Lin applied again in 2020 to the Public Security Bureau, which upheld the previous "correct verdict" (ibid.).

My research revealed that medical reports of sustained injuries are often not considered sufficient evidence for the police and court judges to deviate from mediation and resort to criminal justice. Indeed, victims not only have to pay a high cost to obtain the medical proof of injuries at the hospitals that are appointed and validated by the Anti-Domestic Violence Law, but also are required to prove that these injuries have resulted from the abuser's violence. This is extremely difficult, as the violence often happens in the private sphere of a home without witnesses or surveillance cameras. Even in situations where the violence is captured on surveillance cameras, court judges can still rule that the video fails to prove that the injuries are caused by the violence. This happened to a 28-year-old woman Xiao Lan who worked as a supervisor in a well-known company. In 2019, she was strangled and beaten severely by her husband in the apartment corridor, which was caught by the surveillance camera. She managed to escape to the apartment security office, where security staff witnessed her bleeding body and called the police. She was then sent to the emergency hospital and diagnosed with multiple bone fractures throughout her body. Her injuries were defined in the hospital reports as light injuries, which is more severe than minor injuries, as discussed above (e.g., scalp laceration of more than 40 cm, skull fracture, broken ribs, facial laceration of more than 6 cm, hearing impediment, burning over 20 percent of the body, spine fracture, ruptures of stomach, or gallbladder, or spleen, hip fracture, and penetrating injuries to the eyeballs).[9] The 234th stipulation in the Chinese Criminal Law states that imposing light injuries on others constitutes the crime of intentional harm (Chinese Criminal Law 2020). She hired a lawyer to sue in court for a violence-related divorce, with the evidence of her husband's previous violence, police reports, records of emergency aid at the hospital, hospital reports of the light injury diagnosis, neighbors' testimonies, and videos of his violence against her caught in the apartment corridor. Xiao Lan said:

> The multiple bone fractures [from the violence] made it impossible for me to sit or stand for a long time and gave me many sleepless nights. Even though I presented all the evidence [in court], it was still difficult to pursue criminal charges [against my husband] in court. The judge said what I presented was evidence for domestic violence [not a crime]. He said both of us fought in the video. He said the video couldn't prove that my broken bones were caused by him. By that time, my husband had taken our son away and barred me from seeing him, but the judge couldn't do anything about that either. I felt helpless and gave up pressing criminal charges [against my husband]. My husband didn't have a lawyer, but he put on a theatrical performance of talking, crying, and even kneeling down in front of the judge, appearing to everyone that he was a caring and emotional person, which successfully affected how the judge perceived us and our case. Right after we exited the court, he said to me, "There's no way you'll get anything after our divorce! Look how I'm going to beat you when we get home!" Now one year has passed, I am still waiting for the court verdict about my divorce request.

It was reported that only 1 percent of the second appeal of domestic violence lawsuits were recognized as domestic violence in Beijing City court from 2014 to 2016 (Wang, Jun 2019). The reason for the success of these 1 percent cases was that, in all these cases, abusers admitted inflicting domestic violence on their victims. A lawyer told me, "Courts have very high criteria for recognizing a case as domestic violence. If a victim is beaten just several times, there is not much possibility for that case to be recognized as domestic violence." A court judge told me one reason for the low level of recognition was that "many accusers of domestic violence presented pictures of injuries, but those pictures don't tell the court who did the beating, when the beating happened, and who caused the injuries." As Xiao Lan noted above, the court judge refused to accept the violence caught on the surveillance video as proof that her light injuries were caused by her husband. Another woman Xiao Wang also told me that even though her husband's abuse was captured on the surveillance video in her residential area, the court judge said, "Even though the video showed that Xiao Wang's husband pulled her out of the apartment door to beat her, there was no proof that the injuries were caused by her husband's beating. The proof presented is insufficient." Other women that I have interviewed during my research took pictures of the injuries on their bodies, which were also rejected by the court as the pictures "could not prove that the injuries were caused by the husband."

Moreover, even though the 234th stipulation in the Chinese Criminal Law states clearly that inflicting light injuries on others constitutes the crime of intentional harm (as mentioned above, light injuries include scalp laceration of more than 40cm, skull fracture, broken ribs, facial laceration of more than 6cm, hearing impediment, burning over 20% of the body, spine fracture, ruptures of stomach, or gallbladder, or spleen, hip fracture, and penetrating injuries to the eyeballs), the stipulation is not implemented when the perpetrator is a spouse of the victim. Xiao Lan's lawyer told her that, in general, the perpetrator of domestic violence receives an administrative penalty rather than a criminal charge, except in cases that involve heavy injuries such as paralysis or injuries that are life-endangering.

In 2019, Li from Hefei City, Anhui Province, called the police after her husband's violent episode and requested a police report (Guan 2019). Her request was rejected. She sued in court with a medical report of her sustained injuries including a nose bone fracture and swelling of the surrounding tissues. She later received a court notice that stated:

> The existing evidence cannot prove criminal behavior. Li said her injuries came from her husband's violence, but her husband said Li used a shopping cart to beat him, and then when he dodged, she accidentally fractured her own nose. Although it is a fact that her nose was damaged, there is no written report about the extent of the damage; the existing evidence cannot prove criminal behavior. So we cannot establish it as a legal case.

She appealed to a higher-level court, which upheld the previous court's decision.

Xiao Hui, whom I have interviewed during my research, was a middle-school teacher who had recently given birth. Her husband was her colleague at the school. During the marriage, she was beaten numerous times, but she only reported to the police three times, each time with medical reports of sustained injuries. She was able to secure one Warning Note from the police due to the injuries. The police told her, "You can go to the court for a divorce if you can't live like this." She then sought help from the All China Women's Federation and her residential committee, who told her that they could not interfere due to the fear of her husband's further retribution. In 2019, she decided to hire a lawyer to sue for a divorce. She submitted all the evidence of the violence, including the Warning Note from the police, pictures of sustained injuries from the violence, X-rays, medical reports and medical records from hospitals, and testimonies from both the residential committee and the All China Women's Federation. Her lawyer assured her: "You have demonstrated what we call 'a chain of evidence,' the best testament to the severity of the violence. The Warning Note from the police also has a sufficient legal effect. If this cannot assure a divorce, what can?" Xiao Hui told me that, while in court, she detailed each aspect of the violence—the time, reason, process, location, and result. However, her husband denied everything. Frustrated, she asked the judge, "You're a woman. Does nobody really care enough to approve my divorce until I'm beaten dead or paralyzed?" She told me that, in the end, she was given a verdict that the degree of her sustained injuries and the frequency of the violence were not severe enough to qualify for a divorce. She told me:

> I'm devastated [with the verdict]. I've told the judge that I don't want any possessions from him or from the marriage. All I want is to exit this abusive marriage with a divorce. Even that [request] cannot be granted? The law is apparently not to

protect the weak [victim] but the strong [abuser]. All the evidence that I have accumulated, including the police's Warning Note, now sounds nothing but a joke! I sought help from everyone—the police, court, residential committee, and All China Women's Federation, but received no help or support from any of them. What else can I do except to fight him to the death next time?

The noninterfering inaction that Xiao Hui experienced only exacerbates the violence, and also frequently results in victims' death, as shown in the following numerous cases.

Dong Shanshan, in one of the previously mentioned cases, called the police eight times within a couple of months, but it was only mediated each time (Wu 2020). Her divorce request was also rejected by the court. After she escaped to her mother's place, her husband brought a group of people there and kidnapped her. Her parents reported to the police once again, but the police rejected the kidnap case as they were a couple. With no help from the police or the court, she was finally beaten to death by her husband, for which he received a punishment of six years in prison (ibid.).

In Hebei Province, a wife reported to the police station three times about the long-term violence inflicted by her husband (Huang 2015). Each time the police did nothing but mediate between her and her husband. The fourth time when she reported the violence to the police station, the policeman who was assigned to mediate between her and her husband was not present at the station. When her father stepped out to look for that mediator, her husband killed her and her mother with a knife right at the police station (ibid.).

In Inner Mongolia, Hongmei, the director of the Hangjinqi Broadcasting Company, called the police about her husband's violence that had lasted for fifteen years, but was mediated each time (Wang, Yongqin 2016). She learned from experience that calling the police resulted in nothing but further aggravating her husband and inviting more violence; so she never called the police again. Eventually, in 2016, she was beaten to death by her husband (ibid.). Earlier when she was three months pregnant, her husband had beaten her, resulting in a miscarriage. Her parents, who were teachers, lived in fear of his threats. During the daytime, they dared not ride bikes or walk on the street. During the night, they placed an iron rod underneath their pillows. They justified their fear with two well-known cases that had happened in their town a couple of years ago: a man killed his wife's parents due to her divorce request; a female government worker committed suicide by jumping off a building due to her husband's violence. Dozens of Hongmei's family members and relatives knew about her husband's violence, but they advised her to endure it. Her uncle, who was a policeman, said to her, "It's a family affair. It'll always pass." Her experience of police mediation left her with no alternative but to endure the violence, until she was beaten to death by her husband.

Thirty-year-old La Mu, a Sichuan food channel owner, called and reported to the police multiple times about years of violence inflicted by her husband, but received nothing apart from police mediation (Yuan 2020). When she went into hiding with a relative, her husband beat her sister, causing heavy injuries that required three months of hospitalization, simply because she refused to tell him her whereabouts. Her family members called the police after this episode of violence, but the police, again, took no action. In June 2020, she got a divorce, but the court gave her abusive husband the custody of her two children. In September 2020, her ex-husband attacked her with a knife seven times before pouring gasoline on her body and setting her on fire. Around 90 percent of her body was severely burned and she died sixteen days later. It was the noninterfering mediation approach of the police that, despite her and her family members' numerous calls for help, subjected her to increased violence and ultimately led to her death.

In Shandong, a sixteen-year-old girl, Ruili Yang, submitted a "Help-Seeking Letter" to her teachers and her school, reporting her father's physical violence against her mother and her, including his daily threat of throwing a bottle of sulfuric acid that he held in his hand on her mother (Bei 2019). In response, her teachers told her to do more chores at home and avoid direct conflict with her father. Each time her mother called the police after the violence, she was told that, since it was a couple's conflict, they were not able to arrest the abuser without proof of severe physical injuries caused by him. She sued in the court for a divorce; the police, court mediators, and court lawyers all came to mediate. They claimed that their mediation was successful. In 2019, the sixteen-year-old daughter was beaten to death by the father because she supported her mother's request for a divorce.

In Guangzhou City, a middle-school teacher Xiaoling Zhou was beaten to death in 2019 after her numerous calls for help to the police, her abuser's employer, and the All China Women's Federation were met with nothing but mediation (Chen 2019). An employee at the Power Supply Bureau for five years, 35-year-old Zhou was married to Xiao, during which time she suffered numerous beatings. One time, Zhou was sent to the hospital for medical treatments of the injuries from a severe beating, including multiple tissue injuries throughout her body and injuries to her eyes. After a medical surgery, with a surgical catheter still on her body, she was kidnapped by her husband and taken to a hotel room, where he beat her again and terrorized her with a gun that he said had twenty bullets, forcing her to sign a divorce agreement to the effect that she leave the marriage without seeking any money or custody of their child. Her family called the police about the kidnapping, but the police said it was fine for the couple to negotiate divorce terms. After the divorce, due to his continuous threats and terrorizing attacks, she called the police numerous times for help. In 2019, she sought help from the All China Women's Federation, who told her to utilize legal means. So she went to the police station, with a help-seeking letter that detailed his long-term violence and all the pictures and medical reports of her sustained injuries from his beating. The police rejected all her help-seeking materials and did not make a record of anything she reported. Instead, they told her to go to his employer for help. Zhou then went to his employer, who refused to intervene because it was a "family affair." In June, her husband forced her into his apartment. Her friends and family called the police and his employer multiple times, begging them to check if she was safe at his apartment. Eventually, the police came to his apartment, knocked at the door, and left after no one answered. Shortly after the police left, her abuser called the police, reporting that he had beaten Zhou to death. Zhou was confirmed dead in his apartment, as a result of a cerebral hemorrhage caused by his beating.

Since police mediation usually proved ineffective with deadly consequences, some women decided to hire a lawyer to pursue a divorce. The 32nd Clause in the Marriage Law stipulates that mediation is an indispensable procedure in all divorce cases and that, in violence-related divorce cases, divorce is only granted if mediation is ineffective (Marriage Law 2001). On July 18, 2018, "The Supreme Court Document to Improve Verdicts on Civil Affairs and Reform Work Mechanism" was promulgated (Supreme Court Document 2018). This Document stipulated that, to safeguard family harmony, local courts should increase the use of mediation in all family affairs cases. The Supreme Court Document stated that "local courts should explore diverse mediation methods, innovate new mediation mechanisms, heighten mediation ability, and utilize mediation throughout the entire process of handing all family affair cases" (ibid.).

The principle of court ruling on family affairs cases, according to the Supreme Court Document, is to first mediate before issuing a verdict. Family cases, as it contends, are different from other civil cases in that family cases involve emotions that need to be mediated to resolve family conflicts. Even in cases where the husband has already cohabited with another woman, courts still mediate between them and advise the women to try all means to save the marriage. A court judge told me in an interview in 2020, "If an abuser is remorseful and repentant and the victim forgives the abuser, then the divorce request is withdrawn to offer the abuser a chance. If mediation is proven unsuccessful, if the couple's emotional tie is broken, and if there is sufficient evidence of violence, then divorce is warranted and granted."

Even when court judges did recognize the abusive nature of the case, if the abuser contested the divorce, they focused on mediation and only approved a divorce if mediation was ineffective. This is in accordance with the Marriage Law and the "The Supreme Court Document to Improve Verdicts on Civil Affairs and Reform Work Mechanism," whose goal is to safeguard family harmony and state stability. After Dong Shanshan's husband was released from six years in prison for beating her to death, he married a 23-year-old woman, who sued in court for a violence-related divorce due to his severe violent behavior (Wu 2020). She said, "Only after I sued him in court did I find out that the court never approved this kind of divorce request" (ibid.).

It was reported in 2018 that Dong Fang in Chengdu was beaten by her husband, sustaining injuries that included loss of hearing, but her three divorce requests were all rejected (He 2018). Despite the fact that she obtained the Personal Safety Protection Order prior to her divorce requests, the court judge denied all her divorce requests, citing that "we would rather demolish 10 temples than destroy 1 marriage" and that "her loss of hearing resulted from the couple grabbing and snatching each other (zhuache)," not from domestic violence (ibid.). Indeed, the court judge did not mention anything about domestic violence in his verdict (ibid.). It is important to remind ourselves that not only are the rules and laws biased, but the very culture of the people who implement these rules and laws are also heavily biased in favor of men, following Xi Jinpin's lead of safeguarding family harmony and state stability at the expense of women's well-being.

Indeed, across the country, media extolled court judges for their mediation of violence-related divorce cases. For instance, in 2020, court judges in Gansu were championed for "promoting a harmonious family and a harmonious society" (Ma 2020). It was reported that a victim requested a divorce due to her husband's frequent and long-term violence, but her husband contested the divorce. Court judges mediated between them by educating the husband about the law and advising him to apologize to her. As a result of their mediation, the husband apologized and promised not to beat her again. The two reconciled. Media reports celebrated the court judges' success in mediation in the following manner: "Court judges mediated a couple who were about to confront each other in the court room. In just one day, they successfully corrected the abuser's 10 years of domestic violence. They helped the couple reconcile, thereby contributing to the construction of a harmonious family and a harmonious society" (ibid.).

In 2016, Zhang Huawei, director of the Department of Justice in Xuzhou City, Jiangsu Province, received the commending honor of "Excellent Mediator of the People" and "Excellent Mediating Talent" (Ding 2016). He was celebrated across the country for his one decade of mediation to "resolve couple conflict and safeguard state stability" (ibid.). In one case, a woman Huang approached him at the Department of Justice, showing him all the injuries she had sustained throughout her body, as a result of her husband's violent behavior. Huang explained that her husband had been beating her for years. Severely injured and hurt, she went to Zhang to pursue a legal channel to divorce her abuser. She said to him, "Your Department of Justice has to approve my divorce request; otherwise I'll die right here in front of you." Zhang invited her husband to the Department of Justice to mediate between the two, discussing the law and their emotional ties with each other. As a result of his mediation, her husband promised not to beat her again and asked her to give him another chance. Zhang's mediation led the two to sign the mediation contract. It was reported that, since then, Zhang has created an online video to demonstrate a mediation model to mediate between couples (ibid.).

One theme worthy of note here is the lack of academic freedom in China that has caused Chinese sociologists to base their findings not upon empirical evidence but upon what the state dictates. An honestly, properly conducted sociological survey would be able to show the futility, which has been illustrated here, of police and court mediation. As shown here, police and court mediation does not solve the problem, and may even cause the death of the victim. In a society where social science is not practiced freely because of the dominance of the state over academia, police and court mediation continues in spite of its ineffectiveness, under the guidance of a state-sanctioned order to maintain family harmony and state stability through the sacrifices made by the women.

Violence-Related Divorce Court Cases

Although the Anti-Domestic Violence Law stipulates that courts should reduce or waive lawsuit expenses for victims of violence who have financial difficulties, in practice, it is extremely difficult to implement this stipulation due to the very low rate of recognition of violence in the courts (Xia 2020). It was reported in China that more than 90 percent of the female victims were denied their violence-related divorce requests by courts on various grounds (Shi 2016). Women in my research told me that, even though they were physically threatened by their abusive husbands with guns, knives, and other tools, their divorce requests were still denied in court because "threatening activity has to be frequent in order to qualify for violence." In my interviews with a few court judges, they revealed that light injuries were not sufficient to be recognized as violence, which necessitated a combination of factors that included the extent of cruelty of the violence, long duration of the violence, frequency of the violence, and severe sustained injuries such as body mutilation. Family conflicts and intense quarrels that involved "push and pull," as they told me, were not considered or recognized as violence.

From 2016 to 2017, in a District Court in Beijing, despite victims' multiple appeals for violence-related divorce, only two cases out of eight were eventually approved after court mediation (Wang, Jingzhu 2018). In one of the rejected cases, it was the second time that the wife had sued in court for a divorce. She submitted records of having called the police about the violence and medical reports of her sustained injuries including her severely damaged eyes, all inflicted by her husband, who also severely beat her father. The court judge issued a verdict that determined the nature of the case as "a family conflict" (ibid.). The verdict stated that the way the wife treated the defendant by "avoiding him and calling the police" was not beneficial in resolving the conflict. Hence her second-time appeal for divorce was also rejected (ibid.).

From 2017 to 2018, only 10 out of 102 appealed cases of violence-related divorce in mid-level courts in Beijing were recognized as domestic violence (Huang, Haitao 2019). Even though domestic violence was recognized in these ten divorce cases, court judges still denied victims' requests for a fair share of their possessions, which was in direct violation of the 46th stipulation in the Marriage Law that orders to "take care of the non-faulty party in the case of domestic violence" (Marriage Law 2001).

Like Xiao Hui mentioned above, other women that I have interviewed during my research also told me that their first two requests for a divorce resulted in rejection, and that they could only hope for better luck when they applied the third time. Lin, a woman I have interviewed during my research, for instance, told me that even though she was able to obtain a Personal Protection Order against her abusive husband in 2017 due to her sustained injuries, including a bone fracture, a concussion, and loss of hearing, her subsequent three divorce requests were all denied by various levels of courts on the grounds that the violence was not chronic and that her pictures and medical reports of injuries could not prove that the injuries were inflicted by her husband. Frustrated, just like Xiao Hui, Lin said to me:

> I've got no idea how to prove that it [the violence] was chronic and that my injuries were caused by my husband. Does that mean that I should have installed

a surveillance camera at home so that his numerous beatings were videotaped? But how could I've been able to do that without his knowledge?

My interviews with lawyers and court judges revealed that there were several reasons contributing to this low level of recognition of violence in divorce cases. First, in general, it was the customary practice, following the state-sanctioned discourse, to reject the first divorce request to maintain family harmony and safeguard "family values," including cases with ineffective mediation results, sufficient evidence of violence, and broken emotional ties, which should have qualified for a divorce according to the 32nd Clause in the Marriage Law. As I was told by a court judge in 2018, "The principle of our ruling is to safeguard marriage and protect family harmony. So, the general rule is that we don't approve the first divorce request." Other judges quoted the famous proverb in the interview to explain why they stand by this principle: "We would rather demolish ten temples than destroy one marriage." Second, the denial of divorce requests often arose from the worry that victims would lose their abusers' financial support in a social milieu that lacked a social support system. Third, the perceived occupational hazard as a court judge contributed to the reluctance to approve a divorce. As one court judge told me in 2019, "We have heard of many cases where abusers displaced their anger onto the judges who approved a divorce. Some court judges were threatened and killed due to their approval of a divorce." A few judges that I interviewed cited the case of a Guangxi court judge named Mingsheng Fu who was killed by the defendant abuser in 2017 for approving his wife's divorce request (see also Yang 2017).

It is completely at the judges' discretion as to whether to convict abusers in violence-related divorce cases. Indeed, they pride themselves on persuading victims to drop criminal charges against their abusers. In 2015, a woman in Wuhan was beaten by her husband, sustaining injuries including a shattered broken nose (Yuan 2015). Their daughter was also taken away from her by her husband. Both the Wuhan Civil Affairs judge and the Criminal Affairs judge worked together to persuade the woman to drop her criminal charges against her husband so that her husband would be absolved of criminal penalty. Their success was applauded in the media as an example of how "judges worked together to dissolve hatred and bring about a harmonious ending" (ibid.). The wife's criminal charges against her husband were couched as a result of her "hatred," which was successfully "dissolved" by the judges to achieve a "harmonious" ending.

It was reported in China that, every year, a hundred thousand marriages dissolved due to intimate partner violence (Lian 2012). In the case of child custody rights, court judges often favor the more financially capable party in giving custody of the children, which deterred many women in my research from pursuing a divorce. The Supreme Court Document on Child Custody of Divorce Cases (1993) stipulates that the custody of children less than two years old is generally given to the mother, and the custody of children over two years old is generally given to the party that "benefits children's growth."

Women in my research told me that the party that benefits children's growth is often interpreted by courts as the party that is financially sound with the ownership of an apartment in a better school district. They told me that even in cases where the custody right of the child is awarded to the mother, it is often not implemented in practice. Indeed, courts often award the child custody right to the party that has a better financial situation, regardless of whether this party is the victim or the abuser (Fa 2020). As shown in the above-mentioned case of La Mu, the court gave the custody right of her two children to her abusive husband who eventually beat her to death (Yuan 2020).

In another case in Hangzhou (Zhang, Xiaoya 2016), not only was the custody right of the three-year-old son awarded to the abuser but the victim was also denied visitation rights. The victim Dai Xiaolei suffered long-term violence by her husband Liu Jie. In 2014, Liu beat Dai in public at the city airport, resulting in injuries and bruises in her eyes and her body. His entire beating was caught on the surveillance camera. She called the airport police immediately, who fined Liu 200RMB ($30). Afterward, Liu kidnapped their son, forbidding her to see him. In 2016, both Dai and Liu sued in court for a divorce. Although Liu's long-term violence was recognized by the Hangzhou Court, the court still awarded Liu the custody right of their three-year-old son and divided possessions equally between Liu and Dai. To Dai's demand for a damage fee of 100,000RMB ($15,000) for her years of physical damage and psychological suffering, the court ruled on a damage fee of 5,000RMB ($700). Since then, Liu has refused to pay this damage fee and has rejected her visitation rights. Every year since 2016, Dai has appealed to higher levels of courts to redress her abuser's refusal to pay the damage fee and to apply for the reassignment of child custody rights to her. Her multiple appeals have been rejected each year by various levels of courts. As shown, despite the court's recognition of the abuser's long-term violence, the victim was not given any support, the child custody right was awarded to the abuser, and the division of possessions between the abuser and the victim was equal. Neither the damage fee nor the victim's visitation rights in the court verdict was implemented.

Like Liu, women whom I have interviewed during my research related similar experiences where the divorce ended up robbing them of not only their child custody right, but also visitation rights, with no compensation or support from the criminal justice system. Many women's husbands had transferred money elsewhere before divorce, leaving them little or nothing after the divorce. Some threatened the women, causing them to leave the marriage with nothing. Even in cases where the women were awarded child custody rights, it was either not implemented in practice or their husbands refused to pay child support.

In 2013, Xiao Jie, a dance teacher in Beijing, was awarded the child custody right of their son, after her divorce with her abusive husband Chai Huabei, the CCTV sports news anchor (Gu 2015). Prior to the divorce, her husband beat her multiple times, causing a concussion and multiple injuries throughout her body. Even though the court awarded her the child custody right, her husband Chai took their son away and forbade her to see him. She appealed to the court to enforce the child custody right, but to no avail. In 2014, the Beijing court blacklisted Chai's name from using his ID, which restricted his ability to travel. Chai got around this by using his passport and continued attending activities everywhere. His employer also protected him and refused to "interfere in family affairs" when Xiao approached his company for help to resolve the issue (ibid.).

Even though the 46th stipulation in the Marriage Law states that court judges should "take care of the non-faulty party in the case of domestic violence" (Marriage Law 2001), in practice, this stipulation is often violated. For instance, in a legal case in Beijing, a victim hired a lawyer who helped her receive a Personal Safety Protection Order against her abusive husband for his long-term violence (Lin 2021). Later when she applied for the violence-related divorce, even with the help of her lawyer, the child custody right was awarded to her husband, and she was ordered by the court to pay a monthly child support of 600RMB ($100) to her husband. Moreover, the court awarded her husband most of their bank accounts, the apartment ownership, and car ownership.

This dearth of support by the criminal justice system forced some women to return to their abusers after divorce. Xiao Tong, a woman I interviewed during my research, for instance, after four years of divorce, went back to her abusive ex-husband and asked for a remarriage. Prior to the divorce, although she was beaten by her husband almost every couple of days, at least her livelihood was provided. Even though she had a voice recording of her husband admitting that he beat her dozens of times, the court judge still gave her husband all the possessions and the custody right of their son. Destitute after the divorce, she felt compelled to return to her ex-husband for survival. She told me:

> I'm not financially independent because my deteriorated health condition from his years of beating made it difficult for me to hold a job. After divorce, I found no support from society. My parents also blamed me. I've got nowhere to go but to return to him for survival.

Without any support from the criminal justice system or society, Xiao Tong went back to the abusive marriage. Another woman, Xiao Fang, whom I have interviewed had two children with her husband. After her husband beat her, sustaining several broken ribs, she proposed a divorce. Her husband transferred all their bank money elsewhere, left her, and did not leave her any money. She was sick at home without any economic resource. In a more severe case, Min whom I have interviewed, attempted suicide after she left her abusive husband and became sick and destitute, unable to survive financially.

While concerns about their future livelihood, child custody rights, division of possessions in court, the safety of her natal family, and the lack of social support constitute the deterrent factors, some women in my research also told me that the reason that they did not pursue criminal charges against their abusive husbands was because the long-lasting criminal record would negatively impact their children's future job prospects. Xiao Min, a thirty-year-old bank clerk, gave up pressing criminal charges against her husband's violence. When I asked her the reason, she told me:

> My toddler son dreams of becoming a pilot. After I hired a lawyer to pursue criminal charges against my husband's violence, a policeman said to me, "You

guys are a married couple. If you send him to prison, you won't get any benefit [from it]. Having a father with a criminal record, your child won't be able to pass background checks for future jobs. Nor will he be allowed to take entrance exams to become a government worker." The policeman's words made me realize that I can't do that [press criminal charges against her husband] because it'll crush my son's dream of becoming a pilot in the future. I can't be a selfish mother. As a mother, I have no alternative but to sacrifice myself for my son. So I gave up.

Indeed, in China, if a father has a criminal record, even after his death, his criminal record will prevent his children from access to any administrative or other kinds of jobs in institutions including the government, army, police, military, banks, key enterprises and companies, National Security departments, courts, tax bureaus, and so on. The children will also be barred from entrance exams to schools such as police schools and pilot schools. They can also be easily denied their applications for credit cards. Even if they manage to obtain certain jobs, the possibility of their future promotion is severely reduced. The enduring criminal record will continue to negatively impact the third generation for various job positions (Xiao 2020).

The criminal justice system fails women when it awards the child custody rights to perpetrators of violence, not considering the factor of intimate partner violence in dividing possessions and awarding child custody rights, and not enforcing accountability on abusers who take the children away from victims and deny their visitation rights. In so doing, the criminal justice system perpetuates the violence in the marriage.

Conclusion

The Chinese Criminal Law exhibits deeply entrenched inequities in applying different degrees of sentences to strangers as opposed to family members and male abusers as opposed to female victims. As we have seen in this chapter, the Chinese Criminal Law applies much more severe sentences to violent cases between strangers than to violent cases between family members. As shown, light sentences between six months to six years were given to abusers who had brutally beaten their wives to death, but much heavier sentences between more than ten years in prison and a death sentence were given to wives who had killed their abusers in self-defense. The gender inequity implicit in this legal structure fails to provide victims with the necessary legal recourse to rectify the violence and seek justice. It also violates the Chinese Constitution that guarantees equal protection under the law.

The dearth of legal support fueled suicides among female victims. It was reported by the All China's Women Federation that, every year in China, 60 percent of around 157,000 women who attempted suicide did so as a result of intimate partner violence (Yu 2019). In a more recent case, a 29-year-old mother in Anhui Province, Xiaoyan Yang, suffered years of abuse by her husband who not only beat her up, but also attempted to strangle her often. Both Yang and her husband went to the Civil Affairs Bureau to apply for a divorce, but they were told to observe the newly instituted "thirty-day divorce cooling-off period" that was implemented on January 1, 2021. Yang and her husband were sent home by the officials of the Civil Affairs Bureau. On March 11, 2021, under the threat of her husband, she agreed to leave the marriage without their two children and without any share of their possessions. She also agreed to pay monthly child support for their two children for fear that her husband might refuse her visitation rights down the road. The next day, on March 12, 2021, Yang committed suicide by falling off the twenty-fourth floor of a building with her two children—a four-year-old daughter and a two-year-old son (Shou 2021).

As shown in this chapter, directed by the state-sanctioned principle of family harmony and state stability at the expense of women's suffering and sacrifice, mediation, rather than criminalization, is championed and practiced by police and court judges to mediate between couples to resolve "family conflicts," the term they use to refer to intimate partner violence. Family harmony is deemed pivotal and indispensable to state stability and social security. Following this state-directed principle, the Supreme Court's Directive Document dictates that criminalizing abusers risks dissolving marriages and disrupting family harmony and, therefore, should be avoided. As a result, police and court judges rely on civil mechanisms such as mediation, Written Warning Notes, and Personal Safety Protection Orders. The penalty to abusers involves a fine of less than $142 and an administrative detention of less than fifteen days for a violation of the sanctioned measures or induced "minor injuries," defined according to the Chinese Criteria for Assessing the Extent of Bodily Injuries as a miscarriage, rib fracture, scalp laceration of more than 10 cm, facial burning area of more than 20 cm, eye socket fracture, body burning area of more than 40 cm, traumatic perforation of the tympanic, finger or wrist fracture, nose fracture, and foot fracture (2014). Criminalization is only applied to abusers who inflict severe damages such as mutilation, paralysis, and broken bones. In so doing, the criminal justice system has failed women and, in turn, has perpetuated intimate partner violence.

The Anti-Domestic Violence Law posits itself as a civil law rather than a criminal law in applying civil, soft measures to intimate partner violence cases that result in "minor injuries" (which, as defined above, can include such injuries as a broken bone). In so doing, the Anti-Domestic Violence Law regards intimate partner violence not as a crime but as a civil offense. The Chinese Criminal Law is evoked only to deal with severe cases that involve mutilation and paralysis. In addition, the Anti-Domestic Violence Law fails to include rape within marriage, as the Chinese Marriage Law stipulates that married couples should shoulder sexual obligations and responsibilities toward each other. The Anti-Domestic Violence Law also excludes same-sex couples and divorced spouses, who are barred from utilizing these civil mechanisms and civil penalties to handle abusers in their relationships. This can spawn severe consequences, as seen in La Mu's case in Sichuan—where La Mu's divorced husband continued to threaten, harass, and inflict violence on her. Since divorced spouses fall outside the purview of the Anti-Domestic Violence Law, La Mu was eventually beaten to death by her divorced husband.

As shown in this chapter, the criminal justice system as well as the social system have failed women, because of the lack of social services before and after divorce. This lack of support is enhanced because of the criminal justice system's preference for male abusers in awarding child custody rights and possession divisions, an emphasis on mediation, low issuance of Written Warning Notes, high threshold for Personal Safety Protection Orders, low recognition rates of violence in divorce cases, and high rejection rates of violence-related divorce cases. Outside of the criminal justice system, the lack of support from friends, families, and social services also compelled many women to either stay with, or return to, their abusive husbands after divorce for survival and livelihood. As shown in this chapter, friends, family members, co-workers, community, and neighbors of women such as the female doctor Xiaoyan Zhang, witnessed the intimate partner violence. Not only did they not report it but they also advised the victims to endure it. In some cases, this resulted in the women being beaten to death by their husbands.

In spite of the legal and social constraints that women face, 2021 has witnessed some progress in intimate partner violence training and education at multiple agencies, including the police, the All China Women's Federation, and the courts. Training and education in these key institutional sectors are paramount in disseminating information on modes of intervention in cases of intimate partner violence and institutional implementation of the Anti-Domestic Violence Law. It is critical to build a network among these multiple key sectors to provide both institutional support and legal interventions to protect victims and address their legal concerns and social needs. In spite of these minor attempts to better train incumbent officials and staffs, China still has a long way to go to achieve justice for women in abusive marriages. Until significant changes take place in the area of political and sociocultural violence that undergirds state-sanctioned discourse calling for women's sacrifice for family harmony and state stability, Chinese women will continue to be at risk.

Reflections on the Neglect of Law by Police and Judges in China

As illustrated in this chapter, police and judges make judgments not based upon the law but based upon their personal cultural biases. Indeed, as shown in this chapter, police and judges ignore the law while handling intimate partner violence cases. Why is there such a neglect of law by law enforcement agencies in China? I argue that an acceptance of the rule of authoritarian leaders over the rule of authority of law is deeply rooted in Chinese history.

In the West, a form of law established itself early, initially, among Germanic tribes. This was the tribal tradition. In England, this became the basis of common law, reinforced by court decisions that, over time, established, both in Britain and the United States, rules that embodied basic values. In addition, various bodies created statutory laws; that is, laws that were written down and had the power of the state behind them.

The role of the judiciary in Anglo-America was to interpret this body of statutory and common law as it applied to particular cases. Each of these judicial decisions contributed to the body of law that governed society, providing a large volume of precedents that strictly guided further judicial decisions. In the Anglo-American world, judges worked within a very limited framework. British and American lawyers liked to say, "We are governed by laws, not by men." Westerners generally, because of the prevalence of Christianity, see humans as deeply flawed, victims of Adam's original sin. The structure of the law in the West is meant to shield justice from the caprice of fallible human beings.

There is an alternative pre-Christian point of view expressed by Plato some three hundred years before Christ. In *The Republic*, Plato argues for a philosopher king who will have autocratic power but will not misuse it. Why not? Because Plato believed that evil was a consequence of ignorance. The philosopher king, as the title suggests, would be highly educated in platonic truths, which reject materialism as a value in favor of spiritual riches. He argued that we need not fear the philosopher king because he or she will be grounded in proper nonmaterialist values and will not be corrupted by avarice.

In the Chinese tradition, Confucian values, similar to those of Plato, were not superseded by Christian values. Education in China held supreme value, producing, at its pinnacle, a wise Confucian scholar who could be trusted to provide justice. The law in China is analogous to a situation where an individual might regard (falsely) a red light as an aid to, not a replacement for, a human judgment.

As mentioned, in China, education was of primary importance. Confucius, a teacher, is the most revered figure in Chinese history. However, it would be wrong to think of Chinese education as a free inquiry into the world of ideas. Because truth was absolute and knowable, it was the job of an expert to transfer these ideas into the minds of the students who were not expected to question it. Truth was not up for grabs. Truth was absolute. There was believed to be an objectively true way of seeing the world. This knowledge was passed on by the teacher to the students. Confucius talked about his own experience of becoming wise. It involved a disciplined training and a habit of goodness, until this became a natural response to all situations. The mature Confucian was all wise, as represented by the mandarin class. Their judgment and integrity in carrying out just verdicts were unquestioned, and certainly superior to the rigidity of the conventional law. As suggested above, this process involved a disciplined and long-term exercise of establishing the habit of virtue so that by the time he was in his forties, for Confucius, responding in the correct way to moral challenges had become a natural habit, requiring little thought.

It is often wondered how Communism could be imposed upon a Confucian society with its reverence for tradition and family. Perhaps it is because the deep structure of Confucian thinking includes this notion of an objective truth dispersed by an all-knowing and morally upright expert. The point of convergence may be that, like Confucianism, Marxism also possesses a body of truth that is supposedly based on science. As in Confucianism, this knowledge will make you both wise and moral and trustworthy. For centuries, Chinese society had been accustomed to accepting the authority of a wise man. Communism simply substituted the commissar for the mandarin.

Lord Acton famously said (1907), "Power tends to corrupt, and absolute power corrupts absolutely." As argued above, a fundamental difference between China and the West regarding authority, here expressed by Lord Acton, is that in the West, people believe that they must be shielded from the corruption of human authority with the rule of law.

Chapter 4

MALE PERCEPTIONS AND RATIONALIZATIONS OF INTIMATE PARTNER VIOLENCE IN POST-SOCIALIST CHINA

Few women never get beaten [bu aizou de nvren shao]. Once you're beaten, you need to think about the reason why you're beaten and correct your mistakes. Some women "zui ying" [have a harsh mouth]—they're on the wrong side but they just refuse to listen to reason [benlai jiu budui hai sibu jiangli]. It'd be strange if they didn't get beaten [bu aizou cai guai].

There's a local saying that the dirtiest place in the city is Malan River, and the second dirtiest place is local women's mouths, famous for their uncouth and crude language.

Women love "lao dao" [nagging]. It is extremely annoying, and they'll get beaten for it. If you don't want to be beaten, don't focus on who is right. Even if you're right, you shouldn't "zui ying" [have a harsh mouth]. Otherwise you'll get beaten.

These are excerpts from interviews during my research in Dalian, China, about men's perceptions and attitudes toward intimate partner violence. When asked why husbands beat wives, interviewees, in general, attributed it to men suffering from mental illnesses. Apart from mental illnesses, interviewees invoked women's "zui ying" (literally, harsh mouth) and "you mao bing" (literally, having maladies or physical diseases, and to be at fault) as the root causes that ignited wife-beating or male violence. In this chapter, I will unpack these two discourses.

Studies have attributed intimate partner violence to a plethora of individual factors such as age, education, socioeconomic status, marital conflict, history of abuse in childhood, and alcohol and drug use (Aldarondo 1996, Burgess and Draper 1989; Gelles 1985; Goldstein and Rosenbaum 1985; Dibble and Straus 1980; Song and Xue 2003; Zhang and Liu 2004; Tao 2004; Xu et al. 2005). Attention to individual characteristics, however, reduces this social problem to a private, family issue. An exclusive cultural approach in feminist writings also obscures the political factors and economic conditions that spawn gender inequality in intimate partner violence (Sokoloff and Dupont 2005). Undoubtedly, these are legitimate approaches in the study of this issue. However, in this book, I am more concerned with what is unique in the Chinese political, economic, and cultural context.

I will draw on my ethnographic research in the metropolitan city of Dalian and media representations of intimate partner violence, arguing that intimate partner violence is inexorably linked to structural inequality where the discourse employed to explain intimate partner violence is a regulatory, disciplinary mechanism to control and discipline women's mouths, bodies, and behaviors. Violence against women, in this framework, is not a monolithic phenomenon, but a complex structural problem of multiple forms of oppression growing out of unequal social hierarchy.

Zui Ying ("Harsh Mouth" or "Strong Mouth")

Male interviewees referred to women's "zui ying" (literally harsh mouth, strong mouth), "zui zang" (dirty mouth), "lao dao" (nagging), "zui jian" (mean mouth) as the trigger that provokes male violence. Below are some examples of my interviews with men:

> When marital conflicts arise, women tend to "zui ying" [have a harsh mouth]. How can a man get the upper hand in a quarrel with a woman [nande shui neng chaoguo nvde]? When she continues bickering with her "zui ying" [harsh mouth], he becomes outraged. In an explosion of rage [qidao huotou shang], how can he not beat her? She should shut up; otherwise she'll get a beating.
>
> Men often have a temper. She must "zui ying" [harsh mouth or strong mouth]—have a harsh mouth that choked him [qiang zhao ta le]. In an explosion of fire [huoqi yishang], he can't repress it [ya bu zhu] and start beating. When that happens, you can't blame one party, because both parties are responsible.
>
> I like to play mahjong all night long. Last time when my wife "lao dao" [nagged] and complained about it, I got so enraged that I threw my cell phone into the lower part of her leg. Her leg was so swollen that she couldn't go to work for a couple of days. For a man to slap, push, or throw one or two fists at a woman to release his rage/anger [faxie yixia, chu yixia qi] is a normal part of life, but it becomes domestic violence if he beats her so violently that her bones break. Then they should divorce.

Male interviewees linked women's mouths and wife-beating; they also made a clear distinction between wife-beating and violence. While wife-beating is defined as slapping, pushing, and throwing one or two fists at women, violence (baoli) is described as heavy beating causing broken bones. Interviewees identified women's mouths as harsh, choking, bickering, nagging, and dirty, as in cases where women refused to listen to reason or got the upper hand in a quarrel. Their mouths are pinpointed as the culprit, triggering men's rage that leads to wife-beating. As shown in the interviews, a woman's harsh mouth causes a man to abandon his reason and explode in wrath, which he is not able to control.

As a result, it destroys his self-control and drives him to beat his wife, for which he is not responsible.

This "zui ying" (harsh mouth or strong mouth) discourse is also invoked in popular media to explain wife-beating. A popular publication, *Metropolitan Female Newspaper*, for instance, published a letter from a reader and a formal response by a psychology expert in the advice column. The reader wrote that her husband beat her every time she opened her mouth during a quarrel. The beating, however, was not heavy, she wrote, and he did apologize afterward. She asked the expert why her husband beat her, how to avoid the beating, and whether it stemmed from her mistakes. The expert responded:

> Women's "linguistic violence" can instigate men's "physical violence." In a marriage, if the wife gets the upper hand in a debate and the husband 'zui ben" [has a slow mouth, is inarticulate], it will enrage the husband. At this time, if you continue to nag [die die bu xiu], you will definitely enrage your husband. Under this circumstance, if you are a smart woman, you will act like "Lin Daiyu" [the gentle, physically weak female character in the Chinese masterpiece *Dream of Red Mansions*], your husband will not use violence, as he knows that his wife needs his protection. We hear many cases like yours on our help hotline. In all these cases, the wife's argument is too strong, which is actually a form of "psychological, soft violence" directed at the husband. On the surface, the wife seems to be the "victim" and the husband seems to be the "perpetrator," but this is actually not the case. It is the wife's strong argument that has ignited the angry fire in her husband. Even though the husband knows it is wrong to beat his wife, he cannot control himself. So, a smart wife never provokes her husband. When you see him angry, you should stop talking and be quiet. If you want to tackle the root cause and resolve the issue, you should complain less, nag less, be gentle and understanding, and not give your husband an opportunity to get angry and violent. When a man is faced with a woman who is gentle like water, he will be reluctant to hit her. Wouldn't you agree? (Li 2009)

The psychology expert calls women's harsh mouths "linguistic violence" and "psychological, soft violence," and condemns women's mouths as the root cause of male violence. Like the interviewees in my research, the expert likens male rage to a natural, volcanic fire that, once ignited and instigated by women's mouths, is impossible to stop until it runs its natural course. Depicting male rage as instinctual, biological, and uncontrollable, the expert admonishes women to control their mouths and be gentle: "complain less, nag less, be gentle and understanding, and not give your husband an opportunity to get angry and violent." Indeed, underlying this "zuiying" discourse is the belief that male violent rage is inevitable, immutable, and involuntary, even normative and appropriate when responding to women's harsh mouths. By condemning women's mouths as the culprit spurring male violent rage, this "zui ying" (harsh mouth or strong mouth) discourse puts the blame on the victim (see also Yang 2007).

You mao bing (Literally: Be at Fault)

According to male interviewees in my research, if a woman is beaten, it is a sign that she is at fault. Below are some examples of the interviews:

> The wife must you mao bing [be at fault], otherwise the husband won't beat her. There's always a reason why she gets beaten. She must've had an extramarital affair. As you know, love and passion only lasts three years in a marriage. It's a man's inherent nature not to be satisfied with one wife. One is never enough, and men always want more and desire more. I have many lovers, which is normal nowadays. Even though the lovemaking feels the same with all my female lovers, the temptation is still there, which a man can't resist. However, a woman should always be faithful. If she engages in an affair, it can push him into a corner [bi ji le, bi huo le]. Even a rabbit will bite when it's cornered.
>
> Some women you mao bing [are at fault] because they are blustering, boastful, noisy, and boisterous [dede sese, zhazha huhu]. I don't like this kind of woman. A woman should be gentle and quiet when a man is angry. My wife used to dance at her company after work and often came home late, for which she received a good beating every time. How could she not receive a beating when she has failed to come home at a decent hour?
>
> Some women you mao bing [are at fault] because they're domineering, bossy, and act superior to men [feiyang bahu, gaogao zaishang]. They have their husbands cook, wash clothes, and do household chores, so men have no alternative but to resist and fight back.

Interviewees believe that women who "you mao bing" (have maladies) have extramarital affairs, exercise autonomy, are domineering, bossy, noisy, and act superior to men. A woman is expected to be gentle, quiet, loyal, obedient, at home after work, and conduct all household chores. Nonconforming, "aberrant" women are seen as the source of male violence. As shown in the interviews, women who "you mao bing" (have maladies) typically come home late after work, fail to do household chores, engage in affairs, and do not close their mouths when men are angry. Their transgression from, and failure to fulfil, the gendered roles and wifely duties is perceived as challenging and threatening to men's authority and status in the household, thereby precipitating male aggression.

Associating a wife-at-fault with male violence is also manifested in popular media and official discourse. The state-sponsored *Women of China* magazine, for instance, published readers' reflections on the first TV series on domestic violence titled "Don't Talk to Strangers," which was meant to combat domestic violence. A teacher conveyed her deep compassion for the husband in the TV series, who she believed suffered from mental illness. She contended that he deserved more care and love than a normal person, especially from his wife. She wrote that the wife could have offered him love to make him feel understood and comforted. Instead, she was cold to her husband, which "undoubtedly made her husband's mental illness even more serious." She concluded that the tragedy has everything to do with the fact that she was not a good wife (Deng 2002).

Attributing male violence to a woman at fault is shown not only in this state-sponsored magazine, but also in government officials' advice to female victims. In 2015, a woman in my research called the local government agency—All China Women's Federation, seeking help against her husband's domestic violence. The female government official said to her, "You first need to identify the root cause of your husband's violence. Is it because you are not gentle enough, or because you are not virtuous enough? After your self-reflection, you'll need to make the necessary adjustments to yourself and treat him better so that you can keep your husband's heart." She also advised the woman to plan family activities so that their child could help bring the parents together.

Both the teacher in the state-sponsored magazine and the government official emphasized the inexorable relationship between male violence and an "aberrant" wife. While the teacher attributed male violence to a bad, cold wife, the local government official questioned whether the woman was a gentle and virtuous wife, suggesting that she was the root cause of her husband's violence. The underlying assumption is that it is always the "aberrant" woman who is at fault because she has provoked male anger and violence. Hence, the solution to male violence is a woman's self-reflection and self-adjustments to be more gentle and virtuous and to treat her husband better. This is the key to winning her husband's heart and thwarting his violence.

While infidelity is described as a biological attribute of men, the "you mao bing" (have maladies, be at fault) discourse deems it a malady if a woman was to engage in infidelity instead of following her "biological nature," which is to be loyal and faithful to her husband. As noted in the interview, "It's a man's inherent nature not to be satisfied with one wife. One is never enough, and men always want more and desire more. I have many lovers, which is normal nowadays ... the temptation is still there, which a man can't resist." As he contends, it is a man's biological nature to sexually desire more women and engage in multiple extramarital affairs as they are inherently unable to resist the temptation. Following this rationale, it is women's "biological nature" to stay faithful and it is imperative that they obey their "nature." As illustrated in the "you mao bing" (have maladies, be at fault) discourse, failure to do so is a symptom of a woman having a malady.

Indeed, this discourse represents a biologically determined explanation of gender behavior that governs gender in China. Young women are urged to manage and control men's sexual advances before marriage, satisfy their husbands' sexual needs, and stay clear of extramarital affairs after marriage (Honig and Hershatter 1988). In their study of advice literature, Honig and Hershatter (1988: 53) note that it invariably rests on the shoulders of young women to "channel and control the sexual desires of young men as well as their own and to defer acting on those desires until they [have] reach[ed] the socially appropriate age for courtship and marriage."

In popular media, women are advised to forgive their husbands' extramarital affairs as it is believed it is central to a man's biological nature to engage in extramarital sexual affairs (see also Zheng 2006). An article in a popular magazine *Hers* reads (Lan 2006):

> All men love play. It is their nature. The reason that men can separate love from sex is because they are like animals. They emphasize sensory stimulation, not feelings. They have to depend upon the most basic and the most intimate contact to feel complete release. Men's macho role depends upon their conquest of women. Why does a man pursue pretty women one after another? It is because he wants to prove to everyone that he is capable and he is a man.

In the state-sponsored *Journal of Women in China*, an article titled "Marriage: Women's Rights and Responsibilities," followed by four installments titled "Women Are the Last Defenders of Ethics" (Liu and Xu 2005), emphasizes that a wife, faced with her husband's extramarital affairs, should reflect on her own shortcomings and forgive her husband. One reader, for instance, narrates a story where her husband turns to extramarital affairs because she is not a gentle and womanly wife (Ling 2003). These media discourses exert pressure on wives to take responsibility for keeping the family intact and safeguarding social morality.

Historian Linda Gordon asserts that in Britain and the United States, "it is easier and more 'normal' for men to be lustful and assertive, for women merely to surrender, to be carried away by a greater force" (Gordon 1979: 126). In a cultural milieu that explains men's sexual desires in biological terms, it is not surprising that interviewees in my research have internalized and reiterated this biologically determinist view as immutable natural laws that justify men's uncontrollable infidelity and women's sexual loyalty to their husbands.

The "you mao bing" (have maladies, be at fault) discourse emphasizes expectations that a wife will perform household chores, be sexually loyal to her husband, be gentle and subservient, and stay at home after work. When a wife comes home late, engages in extramarital affairs, and behaves in a domineering, bossy, and boisterous way, she is thought to "have a malady"; that is, she is "unnaturally" transgressing the biologically determined natural laws, violating the established gender norm of propriety, and damaging the honor of her husband. As shown in this discourse, when these expectations are not fulfilled or are even defied by women, men are overwhelmed by emotions that they are unable to control. Their violent rage is justified, uncontrollable, and natural.

Conclusion

Men in my research invoke the discourses of "zui ying" (harsh mouth or strong mouth) and "you mao bing" (have maladies, be at fault) to explain wife-beating. They define wife-beating as slapping, pushing, and throwing one or two fists at women, and distinguish wife-beating from domestic violence, which causes broken bones and warrants a divorce. In this chapter, I argue that the "zui ying" (harsh mouth or strong mouth) and "you mao bing" (have maladies, be at fault) discourses are not just rationalizing frameworks for wife-beating but regulatory mechanisms that blame victims, naturalize, justify, and legitimize male violence, and regulate and discipline women.

Echoed in the popular, medical, and official discourse is the causal relationship between male violence and a faulty wife with a harsh, nagging, and dirty mouth. As admonished by the psychology expert, "when a man is faced with a woman gentle like water, he will be reluctant to beat her." What crystallizes in this discourse is that if a woman behaves properly, she can never be the target of violence. Male violence is thus identified as victim-precipitated. As shown, the discourse condemns women's harsh mouths and labels nonconforming wives as women having maladies, that manifests in their failure to fulfil proper gendered roles and behaviors such as being loyal, gentle, quiet, staying home after work, and handling all household chores. The labeling discourse deems aberrant women unworthy of respect or compassion from others.

Contending that men are biologically unable to control their sexual desires, anger, and violence, the "zui ying" (harsh mouth or strong mouth) and "you mao bing" (have maladies, be at fault) discourses naturalize, justify, and legitimize male violence. The crux of the discourse is that women's deviant mouths and deviations from the expected wifely roles and duties have unleashed the natural, biological male violence. As noted in the interviews, when a woman fails to meet the expected role of a gentle and loyal wife, "it pushes him to a corner (bi ji le, bi huo le). Even a rabbit will bite when it's cornered." The man is likened to a desperate and outraged animal that cannot help biting when cornered. Succumbing to the righteous will of nature or instinct like a cornered animal helps legitimate and justify male violence.

The discourses of zui ying (harsh mouth or strong mouth) and you mao bing (have maladies, be at fault) are disciplinary and regulatory in nature, proclaiming that women's self-discipline and self-constraints can ward off and thwart male violence. These discourses naturalize and rationalize the connections between harsh-mouthed women who are at fault and male violence, thereby subjugating women's mouths and behaviors to scrutiny, control, and regulation. As noted by the government official, the psychology expert, and the interviewees, women should bear the brunt of the issue of male violence and "make the necessary adjustments" to transform themselves to resolve it. Self-transformation includes controlling their speech, staying quiet, observing wifely duties, being subservient, gentle, loyal, and submissive.

Calling on individuals to discipline and transform themselves to prevent domestic violence represents Foucault's technology of the self, accomplished through individuals in charge of their own behaviors, well-being, and improvement. In the neoliberal era of China, the technology of power is less about direct violence or force than about the technology of the self, where individuals alter and change themselves within an internalized, disciplinary discourse. The state is no longer the visible, dominant agent of control. Individuals themselves actively self-monitor, self-scrutinize, and self-discipline through internalized regulatory mechanisms.

The discourses of zui ying (harsh mouth or strong mouth) and you mao bing (have maladies, be at fault) operate as a technology of power and regulatory mechanism to police, discipline, control, and regulate women, and safeguard social stability and national morality. As mentioned earlier, it was the women who were asked to sacrifice for the neoliberal restructuring in China and were, in turn, disadvantaged and negatively impacted. This discourse disguises and masks the political and economic structure that places women at a disadvantage, exacerbates gender inequality, leaving women at the risk of male violence, as the lack of economic resources hinders women's ability to alter the status quo of domestic violence. To sum up, this questionable reasoning makes it impossible for men to be held accountable for any kind of violent behavior against their intimate partners. By definition, male violence is always caused by inadequate behaviors on the part of women.

Chapter 5

EVERYDAY RESISTANCE OF WOMEN AGAINST INTIMATE PARTNER VIOLENCE

Because my husband didn't like the breakfast I cooked, he beat me up so severely that I was sent to the hospital emergency room. My neighbors called the police [about the violence]. The police mediated between us and asked me to sign the mediation note. I asked the police, "I don't understand why you'd only mediate? Does mediation reduce the workload for you? I hope you police can help victims like me. I don't want a divorce but I want him [my husband] to know that there's a price for beating me." I spent half the day negotiating with the police, insisting on a Written Warning Note [to be issued]. In the end, I told him that I'm going to sue him in court if he refuses to issue the Written Warning Note. [Upon my threat], he finally did.

As shown in Chapter 3, according to the 16th stipulation of the Anti-Domestic Violence Law, mediation is an indispensable process for the authorities to deal with intimate violence cases. According to the Law, post-mediation options include a Written Warning Note and/or criticism and education of the perpetrator. In compliance with this stipulation in the Law, the policeman chose the latter—criticism and education of the abuser. Even though the Law does not hold the police responsible for issuing a Written Warning Note, as shown in the interview above, Xiao Jun's persistence and threat to sue the police in court successfully compelled him to issue the Written Warning Note, which she could later use in court as evidence of the abuse in case of a divorce.

Xiao Jun, who worked at the Human Resources Department at a well-known company in a southern city, was well equipped with her knowledge of the Anti-Domestic Violence Law and her financial independence to threaten the police. In addition, if she chooses to do so down the road, she is also financially sound enough to hire a lawyer for a divorce. My research data shows that, even though intimate partner violence takes place across a wide spectrum of class, status, regions, and gender (see also Dasgupta 2013), women from urban areas, in general, enjoy more access to information on intimate partner violence and the available social services including legal counselling and legal representations provided by NGOs and other organizations (see Chapter 6). Women with an independent income are also more financially equipped to hire a lawyer for a divorce, despite the difficulties and complications related to violence-related divorce lawsuits, as illustrated in many individual cases in Chapter 3.

Some resource-poor women in rural areas who killed their abusers or found themselves in desperate situations, as shown in the individual case studies in Chapter 6, sought legal help from the renowned NGO—the Beijing Qianqian Law Firm—for legal resistance and legal justice. These women, in despair, traveled to Beijing seeking legal help to either reduce their death sentence for killing their abusers or obtain legal redress for body mutilations such as having their eyes carved out by their abusers (see also Chapter 6; Lv 2017).

As mentioned above, women's active resistance includes threatening the police, hiring a lawyer for a violence-related divorce, and soliciting pro bono lawyers in reputed NGOs for legal assistance such as legal representations in court. While many of these individual legal cases are elaborated in Chapter 3 and Chapter 6, this chapter focuses on women's everyday resistance against intimate partner violence beyond these legal pursuits for legal justice.

Based on my ethnographic research, this chapter analyzes and explores women's everyday responses to intimate partner violence to demonstrate their everyday agency and resistance. It is important to keep in mind that their experiences of, and resistance against violence, are shaped by structural constraints and inequalities illustrated in Chapters 1 and 3, including police inaction, inadequacies of the Anti-Domestic Violence Law, and the criminal justice system's preference for abusers in court proceedings and court verdicts that thwart and hamper women's resistance to intimate partner violence. In the absence of legal, social, and economic protection, they resort to creative ways to challenge the violence inflicted upon them. This chapter gives voice to the women on the ground by demonstrating their struggles, resistances, and strategies against intimate partner violence, which include, but are not limited to, escape, seeking help from safe houses and NGOs, using informal sources for help, pleasing and avoiding, talking back, fighting back, and murdering and committing suicide. Navigating within the cultural and structural constraints to contend with intimate partner violence, their resistance, oftentimes, is shaped and determined by whatever resources that are available to them.

Escape

Escape is often a luxurious strategy beyond reach for women who are full-time housewives relying on their husbands to survive financially. These women told me that their husbands control the family finances. Without any bank savings to sustain themselves financially, escape is untenable. In the words of a woman with whom I interacted, "If I escape with a baby, both of us will die of hunger." These women, therefore, oftentimes resorted to strategies other than escape. Some, in desperate situations, escaped to Beijing seeking help from reputed NGOs, as illustrated in Chapter 6.

For women who have some savings, limited though it might be, escape is a viable option. The reason that women choose to escape rather than return to their natal family is often due to the shame and disgrace that their return will bring to the family. Below I will recount several representative stories of escape.

Yi's parents strongly disapproved of her marriage to her husband, but she insisted that she chose him herself because he was caring and loving to her and she did not mind his unfavorable financial condition and his faraway hometown. Prior to marriage, he was, in Yi's own words, "extremely good" to her. After marriage, however, Yi found herself abused and tortured by him on a regular basis, including beatings, cursing, turning on the gas to terrorize her, attacking her with a spring knife, strangling her, throwing objects at her, and threatening to kill her with his dagger. When their baby was two months old, he took the baby and threatened to smash the baby onto the floor just because the baby was crying and disrupting his sleep. When she begged him to release the baby, he became more violent, telling her that he was going to kill both her and the baby.

After their baby was eight months old, he took the baby away from her, forbidding her to see the baby unless she was submissive to him. Her first child was born through a C-section surgery and, within less than a year, she was pregnant again. Rather than allowing her to seek a legitimate abortion, he insisted that she jump up and down to induce a miscarriage.

She requested divorce several times, but each time her request was rejected by him and resulted in more physical abuse. Before she escaped, in the last episode of abuse, he believed that she was going to leave him. He asked her to choose one way to die: either being killed by his dagger or being strangled to death. Eventually, however, he released her.

Yi, at the age of twenty-seven and fifty days pregnant, finally managed to escape to a strange city, as she could not bring herself to tell her parents. She was warned by doctors not to get pregnant within one year of her C-section surgery, but she did. Doctors told her that if she insisted on giving birth to the baby, she and the baby might die in the end. Reluctant as she was, in this strange city where she knew no one, she went to a hospital and aborted the child.

Yi later told me:

> This is my own choice. This path was chosen by myself. Whatever it takes, I will finish it on my own.

She insisted that if she returned home, her parents would not be able to face everyone because of the embarrassment. She said:

> At that time [when I was about to marry him], no one liked him. Now they are all proven correct. If I go back, everyone would laugh at my parents.

Yi said that it was her fate, which she had to accept.

Since Yi escaped, her husband has been begging, threatening, and using her child as a bargain to make her return. He threatened to send her relatives nude pictures that he had taken of her in bed. He also threatened to rob her of any opportunities to ever see her child again. Yi said, "My child is my life. It's like killing me if I cannot see my child."

Yi said eventually when the savings run out, she will either go back with a gun or seek help from her natal family. She said, "When I have a gun, I will kill him and then kill myself."

Like Yi, Xuan, a thirty-year-old woman, escaped from her husband. Xuan met her husband online when she was in her mid-twenties. Although he showed great compassion in caring for her when she was sick, after they got married six years later, he changed dramatically. She was deeply hurt by a series of abuses. In the first case, when they argued about when to purchase a house, he beat her up. In the second case, during her pregnancy, because she told him that she was not feeling well enough to iron his clothes, he got furious and beat her up. After that incident, she aborted the child. Half a month after her abortion, she was beaten again because she forgot to bring him chopsticks. In the third case, Xuan suggested that he not overindulge in internet games since he had been playing day and night without eating or sleeping. Infuriated, he spilled a burning hot teapot over her feet, causing her feet to be severely burned.

Xuan's mother died when she was little, and she did not want to burden her dad with her misery. After recovery, Xuan escaped to a city that was 200 kilometers away from home. Although her husband apologized, begged, and did everything he could to make her return, Xuan said she was not returning, as she was afraid of being beaten to death by him.

While Yi and Xuan escaped on their own, other women escaped with their children from their husbands. Ling, for instance, told me that she took her baby with her and escaped to another city. She said she had enough savings for her to hire a babysitter during the daytime so she could look for a job. She insists that women can live without men, and that men are not able to realize what a mistake they have made until they lose everything.

While some women are able to escape successfully without being tracked down by their husbands, other women are not that fortunate. Some women were found and retrieved by their husbands in their attempts to escape, which oftentimes ended in more abuse.

Seeking Help from Safe Houses and NGOs

Xiao Jie, a woman in her mid-twenties, suffered long-term violence at the hands of her abusive husband.[1] She applied for, and received, a Personal Safety Protection Order from the court. Even though after her abuser violated the order several times, he was never punished and the order was never implemented by the court or the police (see Chapters 1 and 3). Xiao Jie was not able to maintain jobs because her husband found her each time at her workplace and continued to harass and abuse her. When she sought help from the police and the All China Women's Federation, they mediated between her and her husband, and advised her to return home (see

Chapter 3). In the vacuum of social and legal help, she was forced to live in fear and go into constant hiding.

Xiao Jie finally escaped. After escaping, she first resided with her relatives and friends. However, her husband found her there. Her relatives and friends were rewarded for their kindness by being beaten by her husband, sustaining serious injuries. Feeling guilty that she had brought this on them, Xiao Jie went to the police for help. After asking her a few questions, the police registered the violence she reported as "common family conflict" (putong jiating jiufen). The police then suggested that she should seek help from relatives and friends. Xiao Jie went to the All China Women's Federation, and there too she was advised to seek help from her relatives and friends. It is important to note here that an assault on a third party is not regarded as an assault and battery by the police (see Chapter 3 for details). As indicated in Chapter 3, China's Criminal Law does not regard a simple assault as a crime unless permanent damage such as broken ribs, skull fracture, and spine fracture is inflicted on a victim.

In the end, she escaped again, this time, to the capital Beijing. She worked at a restaurant as a waitress but was fired a few days later due to her poor health, which was a result of years of physical abuse. Helpless and desperate, she went to the Beijing office of the All China Women's Federation, requesting to stay at a safe house designed for victims of domestic violence.

The officials at the All China Women's Federation told her to go back to her hometown. She cried, telling them that she would never have escaped to Beijing if she had been able to find a solution in her hometown. Then one of them told her that the safe house was located within the social aid station and that the longest duration she could stay was seven days. She gave Xiao Jie the address and information about the bus lines to get there. She then told Xiao Jie:

> We'll contact your hometown. You'll have to return to your hometown to resolve this issue.

Xiao Jie told the official her negative experiences with the local state apparatuses, which had failed to resolve the issue. However, despite her pleas, the official insisted that they would contact her hometown and return her home.

Several hours later, Xiao Jie finally arrived at the reception office of the social aid station. She recorded her experience:

> The moment I entered the office, the receptionist yelled at me: "You! Why are you—such a young girl—coming here?! You must be mentally ill!" I was terrified and dumbfounded by their forcefulness. I murmured: "No. The All China Women's Federation introduced me to the safe house."
>
> The staff member responded: "What safe house? We are a social aid station. Can't you read the sign [on the door]? This All China Women's Federation—they'd push anyone to come here!"
>
> A number of staff members took pictures of me and asked for my ID and my household registration. They then called the police in my hometown. They

yelled on the phone: "How do you guys handle things over there? Do you know that your people have even escaped to our aid station?"

After the phone call, the staff members continued complaining and cursing for a long time. One staff member searched online and got the information of the day I arrived at Beijing by train and my first few days' stay at a hotel.

They interrogated me: "You even stayed at a hotel—what're you doing at our aid station? Do you think our aid station is fun? What on earth are you doing here? How many of you are there? Spare no time and tell us the truth!"

I was so terrified that my whole body started trembling. My eyes welled up with tears. I clenched my teeth to calm myself down.

I answered: "I escaped here on my own. My hometown friend had some surplus balance at that hotel and gave it to me to stay there for a few days so I could look for jobs. I was unable to find a job and ran out of money. It's winter now—I am physically unwell and can't find a place to stay. I thought of the Anti-Domestic Violence Law that stipulates that a safe house can be provided to victims. The All China Women's Federation said that the safe house is located within the aid station, so I came here."

After hearing my answer, the staff members left and never came out for a while. Later, several men and a female garbage-picker came in, requesting help because they had no place to live. The staff members came out and yelled at them impatiently: "What kind of people are you to come to our aid station? All of you are mentally ill—get the hell out of here immediately! We only accept homeless beggars here!"

I was so terrified that I hid in a corner, trembling.

Later, Xiao Jie was taken to the aid station which was 40 kilometers away from the reception office. A staff member told her:

Upon arrival, you need to have your relatives wire you money. You can use that money to purchase the transportation tickets when you leave that place … Once you leave that place, you can no longer enter that place again.

Xiao Jie was put in a room shared by four people, where she had an almost sleepless night. Throughout the night, she was disturbed by the surrounding noise of singing, talking, fighting, and crying. The next morning, she left the aid station.

After she left, Xiao Jie sought help from one of the NGOs in Beijing—Feminist Voice (see Chapter 6). Feminist Voice helped her find a safe temporary place and a job (Xiao 2018). With the support from the Anti-Domestic Violence NGOs in Beijing (see Chapter 6), Xiao Jie was successfully granted a divorce. Even though the NGOs helped her win the child custody rights, her ex-husband has been keeping their child from her (see Chapter 3). Xiao Jie lamented that she has not been able to see their child (Xiao 2018). As shown in Chapter 3, in cases where the women are awarded child custody rights, it is often either not implemented in practice or their ex-husbands refuse to pay child support. The criminal justice system often fails to enforce accountability on abusers who take the child away from victims and deny their visitation rights.

Xiao Jie's story is not only a story of women's everyday resistance, but also a story of structural violence—the unjust criminal justice system and social system that not only fail to protect and help victims of intimate partner violence, but also terrorize and frighten them. As shown in her story, Xiao Jie, even though she exerted her agency to escape intimate partner violence, was dismissed and disregarded when she sought help from the police and the All China Women's Federation. Her abuser's repeated violations of the Personal Safety Protection Order that she successfully obtained in court was also ignored by the court and the criminal justice system.

In the end, Xiao Jie had to forcefully cite the Anti-Domestic Violence Law to the officials of the Beijing office of the All China Women's Federation, demanding protection from the safe house as per the stipulations of the Law. The 15th stipulation of the Anti-Domestic Violence Law states that the police should coordinate with other state departments to help introduce victims to safe houses and aid institutions (2015).

However, in practice, many officials in the police station, the All China Women's Federation, and residential committee have no knowledge about this stipulation or the procedures involved to introduce victims to safe houses (Nan 2019). Although it is deemed the responsibility of the police and other civil departments in the Law, the Law fails to specify the kind of legal consequences these departments will suffer if they fail to perform their legal duties. Without a legal consequence, these stipulations are perfunctory. As shown in Xiao Jie's story, when she called the police for help, the response of the police was mediation, rather than carefully assessing the situation and introducing her to a safe house (also see Chapter 3).

In the safe house/aid station, Xiao Jie was not only yelled at, interrogated, and intimidated by staff members, but she also had an almost sleepless night from the loud surrounding noises. She ended up leaving the next morning. While the Anti-Domestic Violence Law defines a safe house as a place that "provides temporary aid to victims," it fails to specify necessary details such as the amenity requirements, the duration of stay, the operating principles, the conditions under which one must leave, and the daily management (Liu, Xiaodong 2019). The Law also stipulates nothing about the offer of psychological therapy or help from social workers for the victims. The lack of these stipulations in the Law has not only made it possible for safe houses to be established within the social aid station, but also has given victims like Xiao Jie a frightening, terrifying, and disturbing experience.

Safe houses, like the one in which Xiao Jie stayed, are often located within the social aid station (shehui jiu zhu zhan). Social aid stations used to be called custody and repatriation centers (shourong qiansong zhongxin). The custody and repatriation system was established in 1961, for the purpose of controlling the population mobility and safeguarding the household registration system. Due to the flooding of peasants into the cities, the household registration system was initiated by the Maoist state in 1958 to outlaw rural migration (Zheng 2009a: 8).

Three years later, the custody and repatriation system was set up to detain rural migrants in the city before repatriating them back to the countryside (Gao 2009). In 2003, a college graduate Zhigang Sun was detained by the police due to his failure to show a temporary resident card in the city of Guangzhou (Anonymous 2003). He was transferred to the custody and repatriation center, where he was beaten to death (ibid.).

The death of Zhigang Sun prompted the exposure of many other similar cases in the media. With the rising critiques of the system, the custody and repatriation center was subsequently abolished and replaced with the social aid station system in 2003 (The State Department of People's Republic of China 2003). The social aid station, according to this 2003 State Department Order, is a temporary aid to help vagrant beggars in the city (ibid.). It is stipulated that the social aid station should "persuade the person to return to his/her home place" (ibid.). Staff members at the social aid station, according to the Order, "are forbidden to beat, curse at, physically punish, or abuse the person" (ibid.).

In response to the state discourse of "family harmony," victims of intimate partner violence are often forced to return to their abusers, ironically, in order to maintain family harmony and social stability, at the expense of their safety and well-being (see Chapter 3). As shown above, not only the All China Women's Federation, but also the social aid station, called Xiao Jie's hometown to retrieve her. Even though Xiao Jie escaped intimate partner violence from her hometown, staff members at the social aid station took pictures of her, got information on her ID and house registration, and called her hometown. The public phone call not only publicized and revealed her hiding place to her abuser, but also served as an authoritarian attempt to send her back to the violent environment from which she had escaped.[2] Indeed, although the name of the system has changed from the custody and repatriation center to the social aid station, the goal has never changed. The goal, since the inception of the system in 1961, has always been to control population mobility and return the person to his/her homeplace. This goal is one of the reasons that vagrants in the cities are not willing to visit the social aid station for help (Dai 2013).

Although the 2003 State Department Order forbids staff members at the social aid station "to beat, curse at, physically punish, or abuse the person" (ibid.), as we have seen, upon Xiao Jie's arrival at the social aid station, she was interrogated, cursed at, and terrorized by the staff members. Her experience is by no means atypical. In 2013, a journalist named Peng Dai talked to over twenty vagrants in the city of Changsha, Hunan Province. He found out that no one would visit the social aid station for help even though they were homeless and starving. Perplexed, Dai decided to dress up as a vagrant and personally experience the inner workings of the social aid station. Wearing the ragged clothes of one of the vagrants, he appeared on the street. A citizen found him and called the emergency number 110. Two policemen came and took him to the Changsha social aid station.

After the police left, staff members of the social aid station first interrogated Dai coldly whether he was a drunkard or a drug addict. Afterward, one staff member came behind Dai and tightly tied Dai's two hands. Two other staff members pushed Dai to the floor. One pressed his knee against Dai's head and the other one pinned Dai's feet onto the floor. With his head pressed underneath a knee, Dai found himself unable to move or breathe. Nearly fainting, he begged them to let him leave. The staff member who had his knee against Dai's head yelled at him: "Now you want to leave? Too late!" Dai cited the 2003 State Department Order that stipulated that the social aid station is forbidden to limit the freedom of a vagrant if he wants to leave the station. That had no effect either. In the end, Dai had no alternative but to tell them his father's phone number. After his father negotiated his release on the phone, they finally let Dai go.

Two hours after Dai left, another journalist came to the social aid station. He found a vagrant lying on the floor in the reception hall. The vagrant's hands were so tightly tied with a rope that it cut out his circulation and left serious bruises. His feet and legs were tied together with duct tapes. He was unable to sit up, no matter how hard he tried. The blood around his lips had already congealed into scabs. When the journalist asked him if he was beaten at the aid station, he nodded, with tears rolling down his eyes (Dai 2013).

As shown, this violent and hostile environment, together with many other factors, has deterred victims of intimate partner violence and vagrancy from utilizing its services. According to the All China Women's Federation, China has 2,000 safe houses, but only 149 victims in the entire country utilized this service in 2016 (Nan 2019). In Nanjing, only two victims have stayed in their safe houses during a period of eleven years (Wang, Jun 2020). In Shanghai, only two victims have stayed in their safe houses during a period of two years (ibid.). In Beijing, only two victims stayed in their safe houses during a period of three years (ibid.).[3]

To be accepted into the safe house/aid station, as shown in Xiao Jie's case, victims of intimate partner violence are required to present their ID, household registration card, marriage certificate, and an introductory certificate from the All China Women's Federation or the police of their hometown (Chu, Tianjin 2016). This high threshold for the acceptance into the safe house, no doubt, has deterred many victims from seeking help there. Many abusers hide the identification cards and marriage certificates to prevent victims from escaping. Without the cards, victims are not allowed to enter the safe house/aid station. Getting an introductory certificate from either the All China Women's Federation or the police of their hometown can also reveal their hideout, making it easier for their abusers to find them in the safe house. In Xiao Jie's case, after she escaped to Beijing, she was told by the Beijing office of the All China Women's Federation to go back to her hometown to get the introductory certificate. Fearing that returning to her hometown would reveal her hideout to her abuser, she cried and begged before they finally gave her the introductory certificate to the safe house in Beijing.

Safe houses are often located within social aid stations, where victims of intimate partner violence have to share rooms with vagrants, beggars, the mentally ill, and drug addicts, in a hostile and intimidating environment, with ill-equipped living arrangements, often publicly known sites, and a lack of professional services such as psychological, legal, and social aid (Wang, Jun 2020). The fact that safe houses are established within social aid stations means that they are not independent and do not have any financial support. This significantly compromised the secrecy necessary for safe houses (Wang, Zuxin 2018). While safe houses are supposed to be clandestine and secret to protect victims from their abusers, in China, most of the safe house sites are publicly known, as it is clearly announced on the sign outside the building.

As shown, although victims like Xiao Jie escaped her abusive husband's violence and actively sought a safe house for protection, they are further victimized by the structural violence discussed in Chapters 1 and 3, with all the constraints and limitations that undercut their resistance and agency. In Xiao Jie's case, she was fortunate enough to be allowed to stay in the Beijing safe house, far away from her hometown jurisdiction. As per the stipulations of the Anti-Domestic Violence Law, victims of intimate partner violence can only stay in a safe house within their hometown jurisdiction as listed in their household registration card (Wang, Zuxin 2018). While Xiao Jie was lucky to be allowed into the Beijing safe house, if she were with a child, however, her child would not be able to attend schools in the Beijing jurisdiction, as the state policy dictates that children have to go to schools within the jurisdiction as listed in their house registration card.

As shown, when women like Xiao Jie exerted their agency to escape intimate partner violence and seek help, they were met with inaction from the police and the court and a terrorizing and hostile social system that was bent on returning them to the very violence that they escaped in the first place. Indeed, without the support of NGOs in Beijing, victims like Xiao Jie would not be able to find a temporary safe place, a job, or necessary legal aid to resolve the issue of violence in her life (see Chapter 6).

Non-State Network—Women's Natal Family

For some women who enjoy a support system with their family members and relatives, the natal family is an important source of support and help. Oftentimes, it is not until the women realize that their personal strategies prove to be ineffective and unsuccessful that they start seeking help from their natal families. This informal network of the natal family, however, is often only available to women who are not only physically close, but also emotionally tied to their natal families, excluding those whose abusers intentionally isolate the women from their families and friends geographically and through verbal and physical threats. The following two groups of women are often not able to access this informal resource. The first group of women, after marriage, follows their husbands to their husbands' hometown, which often is physically far away from that of their natal family, relatives, and friends.[4] The second group of women marries their husbands despite their parents' disapproval, and hence fear bringing shame and humiliation to their natal family and themselves by seeking their help.

When women seek support from their natal families during a crisis, their family members are able to intervene and control their husbands. Yan is a stay-at-home mom. When she learned that her husband, a government employee, had multiple extramarital affairs, she forgave him. However, he continued to have a mistress—a foot masseuse. One day Yan walked into the house, catching her husband in bed with his mistress. Upset about seeing them together, Yan warned them that she needed to tell his superior about this affair. Angry at her words, her husband and the mistress started beating her. They stripped her clothes and beat her whole body black-and-blue until she lost consciousness.

Her neighbor heard the commotion and called the emergency number 110. She was then taken to the hospital where she was diagnosed with multiple bone fractures throughout her body, including two fractured ribs and two fractured bones in her feet. She subsequently had six stitches on her face.

In the hospital, Yan called her brother for help. Her brother found her husband and his mistress and beat them up so severely that both of them were hospitalized with multiple severe injuries. Her brother commented, "If our father did not pull me away, I would have killed him. I grew up with my sister and we are very close. I will not let anyone bully or beat her." Yan's brother and father confronted her husband, telling him that if he dared to sue them for his multiple injuries and put any one of them in prison, they would beat his entire family to death or paralysis. Their threatening words have been so effective that members of Yan's husband's entire family are in retreat and never dare to provoke any members of Yan's family again. The strong support of her natal family is enough to intimidate Yan's husband into submission. While the brother does provide some kind of justice for his sister, this resembles the blood feud rather than a system of justice maintained by an impartial judiciary system.

Women like Yan told me that men beat their wives because they had never suffered consequences for doing so. They revealed that if a man knows that someone will beat him in response to him beating his wife, he will not dare to beat his wife anymore. As in Yan's case, her husband stopped beating her from then on, as he knew that her brother would beat him up. The fact that a woman has to resort to seeking help from her brother—her natal family member—to curb the violence, once again, evinces the structural violence explained in Chapters 1 and 2; that is, the criminal justice system and the social system fail women and favor abusers.

In another story, Ping's father warned her husband that if he beats his daughter once, he would beat him twice, which is enough to stop her husband from further abuse. Another woman Tan also told her brother about her abusive husband. Her brother immediately brought a number of guys to intimidate her husband, telling him that "If you beat my sister once, we will beat you twice. If you make her lose one hair, we will make you lose a handful of hair. Feel free to try if you don't believe it."

After that her husband never beat her again.

Women like Yan, Ping, and Tan are fortunate to enjoy support from the informal network of their natal families. As mentioned earlier, some women, for various reasons such as being physically apart and emotionally distant from their natal families, are not able to access this support system. Liu, for instance, when her father was alive to confront and control her husband, was able to terminate the abuse. However, after her father died, she lost that support and protection and was once again subject to her husband's physical abuse. For many other women, as shown in numerous individual cases in Chapter 2, their family members not only failed to report or interfere in the intimate partner violence, but also advised the women to continuously endure the violence, ultimately resulting in some of these women's deaths at the hands of their abusers.

Pleasing and Avoiding

Pleasing and avoiding are two commonplace strategies at the initial stages of abuse. To please the husbands, women try to do what their husbands want, apologize to them, praise them, and engage in behaviors that they desire. The purpose of these strategies is to appease their husbands, diffuse the tension, and minimize the abuse inflicted on their bodies. The following story of Chun illustrates this strategy.

Chun, a 26-year-old woman, has a one-year-old baby with her 41-year-old husband. Chun is a stay-at-home mom and a full-time wife. Her husband has been supervising national construction projects such as bridges, skyscrapers, and city squares for more than a decade. She said that her husband appeared gentle and humane to people outside and no one could ever believe that he beats her at home. When Chun's husband is in a good mood, he is really good. He would bathe the baby, wash his dirty clothes, and even wash her clothes or do anything for her. When he is happy, everything is good. However, when he is not in a good mood, anything she does will make him angry. Yelling at her is a daily routine. It is his habit to beat her. He claims that she deserves to be beaten if she is not obedient or submissive to him. He demands that she satisfy him in everything. Otherwise he would get furious and beat her. For instance, he complains that the way she carries the baby is not right. He complains that the way she handles and folds the clothes is not right. He complains that the way she reads a phone number is not right, as the first three digits should be read before the last four digits. In his eyes, these things are not done correctly, so she deserves to be yelled at and beaten. Whenever he beats her, he also rehashes things she did a long time ago. At these times, Chun would try her best to appease him and reduce the abuse by promising that she would correct her mistakes and that it would never happen again.

Chun said that her husband acts like a "master, a harsh supervisor or coach," demanding absolute submission and obedience from her. Whatever he says, it has to be that way. A common complaint by abused women was that their husbands not only beat them, but also demeaned and humiliated them. He would yell out: "Servant girl (Ya tou), pour water for me. Servant girl, I want to drink coffee. Servant girl, massage my back for me." Upon his demand, when he wanted to smoke, she had to hand him the cigarettes. When he wanted to drink, she had to pour water for him. When he wanted to brush his teeth, she had to squeeze out the toothpaste for him. When he wanted to eat sunflower seeds, she had to peel the seeds out of the shells and hand them over to him. When he came home drunk and yelled at her to give him slippers, she had to be agreeable and compliant in taking off his shoes and putting on slippers for him. Besides physical abuse, this humiliation is designed to destroy any sense of self-worth in these women.

Hiding is another strategy Chun uses to avoid abuse. One morning, in the bathroom, she heard him yelling at the baby because the baby was too noisy. This yelling scared the baby, who started crying. Hearing the commotion, Chun knew he was mad. She then avoided him by hiding away.

Pleasing and avoiding are rarely efficacious. As shown in the other sections of this chapter, most women move beyond this early strategy to something else, such as talking back, fighting back, escaping, and seeking help from their families. This is what Chun did later. She switched from pleasing and avoiding to talking back and fighting back. Her husband was surprised at her change in behavior and commented that she was now rebelling against him. She asked him:

> Why do you treat me this way? Is it because you despise me for not working and spending your money? You don't treat me as a wife should be treated.

Her talking back and reasoning with him oftentimes invited more abuse from him. Eventually she requested a divorce, which was enough to scare him into apologizing to her and promising that he would change and would never beat her again.

Chun took the baby with her and returned to her parents' home to stay for a while. She never told her parents about the abuse, as she did not want them to worry about her. Chun said that when she was growing up, she saw her dad hitting her mother's head onto the wall, beating her head, and threatening her all the time. She was scared every day. It was not until she was eighteen years old that her dad stopped beating her mom.

Chun commented that marriage "is sour, sweet, bitter, and spicy, with all kinds of sorrow mixed in it." A short separation from her husband was helpful, she said, and confessed that her marriage is not entirely tragic, and does have some happiness in it.

Chun attributes the abuse to Chinese society in general and her financial reliance on her husband in particular. She said:

> He is habituated to beating me. China, after all, is a patriarchal society. Most men think men and women are not equal and that women should listen to men.

Chun blames the patriarchal society for her husband's abuse. Although she hopes that her husband will stop the abuse as he grows older, she is also prepared to go out to work and be financially independent after the baby gets older so that she can walk out of this violent relationship and stand on her own.

From Talking Back and Fighting Back to Murder and Suicide

Women complain that there is no point calling the police, as they offer no help. As the vignette at the beginning of this chapter shows, Xiao Jun had to threaten the policeman in order to get him to issue the Written Warning Note. We have also seen the general police inaction to phone calls about intimate partner violence and abusers' potentially intensifying violence after such a phone call in Chapter 3. Within such a structural constraint of police nonaction, women often take the matters into their own hands and resist through talking back and fighting back. Like Chun who moved from pleasing and avoiding to talking back and fighting back to resist her husband's abuse, almost all the women with whom I have talked employ both verbal and physical resistance.

Women feel that they have to do something to stop their abusive husbands. Otherwise their violent husbands will become uncontrollable and make beating them a habit. They told me that the reasons for the abuse were usually ridiculous as the husbands would find fault with anything they do. Like Chun, whom I mentioned in the previous section, at the beginning the abused women thought that they had made a mistake, so they apologized to their husbands to please them and diffuse the tension. However, later they found out that even when they corrected the alleged "mistake" and did better to appease them, the abuse continued. Then it dawned on them that they should stop being obedient and subservient and start resisting and fighting back.

As shown in Chun's case, talking back entails challenging the abuse, confronting him about the relationship, requesting for a divorce, and telling him to stop the abuse. Some women tell their abusive husbands that they are animals, scumbags (wang ba dan), mentally ill, and that no one else will be with them. Other women reason with their husbands.

Women told me that talking back helps in venting their repression and frustration. Unfortunately, talking back and reasoning can also result in more abuse by their husbands. The following case is one such example. When Lin and her husband shopped in the mall, Lin spent 200 yuan on food and clothes, which was agreed upon by her husband. On the way back home, however, he suddenly got upset about her spending too much money. Lin talked back, "You had just agreed to spend this amount of money on food and clothes for me. Why are you suddenly upset now?" He responded that he was not worried about the money. Lin continued to ask him, "Then why are you so upset?" Unable to answer Lin's question, he became so infuriated that he dragged Lin into an alley and beat her up. Later, after they got home, he threw all the stuff they had bought onto the floor, pulled her into the bedroom and beat her up again. Although some women such as Lin received more abuse when resisting, they were not deterred.

Some women choose a time when their husbands calm down to talk to them about the abuse. Hong is an example. Every time her talk with her husband leads to him apologizing to her, admitting that he is guilty of losing his temper and beating her. Indeed, he confesses and apologizes after each abusive episode, but his abuse continues without any change. Hong soon stopped listening and just ignored him. He asked if she was mute or deaf, since she had stopped responding to him. Later Hong moved from silence to talking back. She told her husband that he had acted like a patient who has just escaped a mental hospital, and that he was mentally ill.

While talking back entails verbal resistance, fighting back involves using physical force, weak as it may be, to fight against the abuser. As shown in the following two examples, women overwhelmingly lament that they lack the physical strength to effectively fight back. Xiao always fights back when her husband beats her. However, she is not able to injure him, because of her lack of strength. Xiao, a model, just did a photo advertisement of stockings for a store, for which her husband called her a "slut" (sao), complaining that she wore skimpy clothes like a prostitute to be photographed. He beat her face and body with her high-heeled shoes, resulting in two months of hospitalization and an end to her modeling career. Xiao said to me:

> At the beginning I screamed my heart and lungs out and fought back as much as I could, but later with all his beatings, I was not able to let out any sound.

Although she screamed and engaged in physical resistance, in the end she did not have as much strength as he had and was severely injured. Xiao described him as an insane, sick dog. If she had possessed the strength or a weapon, she said, she would have killed him.

Mei used to always fight back, but since her husband's strength was too much for her, she was not able to resist physically as much as she wished. He spent time traveling from city to city and getting massages from women, while she stayed home taking care of the baby. However, he accused her of seducing men. He often used Mei's passwords to check her cell phone and online accounts. One day he left his own mobile phone at home. When he got back and noticed that his boss had not called, he suspected that his wife had had an affair with him. He insisted that she had talked to him and then had deleted it from the record. Mei talked back, telling him that he was mentally ill. He called her "debased" and beat her up. She tried her best to resist and fight back. He beat her across her back with a thick stick until the stick broke. He also used a kitchen knife to cut off her left hand's middle finger. Although her sister took her to the hospital to reconnect the finger, her middle finger was not able to stretch straight. Another time he stabbed Mei's hand, leaving a scar. Each time Mei said she fought back, but was too weak to match her husband's physical strength.

Due to the insufficient effect of verbal and physical resistance, many women contemplate the extreme measure of fighting back—murdering the abuser and then committing suicide. This often occurs when all the strategies such as avoiding and pleasing, escaping, talking back and fighting back are exhausted and to no avail. Killing and suicide are perceived as the last resort in such situations.

Thirteen years ago, Sun married her husband and followed him to a city that is far away from her relatives, families, and friends. During these thirteen years, Sun had been abused by her husband, and found no help from either the police or the All China Women's Federation. As shown in Chapter 3, women face a formidable structural bulwark that includes police inaction, inadequacies of the Anti-Domestic Violence Law, the prevailing method of mediation, the criminal justice system's preference for abusers, and the dearth of legal and social support.

Sun said that anything could trigger his abuse, such as her refusal to have sex with him. Helpless as she felt, she used all her strength to fight back, ready to murder him and commit suicide afterward. She said her principle is "either the fish dies or the net gets torn" (yusi wangpo). She elicits this Chinese saying to indicate that she is determined to engage in a life-and-death struggle with him. She fought back every time when he strangled her. One time, since he often came home late at dinnertime, she only boiled the dumplings enough for her daughter and herself. Enraged that his portion had not been boiled, he cursed her and beat her up. She resisted with a knife and injured him. He became afraid of her and backed off.

Women told me that Chinese law offers light punishment to abusive husbands who murder their wives. As illustrated in Chapters 1 and 3, while women who killed or attacked their abusers in self-defense, in general, received a death sentence or life in prison, their male counterparts, however, were sentenced to three to six years in jail or received no penalty for the murder of their wives (Xing 2011). If it were the same case for women, the women told me, they would all murder their husbands. Yu commented on her husband: "It's not because he cannot control it. It's because there's no consequence for his behavior."

Yu continued to say that if the law punished him, he would never do it again. Yu's words are reminiscent of the exchange theory that postulates that "people hit and abuse other family members because they can" (Gelles in Levinson 1989: 15). The exchange theory posits that family abusers engage in a cost-benefit or risk assessment analysis of their violence. If the negative sanction of their violence is a criminal sentence, it would likely deter and prevent their violence. Social scientists, including anthropologists, have argued with solid evidence that institutional sanctions such as criminalization, which replaced extended family or neighbor intervention as nuclear families became more prevalent in societies, are highly effective in preventing and discouraging family violence (Campbell 1999: 244; McCall and Sheilds 1986; Ventura and Davis 2005; Hautzinger 2007).

Yu's scathing comments pinpointed the lack of criminal sanctions against abusers' violence in China as responsible for fueling the violence that she had to face and deal with on her own in her everyday life. Yu lamented that she is physically weaker than her husband, and that divorce is not viable, as the Justice Department will give custody of her child to her husband since she is financially dependent on him. As shown in Chapter 2, judges tended to favor abusers in court verdicts on child custody rights. In the vacuum of legal and social protection of her rights, Yu said she had thought of killing him and committing suicide dozens of times. She said next time he beats her, she will do all she can to kill him and, then, commit suicide. After all, Yu said, "There is no difference between life and death in my life."

One of the fundamental justifications of state power is the duty to protect citizens, either male or female. As we have seen in Chapter 3, the law failed to provide these protections. Even in the case of men who attacked other men, so long as the injuries were not permanent or severe such as broken ribs, skull fracture, and spine fracture, they were not criminally sanctioned by the Criminal Law. In the case of women, this injustice is even more severe. As we have seen in Chapter 3, women could receive a death sentence or life in prison for exercising their right of self-defense. Whereas men, as illustrated in Chapter 3, often received either a minimal sentence or probation for killing their wives. Even though the Chinese Constitution insists that equal protection under the law should be a fundamental principle, in practice, it is not implemented.

As mentioned before, all the women with whom I have talked sought help from the police and the All China Women's Federation, but to no avail. In their words:

The police and the All China Women's Federation are dog's farts [gou pi].

By calling them "dog's farts," they deemed state institutions and the criminal justice system in China useless and perfunctory in punishing abusers and protecting victims. Indeed, within this structural violence of a lack of legal and social protection for women, their husbands asserted that they could beat them to death without going to prison. As a result, many women told me that they are prepared to take the risk of killing their husbands before taking their own lives (for this kind of legal cases, see Chapters 1, 3, and 6).

This sentiment is represented by the following two women. Ju's husband threatened to kill her entire family if she filed for a divorce. Similar to Ju's case, Hua's husband rejected divorce. When she mentioned divorce once, her husband not only strangled her, but also attempted to kill her daughter by locking them in the kitchen, and turning on the gas. Eventually he released them. Women like Ju and Hua swore to me that one day they would kill their husbands and then commit suicide, although converting this thought into action often involved a great deal of trepidation. Ju said to me:

Every time when I think of killing him and then myself, I think of my child and my parents. What would happen to them if I killed him and myself? These thoughts have been tormenting me with an immeasurable amount of pain. I inquired about all the medications that can cause death, but every time when I was about to use these medications on him and myself, I paused. I felt an immense amount of pain. But then I renewed my resolve and thought: let him and I perish together [tonggui yujin]—this thought is always on my mind.

These women aspire to end the lives of both their husbands and themselves but, oftentimes, the thought of their children and parents stops them. As they related to me, it is selfish to only focus on releasing their own pain through death and not think about the repercussions of their death on their parents and their children. Entangled in these conflicting thoughts, women often go through a number of strategies before taking extreme measures such as killing the abuser and committing suicide. Min said to me:

One day I will repay him ten times the sufferings he gave me. My life has been destroyed by him. I have no fear but hatred now. I just want to make him pay the price. This is life: "If you are not able to walk on a paved path, you have to walk on a thorny small road." I need to treat violence with violence [yibao zhibao].

Indeed, as demonstrated in Chapters 1, 3, and 6, women who killed their abusers accounted for the majority of female inmates convicted with heavy sentences in prison (Chai 2019). In certain areas, 70 percent of the female inmates with heavy sentences killed their abusers (ibid.). For killing their abusers, these female inmates were sentenced to death with a reprieve or a lifetime in prison (ibid.; see also Chapter 6). In Sichuan, for instance, 71 out of 121 female inmates were sentenced to death or life in prison for killing or attacking their abusive husbands (Xing 2011). Since Chinese law recognizes the right of self-defense, this is severe injustice toward women who did not initiate violence, but did respond to violence against them. Once again, we see an unequal application of the law on the basis of gender.

A CCTV program by a reporter Jing Chai recorded her interviews with some of these female inmates in a prison in Shi Jia Zhuang, Hebei Province (Chai 2019). The following three interviewees received life in prison or a death sentence with a reprieve. One interviewee named Hua An killed her abusive husband by attacking him twenty-seven times with a knife (ibid.). Her husband had beaten her for twenty years. One time he threw a beer bottle into her eyes, permanently blinding one eye. Hua An sought help from the residential committee and the All China Women's Federation, but no one dared to intervene. All she could do was to hide outside with their child in the freezing weather for an entire night. She eventually killed her abuser in self-defense. A second interviewee killed her abusive husband who had raped her two daughters and her sister. A third interviewee named Qing Yan was eight months pregnant, when her abusive husband clearly told her that if she gave birth to a girl, he would strangle the girl to death. When she did give birth to a girl, whom he attempted to strangle, she shot him dead. She said there was no other option in that situation. She was sentenced to a lifetime in prison. She said, "For my child, I would even die. It's worth it."

The reporter Chai commented:

> No marriage systems can promise people happiness, but a system should be in place to avoid extreme unhappiness.
>
> In countries with a more developed system of prevention of domestic violence and punishment of abusers, more than 90 percent of domestic violence instances, after being effectively intervened for the first time, stopped reoccurring.
>
> However, in China, a man can still beat a woman, chop her hands off with a knife, throw beer bottles to blind her, press a gun onto her back, rape her sisters, and beat her children. He can even do all of this in front of other people without punishment—all because he is her husband.
>
> When evil is not controlled, it can grow bigger through swallowing others' fear [What Chai means by this is that fear will not allow one to respond to evil].

Chai's commentaries underscored the structural violence—the deeply entrenched gender inequities in the Chinese criminal justice system. As shown in Chapters 1 and 3, the gender inequality implicit in this legal structure fails to provide victims with the necessary legal recourse to rectify the issue of intimate partner violence and seek justice. It also violates the Chinese Constitution that guarantees equal protection under the law.

Conclusion

This chapter debunks assumptions that women who experience intimate partner violence passively and helplessly accept their abuse. Rather, as illustrated in this chapter, some women actively engage in a number of strategies and struggles to resist intimate partner violence in their daily lives. Through foregrounding women's experiences from diverse social locations and giving them voice, this chapter demonstrates that their agency is constrained and hindered by structural inequalities such as economic, social, and legal limits. In the absence of legal protection and social support, whether they stay with or leave their violent husbands not only depends on the efficacy of their strategies and resistance, but also relies on other factors such as their children, their parents, their economic dependence, and their financial constraints.

As illustrated in this chapter, women have exercised a host of resistant strategies including escaping, seeking help from safe houses and NGOs, seeking support from informal networks, avoiding and pleasing, talking back and fighting back, murdering their husbands and taking their own lives. In addition to these strategies, some also choose to temporarily separate from their husbands until things quieten down. Others manage to accumulate and keep all the evidence of the injuries from the intimate partner violence and hope one day these will be helpful in seeking a divorce in court. For many women who are financially dependent on their husbands, however, divorce is not a viable option (see Chapter 3).

As shown in this chapter, while women exert their agency to escape intimate partner violence and actively seek help, they are often met with legal inertia—the inaction of the police and the court to punish abusers' violations of personal safety orders, as well as a hostile and intimidating social system that is intent on returning them to the violent environment from which they have escaped. In compliance with the state discourse of "family harmony" (see Chapter 3), victims of intimate partner violence, are often returned to their abusers in order to maintain family harmony and social stability, at the expense of women's safety and well-being. The emphasis on women's responsibility to ensure family harmony and maintain political stability, as I have argued in Chapter 3, encourages women to endure domestic violence and stay with their abusers. As shown, the harmony discourse prompts various state institutions such as the police and the All China Women's Federation to prioritize mediation as the paramount strategy to resolve domestic violence.

Women are deterred from seeking help from safe houses for a myriad of reasons. For instance, they are required to show the ID, household registration card, marriage certificate, and an introductory certificate from the All China Women's Federation or the police of their hometown. The Anti-Domestic Violence Law also stipulates that they cannot stay at a safe house outside of the jurisdiction as listed in their household registration card. Since safe houses are often located within social aid stations, they have to share rooms with vagrants, beggars, the mentally ill, and drug addicts. Safe houses/social aid stations are often ill-equipped, with a lack of professional services such as psychological, legal, and social aid. They are also often publicly known and announced on the sign outside the building. This public announcement defeats the very purpose of a safe house, which is to protect victims of intimate partner violence, in a secret place, from the knowledge and harassment of their abusers.

As shown in this chapter, some women were able to receive efficacious assistance from various NGOs or their natal family members. With the help from these NGOs, these women were able to find a temporary safe place, a job, and necessary legal aid to resolve the issue of violence in their lives or reduce their sentence in cases where they had killed their abusers (see Chapter 6). Other women were fortunate enough to enjoy the support from the informal network of their natal families, such as their siblings or parents. It is important to keep in mind that while these women are lucky to be supported by their natal family members, many other women's natal families not only failed to report or intervene in the intimate partner violence, but also persuaded the women to continuously endure the violence, leading to their ultimate deaths by their abusers (see Chapters 1 and 3).

Women are self-reflexive when realizing that their husbands are as violent as their fathers. These women grow up watching their fathers beating their mothers. They later marry men who behave similarly. Oftentimes it is by no means their intention to marry someone like their violent fathers but, somehow, they end up with someone just like their abusive fathers. Aware of this unhealthy cycle, some women are brave enough to exert all their efforts to break out of the cycle rather than repeating it.[5]

To the women, their violent husbands are the object of their intense hatred and fantasies of murder. In their imagination, they kill their abusive husbands by burying them alive, slicing them into small pieces, and feeding their dead flesh to the dogs or the field as fertilizers. The "Battered Woman's Syndrome" can be utilized to comprehend victims' understanding of their relationships with the abusers, their perceptions of themselves, and their perceptions of the abusers (see more detailed explanations about the "Battered Woman's Syndrome" in Chapter 6; see also Roberts 1998; Roy 1977; McCauley 1995; White 1985; Walker 1984). One example is that victims tend to perceive their abusers as "omnipotent and omniscient" (Walker and Conte 2017: 53). In one legal case, for instance, a forty-year-old woman Catherine shot her abuser dead. She was not convinced that the shot really killed him, so she took a knife and continuously stabbed his dead body. The Battered Woman's Syndrome was employed to explain why Catherine, even though she had shot her abuser dead, continued to believe that he could still harm her (ibid.: 53). She was subsequently exonerated.

Like Catherine in Canada, in many legal cases in China, women killed their abusers with a myriad of means. For instance, Yan Li cut, boiled, and scattered the remains of her abuser in various places (see Chapter 6). Hua An killed her abuser by attacking him twenty-seven times with a knife (Chai 2019). Liu poisoned her abuser before asphyxiating him with pillows on his face (Lv 2017: 70). Pan killed her abuser by attacking him multiple times with a dagger (ibid.: 75). Zhang first used a hammer and a number of other heavy tools to attack her husband's head and face until he was dead. She then attacked his dead body more than forty times with a knife. She finally cut the penis off his dead body (Yang 2016).

These women, before killing their abusers, resisted hard against domestic violence by reporting the violence to the police, seeking help from the All China Women's Federation, and talking to friends, relatives, and families about the violence (Wang 2013; see also Chapters 3 and 6). However, no one offered any help. No matter how hard they fought, they were not able to get rid of the violence in their lives. In the vacuum of legal, social, and psychological aid, all they could do was to endure the violence, until one day they were unable to endure it any longer and resorted to killing to end this cycle of violence.

In the women's own words, "Injuries on the body can be healed, but injuries to the heart can never be healed." Women lamented to me that they had never received education about intimate partner violence in their schools as they were growing up. Within this restrictive and constraining structural, economic, and legal context, when laws and regulations fail to protect them, women are compelled to bear the brunt of restoring justice through inventing new strategies of resistance and thwarting the violence in their daily lives, even if it means murdering their husbands and taking their own lives.

Chapter 6

ACTIVISM AND INTIMATE PARTNER VIOLENCE

Our Anti-Domestic Violence Network in Beijing—China's only nongovernment organization that has dealt with intimate partner violence—was forced to close down in May of 2014 due to limited funding. Our main objective has been to push for legislation establishing the first Anti-Domestic Violence Law in China. Because nongovernment organizations in China are not allowed to register independently, we had to be housed under the China Law Society in order to be accepted as politically correct so that we can carry out our task.

The China Law Society is associated with the All China Women's Federation, which is directly under the leadership of China's State Council. Members of our Anti-Domestic Violence Network include lawyers, leaders of China's Supreme Court, legal scholars, and directors of All China Women's Federation, who have been instrumental in creating laws such as China's Marriage Law.

Since the ban on foreign aid in 2010, the China Law Society was not able to accept foreign aid, forcing our organization to sever its relationships with them and register with the Chinese Bureau of Industry and Commerce as a company. But we were eventually forced to close due to limited funding.

From 1999 to 2004, our organization first submitted drafts of the Anti-Domestic Violence Law to the National People's Congress Standing Committee. We then advocated a multiagency alliance against domestic violence. We also raised consciousness among migrant workers and college students. We set up training workshops for court judges and local government officials. We also helped with the well-known case where the American educator Kim sued in court against her Chinese celebrity husband who beat and abused her.

I worked in the organization for three years but experienced a heavy sense of failure [cuobaigan tebiezhong]. The government feels there is no need to take up responsibility for the victims [of intimate partner violence]. The government is afraid that if women can unite together to fight for this objective, they can unite together to fight for other objectives as well, such as the independence of Tibet. The system of nongovernment organization is a threat to the government.

Because of these reasons, we never dared to discuss the issue of human rights [renquan]. We only used terms such as "gender equality" [xingbie pingdeng] and "women's rights and interests" [funv de quanyi] to avoid the politically sensitive term "human rights" [renquan].

The above was an interview conducted with Xiao Chen, an activist who worked for three years in the Anti-Domestic Violence Network in Beijing—China's first nongovernment organization that fought against domestic violence. Interviews with her and other activists demonstrate the contributions of their activism to the fight against intimate partner violence in China, as well as the difficulties that they have encountered—what Xiao Chen called "a heavy sense of failure"—on the path of carrying out their activism in China.

Based on interviews with anti-domestic violence activists, this chapter examines the efforts and endeavors that activists and nongovernment organizations in China have contributed to the cause. The nongovernment organizations and activists have made interventions at the grassroots level to provide an alternative route to the institutional impediments that women face in their pursuit of justice. These interventions include counselling, sheltering, and assisting in court cases. While activists are keen to provide services to women who suffer from intimate partner violence, their activism necessitates collaborating with the state. The first section discusses the history of activism against intimate partner violence. The second section details the contribution of activism toward the cause. The third section explicates activists' appropriation of the state discourse to legitimize their activism, which, in the process, ultimately legitimizes state power. This chapter concludes with the strength and limitations of activists' approaches in battling against intimate partner violence.

History of Activism against Intimate Partner Violence

1990–4

In 1990, a conference on China-US Women's Issues was held in Beijing, which generated a published collection of all the papers presented at the conference (Zhong 1991). This conference ushered in an era where domestic violence officially became a scholarly topic in China. In 1991, for the first time in Chinese history, domestic violence was raised as a social issue in an article titled "White Paper on Domestic Violence," published in a state-owned magazine *Chinese Women* (Pi 1991). The author was Xiaoming Pi, who worked as a lawyer in the Department of Women's Rights and Interests (funv quanyi bu) in a district branch of the All China Women's Federation in Beijing. The fact that most of the mainstream media such as *Chinese Women's News* and *Journal on Women's News* refused to publish this article underlines the state's efforts to hide as well as silence this "dark" social issue (Zhang 2008).

Pi credited the acceptance of the article by *Chinese Women* to her long-term friendship with the editor (ibid.).

In the article, Pi testified that domestic violence accounted for 70–80 percent of the divorce cases that she had encountered and dealt with since she started working as a lawyer in the All China Women's Federation in 1985 (Pi 1991). At the beginning of this article, Pi steadfastly declared her position against domestic violence, which was traditionally termed in Chinese as "wife-beating" (da laopo). Recounting heartbreaking stories of victims who had suffered years of abuse by their husbands, Pi refuted the traditional perception that regarded domestic violence as a private, domestic affair. The failure of the existing law to protect women from abuse in a marriage, Pi argued, was the reason that domestic violence continued and society's tolerance of abuse against women persisted. At the end of the article, Pi appealed for a change in the law to punish abusers and terminate violence (ibid.). Despite Pi's call for legal change and public attention to domestic violence as a social issue, her article failed to have the wide impact that it was meant to.

In 1992, the Law of the People's Republic of China on the Protection of Women's Rights and Interests was promulgated nationwide (1992). Drafted in the 1980s by the All China Women's Federation, this law was finally passed by the 7th National People's Congress Standing Committee in 1992. Despite the fact that this law aimed to protect women's rights and interests, it failed to name domestic violence as an issue. The 2nd stipulation contained one sentence that stated, "It is forbidden to despise, abuse, abandon, and mutilate women" (1992). Other than this one sentence, throughout the law, there was no mention of domestic violence, or a definition of domestic violence, or the kind of penalty reserved for the abusers, or any rules and regulations to restrict abusers from violence, or a support mechanism for victims and related matters.

During this time, many court verdicts depicted domestic violence as a "family conflict," in accordance with the traditional Chinese phrase: "An impartial judge will find himself worthless in hearing a case of domestic disputes" (Qingguan nanguan jiawushi). To understand this, we must understand that the traditional Chinese culture did not recognize violence against women as an issue, lacking even the language to describe it, except for "wife-beating" (da laopo) and "abuse" (nue dai). The term "domestic violence" was imported from the 1990 Beijing conference on China-US Women's Issues, but did not resonate with the traditional Chinese culture during that time.

In 1992, the prevalence of domestic violence in China was noticed by Xingjuan Wang, a retired female journalist of the *Chinese Youth Newspaper* who opened the first nationwide Women's Hotline in Beijing, funded by the Ford Foundation, to provide advice and support for female callers. Wang was also the founder of the Women's Research Institute in 1988 that was dedicated to issues of employment and political participation of women, under the auspices of the Chinese Academy of Management Science. Through the hotline, she came to know many desperate callers who suffered abuse from their husbands. These women escaped home only to find themselves having no place to hide. Talking to them made Wang realize not only the severity of the issue of domestic violence in China, but also the ways in which the nationwide All China Women's Federation, in only broadcasting and boasting of China's accomplishments with women's issues, ignored and dismissed the issue of widespread domestic violence (Zhang 2008).

In 1995, she submitted a request to the All China Women's Federation to organize a panel on domestic violence for the United Nations 4th World Conference on Women to be held in Beijing. Her request was rejected by the first secretary of the Beijing headquarters of the All China Women's Federation, as many political leaders refused to admit that domestic violence existed in China. They claimed that the abuse of women only happened in individual cases in China. It was claimed that women's status was so high in China that domestic violence simply did not exist. One must remember that in spite of Mao's proclamation that women hold up half the sky, as Chapter 1 indicates, Chinese cultural history prior to Mao regarded women almost as nonentities. Wang's proposal to organize a domestic violence panel was criticized in a meeting without naming her, saying "some people want to stir up trouble and chaos, saying that our country has domestic violence" (Wang 2012).

As shown above, prior to 1995, domestic violence was recognized as a serious issue by some journalists and lawyers through their experiences of working with female victims. However, in their attempts to raise this issue in public and advocate legal reform and state intervention, they encountered formidable hurdles, including the refusal by news outlets to publish articles on this issue as well as the ban on discussing this issue in a public forum. The fundamental reason for this resistance was that topics like domestic violence exposed the "dark sides" of China, and therefore needed to be silenced and extinguished. Only topics that celebrated women's liberation and women's accomplishments were allowed and encouraged, as they contributed to the state-propagated official discourse of gender equality that had been achieved by the socialist state of China.

The task of addressing domestic violence in China is fraught with problems. The survival of the Communist Party in China is based on two pillars. One is economic prosperity. The other is nationalism. This latter issue is a problem for feminist activists. How do you reform the serious problem without appearing overly critical of Chinese culture? While domestic violence and patriarchy is an issue in every culture, as shown in Chapter 1, it has a particularly fraught history in China. Practices such as foot-binding, clearly a form of abuse, seems particularly onerous to outsiders as well as modern Chinese. It should not be surprising that the Communist government is sensitive to the implicit criticism in any attempt to address the current problem of domestic violence.

Perhaps there is a way to address this problem without igniting the ire of defensive Communist officials. It should be emphasized by Chinese reformers that this is not a Chinese problem but a worldwide problem and, starting with Mao's statement that "women hold up half the sky," it is socialism that can best solve this problem. By identifying China as a potential leader in implementing this reform, the problem is recast as a problem of modern reform over the feudal practice of the past rather than seeing China as the problem.

1995–2004

In 1995, the United Nations 4th World Conference on Women hosted in Beijing marked an historical turning point in the Chinese women's movement, sparking women's activist movement on domestic violence and women's rights in China. The conference introduced to many Chinese female attendees, the new concept of NGOs, pro bono lawyers, civil society, and the issue of violence against women as a human rights issue. It also generated resources of foreign aid that funded Chinese women's activism that followed the conference.

At this conference, violence against women was identified as the sixth among the twelve priority concerns in the comprehensive plan to achieve gender equality, women's rights, and women's empowerment in the Beijing Declaration and Platform for Action. Around 189 government representatives from around the world, including China, signed the Beijing Declaration and Platform for Action (Wang, Qiumeng 2016). This was the first international treaty that post-Mao China had signed (Zhang 2008).

Prior to the conference, as noted above, some political leaders in China refused to admit that domestic violence existed in China and rejected Xingjun Wang's proposal to organize a panel on domestic violence at the conference. Signing the Beijing Declaration and Platform for Action obligated China to acknowledge the issue of domestic violence. Since then, the term "domestic violence" has officially entered the state language in its policy discussions and public recognition of this issue. Incorporating this term in the state discourse marked an historical turning point in opening up social space and political legitimacy for women to engage in activism on domestic violence issues after the conference (Luo 2019; Zhang 2008).

Addressing 17,000 participants and 31,000 NGO activists from around the world, the then first lady of the United States, Hillary Clinton, gave a famous speech titled "Women's Rights Are Human Rights." Her speech was later ranked No. 35 in American Rhetoric's Top 100 Speeches of the 20th Century (Eidenmuller 2009). Hillary Clinton discussed women's rights in her speech in the following way (1995):

> If there is one message that echoes forth from this conference, it is that human rights are women's rights … And women's rights are human rights. Let us not forget that among those rights are the right to speak freely. And the right to be heard. Women must enjoy the right to participate fully in the social and political lives of their countries if we want freedom and democracy to thrive and endure.
>
> Those of us who have the opportunity to be here have the responsibility to speak for those who could not … These abuses have continued because, for too long, the history of women has been a history of silence. Even today, there are those who are trying to silence our words.
>
> Our goals for this conference, to strengthen families and societies by empowering women to take greater control over their own destinies, cannot be fully achieved unless all governments —here and around the world—accept their responsibility to protect and promote internationally recognized human right.

> Every woman deserves the chance to realize her God-given potential ...We also must recognize that women will never gain full dignity until their human rights are respected and protected.
>
> As long as discrimination and inequities remain so commonplace around the world—as long as girls and women are ... subjected to violence in and out of their homes—the potential of the human family to create a peaceful, prosperous world will not be realized.

Hillary Clinton's speech changed forever the future career paths of many Chinese female attendees at the conference. Jianmei Guo, a lawyer as well as the assistant editor-in-chief of the *Chinese Lawyer* magazine, said later: "Hillary Clinton's every sentence in her passionate speech was like a huge fire burning my heart. I was overwhelmed by the excitement and passion that were burning my heart. Her speech lit up the deepest, hidden spark inside of me. I felt then and there that I have found my family" (Zhang, Qing 2016). Wei Pu, a professor of the Chinese Academy of News and Media, said afterward, "Many issues that have troubled me for decades in my life were answered for me by this conference." Yuan Feng, a journalist of the *Chinese Women's Newspaper*, commented later (2019):

> If the United Nations 4th Conference on Women had not happened in Beijing, it would be hard to imagine any women's movement, civil society, or public acceptance of civil society [that had occurred in China because of the conference]. Not only did this conference bring to China the new concept of the NGO and civil society, but it also called on us so-called intellectuals to act and do something. Chinese society did not have this—even though we knew the Chinese terms of civil society and nongovernment organizations, they were, in fact, fake.

As shown, this conference was the first time that these Chinese female attendees had ever heard of these foreign concepts, despite the Chinese state's sudden decision to segregate and move the NGO forums 41 miles away from the conference site—to a faraway town that was not even prepared to host these NGO forums (Zhang 2008). The state's effort to isolate these NGO forums in a remote town failed to thwart Chinese female attendees, who continued attending these NGO forums.

This United Nations World Conference in Beijing was unprecedented in featuring 5 regional NGO forums with 31,000 participants, parallel to the conference sessions. Because the definition of an NGO was an organization founded and organized by activists without government interference or involvement, the concept of NGO and civil society was both foreign and practically nonexistent in China. My interviews with activists showed that participation of NGOs from all over the world introduced this foreign concept to Chinese female attendees and laid the crucial foundation for their later activism in founding NGOs themselves and spearheading the women's movement in China.

The issue of domestic violence arose in the conference not as an individual issue or a family issue, but as a human rights issue that necessitated state intervention (Wang, Qiumeng 2016). For many Chinese female attendees, it was their first opportunity to reflect on the issue of domestic violence. It was at this conference that not only did this issue come to the attention of many Chinese female attendees, but also the human rights framework was introduced to redefine the abuse of women as a violation of women's human rights. Due to the political sensitivity of human rights discourses in China, Chinese female attendees felt compelled to depict domestic violence as a social harm, instead of a violation of human rights, to seek the legitimacy of this issue for state and civil actions. At the NGO forums, they voiced their understanding of domestic violence as a threat to social stability, family integrity, and the welfare of children. They also expressed the pressing need for state intervention and legal reform against domestic violence (Qiumeng Wang 2016; Zhang 2008; my interviews with anti-domestic violence activists).

Chinese female attendees at the conference were mostly from the upper echelons of society, who were researchers, journalists, lawyers, and legal scholars. Activists told me in the interviews that some of these women later went to Europe and North America to visit women's shelters, crisis centers, and NGOs and brought Western ideas, laws, and concepts into China. Exposure to the new concepts of NGOs, pro bono lawyers, civil society, and the issue of domestic violence as a human rights issue at this conference inspired some of them to start their own NGOs with a focus on domestic violence after the conference. Domestic violence, after this conference, became a pivotal issue on the agenda of the women's movement in China.

NGOs in China

As shown above, many Chinese female attendees shared a life-changing, transformative experience at the UN Beijing Conference and the NGO forums. This conference ushered in a new era of the Chinese women's movement, which established a myriad of NGOs to protect women's rights and interests. The following are some examples of these NGOs: Beijing Maple Women's Counselling Center, Media Monitor for Women Network/Feminist Voice, Anti-Domestic Violence Network, and Beijing University Law School Women's Legal Research and Service Center. It is important to understand the threat independent organizations represent to any authoritarian government, particularly the Chinese Communist government. The Party wants to control all sources of power. The existence of independent NGOs is a threat to this hegemony.

Beijing Maple Women's Psychology Counselling Service Center

Xingjuan Wang, the founder of the first nationwide Women's Hotline in Beijing, was punished after the conference for meeting with over forty representatives from home and abroad to introduce the hotline (Wang 2012). After Hillary Clinton arrived in Beijing for the United Nations 4th Conference on Women, she asked to visit the Women's Hotline in Beijing. Government officials summoned Wang's colleague twice to the headquarters of the Chinese Communist Party, asking what kind of organization Women's Hotline was, who Xingjuan Wang was, and why Hillary Clinton wanted to see her. Meanwhile, the sponsor of Women's Hotline—the Chinese Academy of Management Science—also became the target of investigation. After answering countless questions from the National Security Department, they were criticized. Even though the National Security Department later agreed that she could meet with foreign friends, she was still punished. After the conference, they were forced to move out and, afterward, were not able to find anyone who would rent them a place. The Chinese Academy of Management Science also terminated their sponsorship and severed their relationship with them. Their status as a nonprofit corporation was also revoked. In order to maintain its legal status, in 1996, Wang registered it as a company with the Bureau of Industry and Commerce, changing its name from "Women's Hotline" to "Beijing Maple Women's Psychology Counselling Service Center" (Wang 2012).

Media Monitor for Women's Network/Feminist Voice

After the 1995 conference, a group of Beijing journalists of the state-owned *China Women's Newspaper* formed an NGO called Media Monitor for Women's Network in 1996 (Feng 2020b). The objective of this NGO was to promote gender equality and women's rights to voice their opinions in the media. One of the founders, Pin Lv, the previous director of the Department of Women's Rights and Interests of the state-owned *China Women's Newspaper*, quit her job in 2003 (Mi 2021). In 2009, Lv started a weekly *Electronic Newsletter of Women's Voices* that reported activities of women's NGOs and commented on media reports on women and gender issues. In 2011, Lv changed the name of the NGO from Media Monitor for Women's Network to Feminist Voice. From 2012 to 2013, Feminist Voice organized around thirty activities against domestic violence, gender-based violence, and gender-based bias, while pushing for reforms of certain state policies. In 2018, Feminist Voice was closed down (Shi 2019).

Anti-Domestic Violence Network

Yuan Fang, a journalist of the *Chinese Women's Newspaper*, founded the first and only anti-domestic violence NGO—Anti-Domestic Violence Network—after the conference in 1995 (Luo 2019). The Anti-Domestic Violence Network was funded by the United Nations, Ford Foundation, Oxfam the Netherlands, the Embassy of Sweden, the Norwegian Center for Human Rights, and Oxfam Hong Kong. Members included hundreds of lawyers, activists, scholars, social workers, and professors from the Institute of Law, Chinese Academy of Social Sciences, China Women's University, China Public Security University, China University of Political Science and Law, Beijing University, and *China Women's Newspaper* (ibid.).

Activists in this Network told me that the Network formed an informal alliance with other NGOs, including Beijing Maple Women's Counselling Center, Media Monitor for Women's Network, and Beijing University Law School Women's Legal Research and Service Center. By mobilizing women activists in this alliance, the Network advocated and provided social services to victims of domestic violence, raised consciousness of domestic violence among migrant workers and college students at Capital Normal University, promoted multiagency cooperation to interfere in domestic violence, set up training workshops on domestic violence for court judges, police, and local government officials, and helped the American educator Kim Lee win the lawsuit against her Chinese abusive celebrity husband.

In 2000, the Network was housed under the auspices of the China Law Society for political legitimacy. As mentioned in the interview at the beginning of this chapter, the China Law Society was associated with the All China Women's Federation, directly under the leadership of China's State Council. Their members, including lawyers, leaders of China's Supreme Court, legal scholars, and directors of the All China Women's Federation, have been instrumental in creating laws in China such as China's Marriage Law.

Interviews with activists in the Network revealed that it was instrumental for the Network to be affiliated with the China Law Society and to collaborate with the All China Women's Federation. This kind of affiliation and collaboration was beneficial for the Network to carry out its activist work; that is, pushing for the legislation of the first Anti-Domestic Violence Law in China. From 1999 to 2004, the Network submitted drafts of the Anti-Domestic Violence Law to the National People's Congress Standing Committee, which was eventually passed in 2015 and enacted on March 1, 2016. On the one hand, the Network relied on its affiliation and collaboration with these state institutions to succeed in its goal to pass the first Anti-Domestic Violence Law in China. On the other hand, activists in the Network told me that this kind of instrumental affiliation and collaboration led to the high turnover of staff members. One activist told me:

> Our directors come and go. Our staff members also come and go. Our team membership [ren li ren yuan] was very unstable.

With few members committed to the Network and the ban on foreign funding, the Network was compelled to close down in 2014.

Beijing University Law School Women's Legal Research and Service Center

Inspired by Clinton's speech as well as the conference, Jianmei Guo, a Beijing University Law School graduate, quit her job as the assistant editor-in-chief of the *Chinese Lawyer Magazine* after the conference, which was a coveted "iron rice bowl job" at a state-owned institution (Wen 2020; Huang, Jian 2019). In December 1995, Guo founded the first nongovernment legal organization called Beijing University Law School Women's Legal Research and Service Center, funded by the Ford Foundation ($30,000), to provide free legal aid to vulnerable women with no social or economic resources.

In so doing, Guo became the first pro bono lawyer in China. She said:

> China has 150,000 lawyers in total. That's about 1 lawyer for 10,000 people on average. Now 90 percent of the lawyers work for only 10 percent of the

population. Someone has to speak for those vulnerable populations who do not have money or social status, have been bullied due to inequality, and cannot fight back due to inequality! (Bei 2020)

As per the rules in China, Guo sought after, and successfully secured, the sponsorship of the Law School at Beijing University, thanks to her personal and institutional connections. However, her center was a one-room, cramped office borrowed from the university (ibid.).

Guo later reminisced that, although she was able to overcome the myriad risks, pressure (financial, political, and social), and threats that she encountered while handling the legal cases, she was unable to surmount others' misunderstanding and slander (Liu, Ruhua 2019). While Guo chose to be a pro bono lawyer with passion and ideals, others saw it as her means to seek fame, court publicity, obtain more cases, and strive for political advancement. She was also slandered as incapable, having no choice but to be a pro bono lawyer. Guo used to be regarded as an elite, working as a lawyer and journalist at top state-owned institutions such as the All China Women's Federation and the *Chinese Lawyer Magazine*. Ever since she started her career as a pro bono lawyer, she felt she was

> falling from the sky into an ice hole, always begging for help everywhere, with no one responding. It was an unimaginable feeling of loss that I was unable to release myself from. (Liu, Ruhua 2019)

The experience of social pressure, work pressure, and the overwhelming cases of violation of women's rights pushed her into depression. After a break of half a year to treat her depression, she went back to work and, later, remarked:

> I saw strength from the women we have helped—the kind of strength arising from their inside in the face of tremendous difficulties. I saw an awakening public. I saw the brightest sight in life—the light of human nature. When I encountered difficulties, I thought, it was nothing compared with these women. From them, I absorbed a nourishment. They reminded me not to only look at the dark corners. (Liu, Ruhua 2019)
>
> I feel that these women are the true nameless heroes. Many women we have helped eventually lost the case, having sacrificed tremendously for the lawsuit, even losing everything. Without these women, the ambiguous and gray areas in the laws would not have aroused public attention. These are hundreds and thousands of ordinary women who have pushed for Chinese legal progress.
>
> When I faced difficulties, because I knew that what I was doing was to seek justice, to push for legal progress, I was able to throw myself into the guillotine as Hulan Liu did [a famous Chinese Communist female martyr in the 1940s who defied her Nationalist oppressors and refused to relent in exchange for life, fearlessly laying herself at the guillotine and asking the killer to set the guillotine correctly prior to cutting her head off] … This forged a strong heart, making me a rock [shitou]. (Ruo 2020)

When she started the center, Guo required her four or five colleagues to handle at least twenty cases per person. Later she changed from the focus on the number of cases to only select those cases that could raise certain critical gender issues in public and, in turn, push legal reforms in issues such as domestic violence. In 2009, her center established China's Pro Bono Lawyer Network, attracting over four hundred lawyers. Since 1995, Guo and her colleagues in the center have provided free legal consultation for over seventy thousand women, handled about three thousand legal cases, submitted over seventy expert opinions about laws and regulations, and organized over eighty training sessions and seminars on women's rights and interests (Huang, Jian 2019; Liu 2019). Guo was nominated for the Nobel Peace Prize in 2005. She was awarded the Simone De Beauvoir Prize in 2010, the International Women of Courage Award in 2011, and the Right Livelihood Award in 2019 for her lifetime work to safeguard women's rights and interests in China (Gong 2020; Liu, Ruhua 2019). As noted later in this chapter, her NGO was forced to close down in 2016.

2005–15

A decade after the United Nations 4th Conference on Women, women's NGOs and activism in China continued developing and expanding, with the fast development of the civil society (according to my interviews with activists in 2020 and 2021). Previously established NGOs flourished with a profound impact on Chinese legislative changes and protection of rights and interests of the vulnerable populations of women. New NGOs started mushrooming. Especially since the Wenchuan, Sichuan Earthquake in 2008, more funding opportunities opened up within China to invest in grassroots NGOs and in the development of a civil society (according to my interviews with activists in 2020 and 2021).

In 2005, Bin Xu formed Tong Yu, an NGO dedicated to advocating the rights and interests of the LGBTQ group and pushing for legal reforms to protect the LGBTQ group from violence, prejudice, and discrimination. My interviews with an activist in Tong Yu revealed the arduous work they have undergone in order to change the draft of the Anti-Domestic Violence Law submitted to the National People's Congress to protect the LGBTQ population:

> One of our goals was to get involved in influencing state policies and laws and regulations. [In order to do that,] we have to first understand how the system of legislation through the National People's Congress works. Every five years, they [the National People's Congress] have a meeting to make a five-year-plan for new laws to be passed in five years.
>
> When we learned that the alliance of the Anti-Domestic Violence Network and the All China Women's Federation submitted the draft for the Anti-Domestic Violence Law [to the National People's Congress], we [Tong Yu] went through an emergency campaign to expand the purview of protection in the law. The draft of the law only protected married spouses. We decided that our contribution would be to define victims of domestic violence as not just those

who are married spouses, but among intimate partners, with no limitation of gender.

This change [to the law] would ensure legal protection of the LGBTQ group. It is a customary practice that the National People's Congress, prior to passing a new law, collects public opinions ranging from one to three times. All the NGOs and individuals can provide their opinions.

We [Tongyu] spent three months completing an emergency [online] survey of domestic violence in the LGBTQ group. The result showed a higher domestic violence rate among intimate partners than married spouses. 68.97 percent of the [LGBTQ] group has experienced either intimate partner violence or domestic violence from their parents.

It [the online survey] also showed that 33.54 percent of the [LGBTQ] group has experienced intimate partner violence. We sent our research findings to researchers and experts who were directly involved in the legislative process in the National People's Congress.

Afterward, representatives in the National People's Congress held an internal meeting where they discussed the higher rate of domestic violence among intimate partners [in Tongyu's research reports]. They [the National People's Congress] eventually supported the change.

When the [Anti-Domestic Violence] Law was passed in 2015, the 37th stipulation states, "People who cohabit together can use this law to protect themselves."

The triumph of our campaign was inspiring to us. It opened a door for us. We realized that ordinary people can also affect the law. In the past, we thought laws were only passed by the legislatures in the government. Now we realized that public participation and public campaigns can also work in China.

As shown in the interview, prior to Tong Yu's activist intervention, the draft of the Anti-Domestic Violence Law only protected victims who were related to their abusers either by blood or marriage. Tong Yu took the initiative to conduct emergency surveys and research in a period of three months. They presented and submitted their research findings to the scholars and experts who were directly involved in the legislative process in the National People's Congress. Their efforts successfully pushed the law to change its purview of protection. Their research findings were eventually accepted by representatives in the National People's Congress. The final Anti-Domestic Violence Law passed in 2015 specified that "intimate partners who cohabit together, or are in a relationship, or used to be in an intimate relationship" should be included in the protection purview. In so doing, the rights and interests of the LGBTQ group were safeguarded by this law.

Activists I interviewed told me that this ten-year period represented a steady progress and success of the women's NGOs, the women's movement, and the creation of a civil society in China. Many women activists were able to travel abroad to learn about other countries' laws and regulations as well as the social services available for victims of domestic violence. Such international exchanges made it possible for them to compare laws and situations in China with those in other countries. These activists, in turn, got involved in politics, pushed for legislative changes in China, and succeeded in getting the Anti-Domestic Violence Law passed by the National People's Congress in 2015 to protect all intimate partners including the LGBTQ group, not just married spouses.

2015–Present

Activists told me that, since 2014, the government started surveillance and control of NGOs, prohibiting foreign funding, as a result, forcing many NGOs to close down. In 2015, No. 12 of the Standing Committee of the 12th National People's Congress publicized on its website a draft of the Law of the People's Republic of China on the Administration of Activities of Overseas Non-Governmental Organizations within the Territory of China, which was later passed on April 28, 2016 (2016). This law prohibits overseas NGOs from conducting political or religious activities in China. It stipulates that the Public Security Bureau and relevant state-owned departments are responsible for designing the areas of activities and lists of projects for overseas NGOs. These activities must be conducted in collaboration with the Chinese state authority departments, state-owned organizations, and state-owned institutions. These state-owned organizations and institutions must seek approval from higher state authorities for these activities fifteen days prior to the time of the activities. In addition, on January 31 and December 31 of each year, NGOs must send their annual report of the previous year and the annual plan for the next year to state authorities for annual checkups, including a detailed list of their activities and use of funding. Clearly NGOs, up to this point, have helped advance the rights and interests of Chinese women. However, they also threatened the hegemony of the Chinese government, thereby causing the government to respond by limiting the power of the NGOs.

Even though the law names overseas NGOs, the 52nd and 38th stipulation state that it applies to Chinese individuals, Chinese legal persons, Chinese grassroots social organizations, or other organizations in China (2016). As per the law, the Public Security Bureau has set up a specific office called Overseas NGOs Management to manage all NGOs in China. As a result of this new law and the new operational office at the Public Security Bureau, many NGOs that were funded by foreign aid or were unable to find a state authority department as a collaborator were forced to close down. For instance, on May 18, 2014, the Anti-Domestic Violence Network, which relied on foreign funding, closed down.

Activists told me that, in 2020, only two out of the seven NGOs that had been instrumental in the legislation of the Anti-Domestic Violence Law survived. The year 2020 served the heaviest blow to these NGOs, whose work has come to a halt. According to the activists, in 2021, nationwide, less than five social work organizations continue to provide service for victims of intimate partner violence due to limited funding. One activist told me:

> Ever since foreign aid was revoked [by the law], there has been very limited funding. We have been exploring how we can continue to survive. Now the

government implemented the "procurement of service." That is to say, the government departments provide certain organizations with funding through procuring their social services.

However, while they [government departments] have been procuring [and providing funding for] social services in areas such as HIV/AIDS, left-behind children in the countryside [liushou ertong], and senior citizens, intimate partner violence has never been an area for state funding [or procurement]. Without funding for intimate partner violence, the current situation in China is that there is no professional training, no prevention system, and no appraisal or assessment of volunteers' work in the area of intimate partner violence.

In China, Measures for the Administration of Government Procurement of Services was passed by the State Council and Ministry of Finance on March 1, 2020 (2020). According to the Measures, state authority departments make payments to service providers for services that fall within the purview of their own responsibilities (2020). Article 3 states, "Government procurement of services shall follow the principle of budgetary constraints, fees based on the service items, and selection of public services based on their merits, good faith, and performance" (2020). Article 4 stipulates that the Ministry of Finance will be responsible for the procurement service system, "guiding and supervising the government procurement for all regions and all departments" (2020).

According to the activists that I have interviewed, intimate partner violence, gender issues, and feminism have never been the services that state authority departments have ever procured. As a result, activists of NGOs that focus on these issues have been struggling to survive. An activist said to me:

> Ever since the five feminists were arrested in 2015, women's issues have been considered overseas-infiltrated topics [jingwai shentou yiti]. We NGO activists have to keep up with international politics and the ways in which it affects inland practices in China.

As noted in the interviews, issues related to feminism, gender, and intimate partner violence became taboo topics twenty years after the United Nations 4th Conference on Women. Because NGOs that focus on these issues were largely funded by foreign aid, these NGOs have become the target of state suspicion, surveillance, and control. Pin Lv, the founder of Media Monitor for Women's Network/Feminist Voice, analyzed the reason that topics of feminism and gender had become a "criminalized minefield" that was censored:

> First, feminism, after all, is criticism and interrogation. Second, any organizing and mobilizing power is taboo. No matter what it pursues. Third, when public space collapses, feminism does too. When different opinions were all obliterated, this included, of course, feminism. (Lv 2018)

According to the Law of the People's Republic of China on the Administration of Activities of Overseas Non-Governmental Organizations within the Territory of China (2016), the Public Security Bureau and relevant state-owned departments are responsible for designing the areas of activities and lists of projects for overseas NGOs. Activists told me that the involvement and interference of the Public Security Bureau and the State Security Department in the work of NGOs has not only led to a loss of employees who have decided to change careers but has also instilled fear among activists, impeding their ability to make plans and carry out activities. One activist said to me:

> We can only conduct our work after seeking the government's approval first. There has been much time, effort, and energy wasted from negotiating and talking with the police. Each time after we communicated with them [the police], we were told to cancel our activities and redo the planning. This is really not something that we are interested in investing our time and energy in—that is to say, dealing with the police all the time [instead of doing our work].
>
> We are currently just barely surviving in the gray area after registering our NGO with the Bureau of Industry and Commerce as an enterprise. It has been very challenging. Although it has been an arduous journey, we have been exhibiting much creativity to cope with the situation.

Another activist told me:

> Because our NGO has a world reputation, we have been watched and under surveillance on a daily basis [by the police]. If we plan on an activity, we have to report it to the police for approval. Our difficulties stem from the police, creating a tremendous amount of psychological pressure.
>
> Our colleagues, one after another, have ended their careers here. It's not a healthy development [jianquan fazhan] or a flourishing [xinxin xiangrong de jumian] situation [for NGOs]. Faced with this challenge, we have to invent new resolutions.

Activists told me that they have to submit their annual plans of activities to the police for approval. One activist said to me:

> It's been terrifying. We have to report to the police our monthly plan of activities, how we have used the funding, and whom we have supported. Our monthly updates are required to be approved [by the police] in order for the government to continue to support us NGOs. It's been really horrifying.

Another activist said to me:

> Since 2015, repression has been nonstop and constant. Our funding has shrunk in half and our size has shrunk in half. Since 2019, the police have been checking

the background information of all our full-time employees. Our full-time employees are required to report to the police issues concerning their individual privacy information, including their sexual orientation, which can negatively affect their family relations. [Because of that,] we don't want to have too many full-time employees. We prefer flexible employees, not full-time employees.

Faced with political risks, we have been under tremendous psychological pressure to find techniques to deal with the police. When candidates sought employment at our NGO, we asked them to give it more thought, since they would not only make little money without a stable financial situation, but also may be destroyed politically without political safety.

Now is the time for us to seek survival. We have been holding meetings to discuss how we can continue our survival.

In my conversations with them, activists lamented that the decade after the United Nations 4th Conference on Women was the "golden decade" for NGOs in China, when NGOs flourished and activists had a great deal of exposure to, and exchange with, the outside world. Trips to other countries brought them knowledge of how other countries have dealt with intimate partner violence via laws and social services. Returning to China, they were eager to translate these into practice in China through legislation, policy, and social services.

These international exchanges, as activists told me, came to a halt in 2015. As mentioned, under this new Law of the People's Republic of China on the Administration of Activities of Overseas Non-Governmental Organizations within the Territory of China, foreign funding has been banned and NGOs have been the target of systematic control, management, and surveillance by the police. The organizer of the movement implemented by the five feminists, who were arrested in 2015, was forced into exile afterward. One activist told me:

Personal safety of us activists in the NGO field is endangered. In the past ten years, a lot of us were arrested and have not been released yet. Some were in exile to evade imprisonment. Most of us don't have the resource of language to study abroad. Those who do are pursuing their PhD degrees in the US. Those who don't have the necessary language skills have remained in China.

As mentioned in Chapter 2, the recent #metoo movement in China, led by female university students, encountered insurmountable political crackdowns and institutional constraints. In 2015, five female university students were arrested, detained, and jailed by police for planning to disseminate stickers about sexual harassment on public transportation to commemorate International Women's Day in Beijing, Guangzhou, and Hangzhou (Wang, Ping 2015). They were charged with "the crime of creating disturbances" and "gathering crowds to disrupt public order" (ibid.). Prior to the arrest, they staged "the wounded bride" as street art in 2012, which was the first public protest against domestic violence in China. During this protest, they stood in the streets, dressed in white wedding gowns with red paint signifying blood splashed on them, holding billboards with the words "no tolerance for domestic violence," "love is not an excuse for violence," "violence is right next to you, are you still silent?" (Zhou 2012). In 2012, they also performed a street art by "occupying men's restrooms," protesting against the gender inequality implicit in the construction of more public restrooms for men than women (Liao 2012). This also critiqued the gender-stereotyped assumption that more men were in the public sphere than women (ibid.). While in prison in 2015, one of the five feminists suffered a heart attack due to police interrogation, another was initially denied medication for her hepatitis B, still another was verbally abused and locked in a hotel room for eight hours (Yu 2015). Even though they were eventually released after thirty-seven days, they have now been under strict police surveillance for an entire year, and are subject to questioning and harassment at any time by the police (ibid.).

Four months after the arrest of the five feminists, more than three hundred rights-protection "lawyers and activists from across the country were targeted, with 27 forbidden to leave the country, 255 temporarily detained or forcibly questioned and 28 held in government custody" (Palmer 2017). This was called "709 Repression" because these lawyers and activists were arrested on July 9, 2015 (Chu, Bailiang 2016). In 2015 and 2016, a number of NGO employees in Guangdong Province were arrested, and several rights-protection activists were charged and convicted of "gathering crowds to disrupt public order" (Zhou 2018).

In 2014, Media Monitor for Women's Network/Feminist Voice (hereafter Feminist Voice), the NGO that was founded after the United Nations 4th Conference on Women, planned to start an eight-week summer Feminist School for students and principals who enrolled (Yu 2015). Before the official start of classes, Feminist Voice received several warnings from the police not to host those classes. On June 29, the police occupied the office of Feminist Voice to "prevent unlawful social gatherings" (ibid.). The organizer Pin Lv gave her laptop to a colleague for fear that the police would access her documents in case of an arrest (ibid.). After the arrest of the five feminists in 2015, Lv, who was in the United States attending the United Nations Commission on the Status of Women, learned that the police visited her apartment in Beijing. Lv decided to stay on in the United States and pursue a PhD degree in Women and Politics at Rutgers University in 2020. In an interview, Lv said:

> We don't have any means to oppose our government. That's not our objective either. We want to look for a different space, a more flexible space, a diverse space to develop our movement, but not directly oppose the government. That's not what we want to do. (Shi 2019)

During the arrest of the five feminists, many female activists were called by the police for a talk (Zhou 2018). Due to the uncertainty and fear, Feminist Voice employees moved out of Beijing. One activist said:

> I get nervous every time I hear someone at the door. I get nervous every time I hear the voice of the mailman. Mostly, I worry. I worry about those who have been arrested, wondering how they are doing. (Zhou 2018)

Even though Feminist Voice moved back to Beijing after the release of the five feminists, they found a worsening environment where not only street performance arts were impossible to continue, but also activities and public forums on the topic of feminism were restricted. In 2017, Feminist Voice was blocked for thirty days by the Chinese equivalent of Twitter—the Weibo website (Di 2017, Gan 2021; Williams 2021). The Chinese Weibo website sent them a notice that read as follows: "Because the content you recently posted violates national laws and regulations, your account will be banned for 30 days" (ibid.). Prior to the block, the last online post by Feminist Voice was about the Women's March on March 8 in Washington DC (ibid.). On March 18, Xiong, the editor of Feminist Voice, was called in for a talk by the police (Zhou 2018). The police inquired about the nature of Feminist Voice organizing, its funding source, and its employee information. The police said:

> About the #metoo movement, people at the top don't like the word 'movement,' not to mention that it is a movement from abroad.

The police asked what Feminist Voice had posted about the #metoo movement. After Xiong responded that they had published many posts on the subject, they told her not to "stir up trouble" anymore (Zhou 2018).

On March 6, 2018, Feminist Voice posted an article on the two largest Chinese social media platforms—Wechat and Weibo—to introduce an online anti-sexual harassment activity on International Women's Day, titled "A Guide on How to Spend the Strongest Women's Day" (Guo 2019). This article was a follow-up of the Chinese #metoo movement that was initiated by a PhD graduate Qianqian Luo, who exposed online her experiences of sexual harassment by her advisor Xiaowu Chen twelve years ago. Inspired by Luo, over eight thousand students and alumni from over ninety universities signed an online letter, urging the Ministry of Education to establish a campus prevention mechanism against sexual harassment.[1] Feminist Voice posted an article that called on women to post online their experiences of, and declarations against, sexual harassment to promote public awareness. This article was deleted by both Wechat and Weibo on March 8, citing that "this content violates the Cyber Security Law of the People's Republic of China" (ibid.). With the deletion of the article, Feminist Voice was permanently blocked by both Wechat and Weibo, losing its 180,000 followers (ibid.). Other accounts that supported Feminist Voice were also blocked. Feminist Voice hired a lawyer to sue the companies in two different courts. They also sent letters to the Chinese Cyber Security and Leading Information Office, demanding a reason for the blocking of their account and asking for a public announcement of their criteria in censoring gender equality discourses. Supporters of Feminist Voice also wrote letters to 123 representatives of the National People's Congress, 90 members of the National Committee of Chinese People's Political Consultative Conference, and the Cyber Management Offices, asking them to release the detailed regulations upon which Feminist Voice was blocked. They received no response. Feminist Voice also received no response from the courts or the Cyber Office (ibid.).

In 2010, Beijing University Law School Women's Legal Research and Service Center, the NGO that was founded after the United Nations 4th Conference on Women, was notified of its termination by Beijing University (Ding 2019; Wu 2010). Beijing University explained that the reason for terminating it was its source of foreign funding and its involvement in sensitive legal cases (ibid.). As noted earlier in this chapter, during the past fifteen years, Women's Legal Research and Service Center, founded by Jianmei Guo, provided over seventy thousand free legal consultations, handled around three thousand legal cases, submitted over seventy expert opinions on laws and regulations, and organized over eighty trainings and seminars on women's rights and interests. After the forced termination, Guo registered with the Bureau of Industry and Commerce an enterprise under a different name "Beijing Zhongze Women's Legal Consultation Service Center." However, in 2016, Guo was told by the government to close it down (Di 2016). The year 2016 also witnessed the "790 Repression," with around 250 rights-protection lawyers and activists being detained, interrogated, and sentenced (Chu, Bailiang 2016). Ever since Guo followed the state order and closed down the Center, she has continued providing the service to the vulnerable population through her pro bono lawyer firm that she established in 2009—"Beijing Qianqian Law Firm."

Contributions of NGO Activism

Activists at these NGOs have exercised a collective agency in promoting legal reform, providing free legal aid, and advocating public awareness of intimate partner violence in society. Their collective activism has produced many more positive legal reforms and social changes than individuals could have achieved on their own. Their collective agency has demonstrated their shared drive and steadfast commitment to fighting against gender-based violence and building a society that ensures gender equality and social justice for vulnerable populations in Chinese society. Unfortunately, these advancements have been at risk since 2015.

Promoting Legal Reform

Over the years, activists working in NGOs came to realize the significance of the law as a weapon to protect women's legal rights and interests. They have devoted their efforts and energy to the cause of promoting legal reforms. Activists, through their organized NGOs, collectively engaged the legislature, aiming to effect legal reforms to protect women's rights and interests. However, it is important to remember, as discussed in Chapters 1 and 3, the historical fragility of the concept and practice of law in China. We may see the frustration due to lack of progress as the rule of authority figures over the rule of law has reasserted itself since 2015.

Since 1992 when Xingjuan Wang founded the Beijing Maple Women's Counselling Center, the large number of calls from wives to complain about their husbands' abuse made Wang realize how widespread this social issue is (Wang, Zheng 2015). It also drove home the lack of protection for victims under the existing laws (ibid.). She invited numerous court judges, lawyers, and legal experts to analyze the legal issues, the blind spots in the laws, and the implementation problems that have crystallized from the calls that their Center has received. They collectively submitted their report titled "Study of Legal Consultation of Women's Hotline" to the Party Secretary's Office of All China's Women Federation Headquarters and the Women and Children's Unit of China's legislative institution—the Internal Affairs and Justice Committee of the Standing Committee of the National People's Congress (ibid.). In 1997, learning that the Chinese government was going to revise the Marriage Law, Wang, once again, galvanized other activists to write up another collective report titled "Let the New Marriage Law Be a Protection Umbrella for Abused Women." They submitted the report to the legislature for their consideration (ibid.).

After the United Nations 4th Conference on Women in Beijing in 1995, several activists of newly founded NGOs such as the Beijing University Law School Women's Legal Research and Service Center invited a number of scholars, lawyers, court judges, legal professionals, and officials of the All China's Women Federation to discuss a collective agency, committed to the cause of fighting against domestic violence (Rong 2006). Over the years, galvanizing support from governmental, institutional, and societal levels has proved highly effective in helping to pass the Anti-Domestic Violence Law and promote legal reforms.

A member of the Anti-Domestic Violence Network commented, "The Anti-Domestic Violence Network allowed numerous NGOs to come together and share resources in a joint effort to deal with domestic violence" (Dong 2014). As noted in the previous section, after 1995, activists in the Anti-Domestic Violence Network formed an informal alliance with other NGOs, including the Beijing Maple Women's Counselling Center, Media Monitor for Women's Network, and Beijing University Law School Women's Legal Research and Service Center. This collective agency was instrumental in mobilizing pooled resources, including organizational, financial, research, and intellectual, to collaborate on the joint goal of fighting against domestic violence.

The Anti-Domestic Violence Network—a coalition of seventy-one activists from grassroots organizations and hundreds of legal scholars, psychologists, social workers, journalists, and professors—drafted one of the laws emanating from Chinese civil society in Chinese history (Lv 2018). Since the Network was founded, promoting an Anti-Domestic Violence Law has been a priority for the Network, which ascertained that "the major direction of China's anti-domestic violence enterprise is the making of laws" (Rong 2003). To achieve this goal, they must overcome several hurdles. One impediment was the lack of legal recognition of "domestic violence" in Chinese Law. Another impediment was the ubiquitous judicial perception of domestic violence as a private affair in the criminal justice system in China (Zhang 2008).

In 2001, the government planned to make amendments to the Marriage Law and the Law on the Protection of Women's Rights and Interests. The Network seized this opportunity to exert their influence on the expert committee to write the term and concept of "domestic violence" into these laws. Indeed, several legal scholars in the Network, such as Mingxia Chen from the Institute of Law of the Chinese Academy of Social Sciences, served on the expert committee to draft the amendments (Zhang 2008; Chen 2013). These legal scholars were instrumental in inserting the term "domestic violence" into the amendments of both laws (Qin 2014). Despite the success in legitimizing the term and concept of "domestic violence" in the laws, the additional clause of "forbidding domestic violence" failed to provide a comprehensive definition of domestic violence or effective ways to protect women's interests (Zhang 2008).

To redress the problem and push the law further, in 2002, the Network produced the nation's first anti-domestic violence street advertisement (ibid.). In 2003, the coalition in the Network collectively drafted the Anti-Domestic Violence Law and submitted it to China's legislature—the National People's Congress—for review and consideration. The drafted bill quoted the definition of domestic violence as gender discrimination and human rights violation of the international treaties that China had signed, such as the Convention on the Elimination of All Forms of Discrimination against Women (1979), the Convention on Children's Rights (1989), the Declaration of the Elimination of Violence against Women (1993), and the Beijing Declaration and Platform for Action (1995). The drafted bill asserted that

> to prevent and stop domestic violence requires a comprehensive social law whose immediate goal is not to adjust citizen's marriage and family relations, but to offer direct support for citizens' rights to their body, to life and health, and to freedom and human dignity, and with these, we can facilitate gender equality, guarantee healthy and secure family life and stimulate society's civilization and sustainable development. (Chen et al. 2005 cited in Zhang 2008)

After two decades of hard work, this coalition of activists and NGOs succeeded in pushing for the final passage of the Anti-Domestic Violence Law in 2015. Prior to the passage of the law, Pin Lv, one of the founders of Media Monitor for Women's Network, was responsible for advertising the proposed draft bill through the media during China's Two Sessions—the annual plenary session of the National People's Congress and National Committee of Chinese People's Political Consultative Conference. Lv took advantage of the proliferation of media attention during the Two Sessions to introduce to the reporters the background information on domestic violence as well as the proposed bill to advocate the drafted bill to the public and promote awareness of the proposed bill (Lv 2018). Activists also issued a public petition with 12,000 signatures that demanded the following:

> We don't want a hollow, empty and only symbolic domestic violence law … we want a law with actual power … we hope to be informed of, take part in, and monitor the lawmaking process. (Lv 2018)

After the Network closed in 2014, other NGOs continued promoting legal reforms to protect women's rights and interests. Jianmei Guo, the founder of the Beijing University Law School Women's Legal Research and Service Center, commented:

> The current legal system is not at all adequate. From the legal perspective to the social perspective, it is an extremely inadequate system in terms of the psychological aid, medical aid, and legal aid from offices of the police and other legal institutions. We can say that no system like this even exists. (Rui 2013)

The Center under the leadership of Guo implemented a dual approach of providing free legal aid to individual women and "protecting women's rights and interests through advocating legal reforms and systematic changes" (Lv 2021). To achieve this dual goal, Guo shifted her strategy from accepting all individual cases to focusing on public interest litigation and choosing cases that could potentially push for reforms and changes in the existing laws and policies (ibid.).

Since the implementation of the Anti-Domestic Violence Law in 2016, Guo, together with other activists in her Center, have advocated changes to the law (Lv 2017: 191). In 2017, they drafted and published a diagram that contained detailed changes as well as a list of detailed reasons for the changes to every single stipulation in the Anti-Domestic Violence Law (ibid.: 190–209). For example, they proposed expanding the definition of domestic violence to include violence perpetrated by ex-partners, ex-spouses, and cohabitors, financial control, mental harm, and sexual abuse. As shown in Chapter 3, this was deemed necessary because violence perpetrated against other people that does not cause permanent damage such as broken ribs, skull fracture, and spine fracture is not a felony according to the Chinese Criminal Law. They also suggested providing psychological therapy and behavioral correction for the abusers. They advised that the appointed medical institutions to assess injuries should "reduce the assessment fees or provide the medical assessment free of charge." They recommended that the court, in emergency situations, should issue the Personal Safety Protection Order immediately, rather than within forty-eight hours. They proposed that during the effective period of the Personal Safety Protection Order, the abuser should be ordered to move out of the cohabited dwelling and be forbidden to be within 200 meters from the victim. The abuser was also not to be allowed to transfer mutual possessions elsewhere. For victims without a stable financial income, the abuser would be required to pay for their living expenses, child support, and children's education fees, etc. (ibid.: 190–209). They also proposed revising the ambiguous descriptions of the duties of law enforcement authorities to more detailed, spelled-out responsibilities. For instance, the proposed revision specified clearly that the Public Security Bureau *should* issue Written Warning Notes, not "*or* issue written warning notes" as stipulated in the current law (ibid.: 199).

Provide Legal Aid

Among NGOs that aim to provide free legal aid and assistance to vulnerable women, the most reputable one in the country is the Beijing University Law School Women's Legal Research and Service Center, founded in 1995. The founder Jianmei Guo has recruited and employed pro bono lawyers and legal aid activists as her colleagues to work in the Center to provide free legal assistance and legal counselling to vulnerable women. As noted earlier in this chapter, in 2009, Guo founded "China's Pro Bono Lawyer Network," employing over four hundred lawyers. As mentioned above, since 1995, Guo and her colleagues in the center have provided free legal consultation, handled legal cases, and organized training sessions and seminars on women's rights and interests (Huang, Jian 2019; Liu, Ruhua 2019). As illustrated, Guo was nominated for the Nobel Peace Prize in 2005. She was awarded the Simone De Beauvoir Prize in 2010, the International Women of Courage Award in 2011, and the Right Livelihood Award in 2019 for her lifetime work to safeguard women's rights and interests in China (Liu, Ruhua 2019). After her NGO was closed in 2016, she continued her work for the vulnerable population through her pro bono lawyer firm that she established in 2009—"Beijing Qianqian Law Firm."

Through decades of work as pro bono lawyers, Guo and other activists became representatives of vulnerable women in the fight for women's rights and interests through the use of the law. They helped victims use the law to obtain the Personal Safety Protection Order and Written Warning Notes, secure child custody rights, and reduce sentences for victims who killed their abusers. They also helped victims fight for the monetary compensation for physical injuries and mental abuse inflicted by their abusive husbands. Their efforts were at times met with failure. For instance, their claim for monetary compensation was often rejected when the victim's marriage was not dissolved. At times when they helped a victim win the child custody right in court, the verdict failed to be implemented for years during which time the abuser kept the child in his custody. Even though court judges were aware that the abuser failed to comply with the verdict, they chose to let the situation continue instead of applying compulsory means to stop the abuser (Jie 2015). As shown in Chapters 1 and 3, once again, we see the historic preference for the decisions of individual authorities rather than respect for the law.[2]

Activists have encountered a variety of hurdles and adversities. Jianmei Guo discussed how, while handling legal cases, she and her colleagues were harassed and threatened by abusers (Ju 2020). Guo also commented that in many cases, judges did not even follow the basic legal procedures due to the large gap of social status and gender difference between the plaintiff and the defender (Xiao 2019). She discussed the first legal case where she represented a poor woman whose wounded body expelled a strong odor (ibid.). The court judge asked her, "Are you really a lawyer? How can you handle cases for this kind of person?" (ibid.). While in court, Guo was not allowed to read her 8,000-word speech that she had prepared. The judge threw the verdict onto the floor in front of her and declared that she had lost the case. Guo related another court case that involved peasant women who were deprived of monetary compensation for their land; an employee of the court pointed at her, yelling, "Don't stir up clients' emotions! Otherwise I'll arrest you with a criminal charge of assaulting the national government!" (ibid.).

Even though faced with such a myriad of challenges and adversities, Guo and her pro bono colleagues represented vulnerable women in about three thousand legal cases. One of the breakthroughs in these legal cases involved changing the traditional sentence of execution of victims who killed their abusers in self-defense.

One important strategy to accomplish that goal was to employ the "Battered Woman's Syndrome" theory by an expert witness in court.

The Battered Woman's Syndrome was a Western theory that was introduced into China by Min Chen. When Chen studied Feminism Law in the British Columbia University in Canada, she learned that the Battered Woman's Syndrome was presented by an expert witness in court to reduce prison sentence or exonerate victims of abuse who killed their abusers in self-defense[3] (Pan 2018; McClauley 1995). The Battered Woman's Syndrome refers to a collection of post-traumatic symptoms as a result of intimate partner violence, as well as the "negative alterations in cognition and mood" established in the post-traumatic symptom diagnosis stipulated in the Diagnostic and Statistical Manual of Mental Disorders (Walker 2006; Walker and Conte 2017). The symptoms include "(1) intrusive recollection of the traumatic events; (2) hyperarousal and high levels of anxiety; (3) avoidance behavior and emotional numbing (e.g., minimization, dissociation, depression); (4) disrupted interpersonal relationships; (5) body image distortions and somatic complaints; and (6) issues with sexual intimacy" (Walker and Conte 2017: 53).

Chen, during her graduate studies in Canada, read legal cases where the Battered Woman's Syndrome was used by an expert witness in court, leading to the acquittal of victims who had killed their abusers. In 1999, Chen returned to China and started activist work in protecting women's rights and interests. In 2000, she first introduced the theory in China with her article titled "Battered Woman's Syndrome" in the *Chinese Women's Newspaper* (Pan 2018). Thereafter, she has been spreading this theory in the criminal justice system, trying to hold the abusers accountable and reduce the criminal sentences of victims who had killed their abusers (ibid.).

Realizing that women's rights and interests were not protected by the current system, Chen was determined to work within the system to change it. In 2007, Chen worked as the director of the Gender and Law Office in the China Institute of Applied Jurisprudence (Pan 2018). In 2014, it was the first time in China's history when she, as an expert witness, was invited to appear in court (Hu 2016). She applied the Battered Woman's Syndrome and other professional information on intimate partner violence to a case where a victim killed her abusive husband (ibid.). Since 2014, Chen has served as an expert witness for six cases where victims killed their abusers.

Chen pointed out that many court judges were not familiar with the "unusual mental state and behavior patterns of victims of intimate partner violence" (Hu 2016). In this context, as she contended, an expert witness should be called in court to provide professional knowledge that would make up for court judges' lack of knowledge and experience of intimate partner violence (ibid.). Chen explained that these expert witnesses could be clinical psychologists, psychiatrists, social workers, sociologists, researchers, and the police who had direct contact with victims for at least a year (ibid.). Only these experts who had studied intimate partner violence or victims could understand the long-term psychological effect the violence had on victims. Because intimate partner violence was often hidden and took place in private spheres, evidence of violence was often times indirect, such as police records, pictures of injuries, or testimonies of witnesses. With the help of a professional expert witness in court,

> an expert witness is an effective method to resolve the issue of evidence. Otherwise, judges, lawyers, and prosecutors could only see scattered evidence, but not the issue behind the evidence … The court judge can decide from the statements [of the expert witness] and other evidence whether domestic violence exists in the case ... The judge can then make a final verdict that reflects gender equality and social justice. (Song 2016)

In court, Chen, as the first expert witness in a Chinese court, contended that a victim, upon the threat of her life, would respond with the most extreme form, which was to kill the abuser (ibid.). Due to "cultural, psychological, and economic reasons," she explained, "victims were faced with a very limited menu of 3 choices: being beaten to death by the abuser, committing suicide, or killing the abuser" (Hu 2016). Women's resistance usually does not happen during the abuse, because they are not a match for their abusers. Their resistance is often in other forms such as "poisoning their abusers after the abuse," Chen stated in court (Song 2016). "Fear is the motivation of victims' resistance," Chen explained in court (ibid.). For cases where victims used a knife to continuously attack the abuser's dead body or burn the dead body, Chen commented that some victims were still in fear even after they had killed the abusers—Which is why they would exert revenge on the abuser's dead body that had previously caused them suffering (ibid.).

Prior to the introduction of an expert witness in court, the death sentence was often given to victims who had killed their abusers in self-defense, and the execution was often times immediate (Yong 2016). Since the expert witness was introduced in court, less severe sentences have been given. For instance, in 2015, a victim in Sichuan poisoned her abusive husband (Song 2016). Afterward, she used a cleaver to dismember his body. Min Chen was called to court as an expert witness. After she gave her professional statement about intimate partner violence, the court judge adopted her expert opinion and sentenced the victim to five years in prison. This was a testament to the great stride that activists like Chen have made in the field of legal reform and legal aid that is made available to vulnerable victims of intimate partner violence in China.

Case Study of Legal Aid

As mentioned before, women activists in NGOs not only helped victims obtain Written Warning Notes and Personal Safety Protection Orders, but also represented them in court proceedings to protect their rights and interests. The Anti-Domestic Violence Network, for instance, helped a victim who suffered a rupture, and eventually removal, of her spleen as a result of her husband's beating (Qin 2014). With the help of the Network, the victim's abuser was sentenced to four years in prison (ibid.).

One of the most famous court cases that the Anti-Domestic Violence Network helped with involved the American educator Kim Lee, whose Chinese husband Yang Li—a celebrity—physically abused her multiple times, as mentioned in Chapter 1 (Lv 2018). Yang Li became a celebrity in 1999 for inventing a unique method to study the English language called "Crazy English," which taught students all over China to speak English crazily and read English crazily, including yelling out English sentences and phrases on the street without shame or shyness. His famous teaching philosophy was "I enjoy losing face" (Zang 2018). Kim Lee, an American educator, lived with Yang Li in 2000, working as the editor-in-chief of Li's "Crazy English" teaching enterprise. She wrote books, recorded audios and videos, and trained students. In 2006 and 2011, Kim posted pictures of her injured head, ears, and legs online caused by Yang's beatings (ibid.). Yang, who controlled all the earnings of their teaching enterprise, stopped providing living expenses for their three children and threatened Kim with texts such as "You're a total bitch! Hell is your place! In America, you should be killed by your husband with [a] gun, this is the real American way. You're so lucky to be in China!" (Xin 2012).

Kim wrote letters to activists in the Anti-Domestic Violence Network about the domestic violence that she had suffered (Fan 2011). She wrote:

> Using family harmony to ignore domestic violence can only make our next generation suffer the same pain ... In the lack of a law, the most powerful response is the public's refusal to tolerate domestic violence and recognize the fact that domestic violence is not culture. Domestic violence is a crime! (Fan 2011)

Activists in the Anti-Domestic Violence Network provided steadfast support and helped represent Kim in court for a divorce. This court case that involved an American citizen and a Chinese celebrity dominated the news all over China for an entire year. With the help of activists in the Anti-Domestic Violence Network, the court eventually recognized domestic violence and Kim won the case. Kim was awarded the divorce, child custody rights, child support, and a 50,000RMB compensation—the highest compensation for spousal abuse in a divorce case in China's legal history (Lu, Pin 2018).

In 2019, Kim posted online an open article with family pictures with Yang, stating, "I love my husband forever," and "I have forgiven my husband" (Lina 2020). Harsh responses to her post were visible on the internet. For instance, one response read:

> Kim's forgiveness is her individual choice. It is also a betrayal of the collective. In previous years, she and many activists helped push for China's Anti-Domestic Violence Law. Now she has utilized her individual power to weaken the fruit that the collective has won. Rather than posting an open letter to everyone [about how she has forgiven and loves her husband forever], she should ask for forgiveness from those activists who had helped her in those years. (Di 2019)

Despite such lamenting responses, the triumph of Kim's court case with the help of activists in 2013 marked a historical milestone in domestic violence cases, shaking the nation with the its first Personal Safety Protection Order, raising public awareness of domestic violence across the nation, and pushing forward the passage of China's Anti-Domestic Violence Law in 2015.

Another famous case that activists helped involved Yan Li, a victim in Sichuan Province, who killed her husband, and then cut, boiled, and scattered the remains in various places, as mentioned in Chapters 3 and 5.[4] (Duan 2012, Zhou 2015; Luo 2019). In 2011, Li was sentenced to immediate execution. Li appealed, but her appeal was rejected by the Sichuan Provincial Supreme Court. Li's brother, before taking a trip to Beijing to petition to the Supreme Court, read newspapers and came across a similar legal case handled by the NGO Beijing Qianqian Law Firm, originally founded by Jianmei Guo (Luo 2019). He made a phone call to the Qianqian Law Firm and explained the case. A young lawyer told him on the phone that the sentence was obviously too heavy (ibid.). That response gave Li's brother hope, prompting him to ask the Qianqian Law Firm to handle Li's case.

In 2013, Jianmei Guo and Weihua Xu, learning that it was the critical time of Li's death penalty review, flew to Sichuan Province to visit Li at the detainment center (Luo 2019). At the detainment center, Guo and Xu encouraged Li to talk about the violence she endured in marriage. Li explained that, after marriage, she was beaten several times a month by her husband, including having one of her fingers chopped off—which he disposed of before it could be reattached. He also kicked her, starved her, locked her outside in the freezing night, slapped her, used cigarettes to burn her face, her breasts, and her vagina, and used a stainless steel hanger to beat her, and banged her head onto the wall (Zhou 2015). After each beating, her husband forced her to have sexual intercourse, while burning her body parts with cigarettes, including the night after Li had a long, painful abortion procedure. He also frequently raped her daughter from the previous marriage, while forcing her to watch. His years of abuse left Li with psychological trauma and physical injuries. Although Li sought help from the residential committee, officials at the All China Women's Federation, the police, and the court, no one provided any help. The police, upon her calling, hung up as soon as they learned that it was a "family issue" between a married couple. In 2010, her husband hit her feet with a rifle, breaking off one of her toenails, threatening to kill her. She resisted and killed her husband.

In 2014, the suggestion of utilizing expert witnesses in court for this case was denied by the court. In the review of the death penalty sentence, Guo and Xu represented Li, trying to convince the judge and the audience that Li suffered long-term domestic violence and acted in self-defense against her long-term abuser. In court, Xu asked Li to show the audience her left hand with a missing finger that had been chopped off by her husband. However, at the same time, Guo and Xu were confronted with insults and curses against them by Li's in-laws and relatives in the audience (Zhou 2015). Guo argued in court that Li was a victim of severe domestic violence and killed her abuser out of self-defense, a behavior that did not have or cause harm to society (Rui 2013). Causing harm to society is a crucial element in determining a heavy or light criminal sentence in the Chinese Criminal Law (2020). Guo argued that Li did not start a fire or kill people in society, which would have caused harm to society. Also, she argued that the fundamental reason for her killing her abuser was the lack of social aid mechanisms for victims (Rui 2013).

Meanwhile, activists in the Anti-Domestic Violence Network worked hard to make sure that Yan Li's legal case was publicized nationwide. It received an unprecedented amount of media attention. Because of their galvanizing activist work, around 136 scholars, lawyers, and NGO activists from both home and abroad jointly posted an open letter online, appealing to save Li's life (Luo 2019). Over two hundred feminists and activists also sent an emergency appeal letter to the Sichuan Provincial Supreme Court (ibid.). Internationally, the famous human rights organization Amnesty International also appealed to China: "Tell China: do not sentence victims of domestic violence to death" (ibid.). Volunteers staged performance art in front of the city courts of eight cities, including Guangzhou, Shanghai, Wuhan, Beijing, and Xi'an. In these eight cities, volunteers lay in front of the city courts, wrapped themselves with white cloth into a white cocoon, showing that they were not able to struggle out of this cocoon no matter how much they tried. Next to them were large papers with the words on them: "I will not become the next Yan Li" (ibid.).

Eventually, in 2015 with pro bono lawyers Guo and Xu's help in proving the domestic violence that Li suffered, the final court verdict was released. The new verdict stated that the previous verdict did not recognize the existence of domestic violence. In view of the new evidence of domestic violence, the old verdict was revised to a death sentence with two years' reprieve. This legal case was celebrated as one of the most influential ten court cases in 2015 by a number of organizations and media outlets.

In 2019, Guo commented on the legal cases of victims killing their abusers:

> There have been, and still are, a lot of cases of victims using violence to deal with violence. Because Yan Li's case took place at the critical historical period of the drafting of China's Anti-Domestic Violence Law, her case received nationwide media attention, generating extensive concern and public discussion on legal cases of this nature. However, nowadays, cases of this nature no longer enjoy the same kind of attention and concern. (ibid.)

As mentioned above, the Beijing Qianqian Law Firm founded by Jianmei Guo, over the years, has handled about three hundred legal cases like this, representing vulnerable women and protecting their rights and interests. The following legal case is one more example. In Hubei Province, Xia's husband used a screwdriver to carve out both her eyes during her sleep, seventeen days after her giving birth to their son (Lv 2017). The reason for his cruelty was that she had previously refused sex. Her husband was sentenced to eight years in prison, and compensation of 56,136RMB ($9356) was to be paid to her. However, this payment never materialized, despite her triumph in the court case. During the following years, Xia appealed to the court many times but each time the court responded that her husband's obligation could not be met because he was unable to pay. Out of desperation, Xia sought help from the Beijing Qianqian Law Firm.

After learning about this case, the Qianqian Law Firm sent pro bono lawyers to local courts to procure information about the case and its execution. After learning that the compensation could not be paid , the Firm cooperated with the local All China Women's Federation and national media to look for multiple strategies for aid. In 2006, the Firm worked together with the Beijing Maple Women's Psychology Counselling Service Center to organize a forum titled "A Forum on Anti-Domestic Violence Legal and Psychological Aid." In the forum, they invited Xia to introduce herself and talk about her experience of domestic violence. Her story caught the attention of the media, as well as scholars and experts. A few days later, the Firm took Xia to the annual meeting of the Anti-Domestic Violence Network, where Xia narrated her story again. After the meeting, donations from attendees came to about 5,000RMB ($1,000). Xia was also promised jobs by activists from NGOs in Hubei Province. After her story was reported nationwide in the media, a German glass eye company offered her their highest-quality prosthetic eyes free of charge. Meanwhile, the Hubei Supreme Court learned the news from the media and ordered lower courts to execute the compensation fee. In 2007, three lower courts collectively paid Xia an advance of the compensation fee. In 2009, when Xia sought help from the Firm again, the Firm utilized the internet to search for donations to pay for her follow-up treatments of her prosthetic eyes (Lv 2017).

Public Awareness

Activists in NGOs consider it paramount to conduct training of law enforcement and justice workers about domestic violence, promote public awareness, and critique victim-blaming perceptions in the mass media. Through raising public awareness, activists believe that women can arm themselves with the knowledge about the law to be proactive in collecting evidence and pursuing justice through the law. This allows law enforcement workers to better implement the law and provide necessary aid and assistance to victims.

Various NGOs, including the Anti-Domestic Violence Network and the Beijing Qianqian Law Firm, have organized training sessions for court judges and the police. One activist told me,

> One of the main obstacles to implementing the Anti-Domestic Violence Law is the ignorance of law enforcement and justice workers about the meaning of domestic violence. Some think domestic violence has to be long-term. Some think domestic violence has to be physical with a consequence of severe injuries. We have the responsibilities to inform them and the public that domestic violence can be physical, mental, or financial, and that it does not have to be long-term [to qualify for domestic violence].

Like this activist, NGO workers are cognizant of the crucial importance of training court judges and police in the spirit and meaning of domestic violence in order to ensure the proper implementation of the Anti-Domestic Violence Law. In 2019, for instance, the Beijing Qianqian Law Firm organized a "Domestic Violence Seminar," attended by the police, lawyers, social workers, and staff members of the All China Women's Federation (Ji 2019). The seminar provided training materials and training sessions for the attendees about the legal responsibilities of law enforcement workers toward victims of domestic violence, including issuing Written Warning Notes and Personal Safety Protection Orders. In 2019, activists from NGOs in Hubei also organized a couple of training sessions for 132 newly recruited police personnel in the province (Song 2019). These training sessions introduced the complicated nature of domestic violence, provided the police with technical skills to handle domestic violence cases, and stressed the necessity of collaborating with multiple agencies to offer victims aid and assistance (ibid.).

Activists in NGOs, such as the Media Monitor for Women's Network/Feminist Voice, emphasized the crucial role mass media played in promoting public awareness of domestic violence, critiquing the victim-blaming rhetoric, and advocating gender equality. Media Monitor for Women's Network/Feminist Voice, for instance, since 1995, has set its goal to expose gender prejudices and discriminations in society and advocate gender equality and women's right to voice their opinions in the media. Believing that one of the root causes of domestic violence is gender inequality, they see it as their primary responsibility to promote social and cultural consciousness of gender equality (Cai et al. 2001). As the founders Yanqiu Guo and Yiping Cai wrote, "Mass media, rather than an objective reflection of reality, helps form public perceptions of the world. The way information is reported in the media has ramifications in formulating public perceptions of society" (2000: 169).

Over the years, activists in these NGOs such as the Media Monitor for Women's Network/Feminist Voice have collected, analyzed, and critiqued news reports on gender-related issues. Prior to its closedown in 2018, two staff members of Feminist Voice, for instance, managed their online Weibo account (similar to Twitter) through posting their analysis and criticisms of news reports related to gender (Yu 2015). As mentioned earlier, from 2012 to 2013, Feminist Voice organized around thirty activities against domestic violence, gender-based violence, and gender-based bias (Shi 2019). By the time of its closedown, Feminist Voice enjoyed as its fruits of labor 180,000 followers.

Activists in NGOs organized a variety of street performance arts to promote public awareness of gender inequality and domestic violence. As mentioned before, to support the legal case of Yan Li, volunteers staged performance art in eight cities, where they lay in front of the city courts (Luo 2019). They wrapped themselves in white cloth and curled into a cocoon, attempting to struggle out of it but in vain. Next to them were large words: "I will not become the next Yan Li" (ibid.). In another street performance, they walked on the streets in white wedding gowns with red paint splashed on them, representing blood from domestic violence (Zhou 2012). They raised in their hands large bulletin boards that read: "No tolerance for domestic violence," "Love is not the excuse for violence," "Beating is not care and swearing is not love," and "Violence is right next to you, are you still silent?" (ibid.). In 2012, activists staged another important street performance, "Occupying men's restrooms" (Liao 2012). This activity protested against the fact that there were more public restrooms for men than women, manifesting gender inequality and gender stereotypes that more men were expected to be present in the public sphere than women (ibid.).

Activists in NGOs spoke out in the media, critiquing the victim-blaming rhetoric in the media for domestic violence and raising public awareness to change policies and provide necessary aid and assistance to victims. Pro bono lawyers Xiaoquan Lv and Jianmei Guo from the Beijing Qianqian Law Firm, for instance, when talking to the media about the legal case of Yan Li, emphasized that many victims, like Li, fought hard against domestic violence by reporting the violence to the police, seeking help from the All China Women's Federation, and talking to friends, relatives, and families about the violence (Wang 2013). However, no one offered any help to Li and other victims like her. Victims like Li, as Lv contended, no matter how hard they fought, were not able to get rid of the violence in their life. Within this vacuum of help in the society, as Lv told the media, all they could do was to endure the violence, until one day they were unable to endure it any longer and resorted to killing to end this cycle of violence.

Pro bono lawyer Jianmei Guo, founder of the Beijing Qianqian Law Firm, explained to the media that the reason that victims like Li killed their abusers was because of the lack of social aid, psychological aid, and legal aid (such as the police) in society (Wang 2013). Guo ascertained: "The fundamental reason [for Li's killing of her abuser] was the inadequacy of the Anti-Domestic Violence Law and the inadequacy of the social aid system" (ibid.).

While Lv and Guo put the blame on the void in the area of social aid, Pin Lv, one of the founders of Feminist Voice, criticized the media's victim-blaming rhetoric:

> Whenever mass media reports a case of a woman as a victim [of domestic violence], it often reads: "She does not understand the law. She is too weak. The fact that she has failed to resist [the violence] results in the tragedy of herself as the victim." When mass media reports a case of a victim killing her abuser, it often reads: "She does not understand the law [and resists against the law], resulting in such a tragedy." Mass media often simplifies this issue with a critical attitude. We should avoid such discourse in reports on domestic violence, as such discourse blames victims. We must gather from their own life experiences and life situations to understand why they do not resist or do resist, rather than judging them from a top-down view. If we can understand them and support them, they will be able to speak out about their suffering and come to the recognition that their suffering is not a shame. They can be empowered to resist. Blaming victims cannot empower victims.

Activists like Xiaoquan Lv, Jianmei Guo, and Pin Lv are fully conscious of the importance mass media plays in promoting public awareness of domestic violence and in pushing for a social aid system for victims. While criticizing the media's depiction of victims of domestic violence as weak and ignorant of the law, they pointed directly at the void of a social aid system as the main culprit of the issue. In order to ameliorate the situation and change policies, activists in various NGOs have been working hard to train law enforcement and justice workers on domestic violence, build public consciousness of domestic violence and gender inequality through a variety of street performances, protests, and online article postings, and empower women to collect evidence and pursue justice in court.

Appropriating the State Discourse

As I have argued elsewhere (Zheng 2015), NGOs in China, in general, share a nonconfrontational and non-oppositional relationship with the state. As I will show in this section, activists in NGOS feel that they have no alternative but to actively collaborate with the state and appropriate the state discourse in order to legitimize their activism and implement their agenda to fight domestic violence and gender inequality. To do so, in addition to cooperating with the state discourse of "family harmony" and "social stability," they continued the rationale of the linkage between women's social status and the global reputation and status of China as a nation.

From a Symbiotic to a Hierarchical Relationship with the State

Since these feminist NGOs were founded in 1995, activists have been carrying out their agenda of fighting domestic violence and advancing gender equality through working within the state apparatus. As shown in the previous sections, before the collaboration was terminated by the newly instituted law against a foreign funding source, many NGOs had been housed under the auspices of a state apparatus. For instance, the Anti-Domestic Violence Network was housed under the auspices of the China Law Society for political legitimacy. The Women's Legal Research and Service Center was housed under the auspices of the Law School at Beijing University. The Beijing Maple Women's Psychology Counselling Service Center was housed under the auspices of another state apparatus—the Chinese Academy of Management Science.

In this symbiotic relationship between the NGOs and the state, activists work in a nonconfrontational framework with the state (see also Zheng 2015, Spires 2011). As Pin Lv, one of the founders of Media Monitor for Women's Network/Feminist Voice, said,

> We are not that powerful. We have no means to oppose our government, which is by no means our goal. We need to look for a different space, a more flexible space, a more diverse space to develop our campaign, but not a direct opposition. It [a direct opposition with the state] is by no means what we want to do. (Shi 2019)

As shown, activists such as Pin Lv depoliticized their activism and avoided challenging or opposing the state in order to survive the political environment and the increased surveillance on NGOs. Through this strategic depoliticization and a non-oppositional relationship, activists seek to bring about policy changes and legal reforms through engaging with state institutions, accessing state mechanisms, and confining their strategies within the state framework.

The Anti-Domestic Violence Network, for instance, had been in collaboration with a variety of political and administrative apparatuses, including the All China's Women's Federation, the Public Security offices, and the prosecution and law departments all over China in order to put forward legal reforms and policy changes (Dong 2014). One of its activists told me:

> We were housed under the China Law society, which was a government agency. Having this government sponsor helped place us within the political system. For us, getting legislation of an Anti-Domestic Violence Law passed was one of our important missions. The China Law Society, as a state agency, had key access to the essential government branches such as the legislative, judicial, and public security offices. Officials at these branches also trusted people at the China Law Society. As you know, NGOs in China were strictly regulated by the Civil Affairs Department and they were not trusted unless they were affiliated with a government agency.

As stated by this activist, the Anti-Domestic Violence Network, due to its limited access to the state, strategically used its connection with the government to advance its agenda of effecting legal reform and policy changes, from within the system (see also Qin 2014). This pragmatic, strategic alliance with different government agencies was successful in accomplishing the Network's goal. In 2015, the Anti-Domestic Violence Law that they drafted and proposed was finally passed, marking a historical milestone of being the first law against domestic violence in Chinese history.

One of the government agencies with which the Network collaborated most closely was the headquarters of the All China Women's Federation, as well as its provincial and municipal branches across the country (Zhang 2008). In fact, one of the special advisors for the Network was the director of the Rights and Interests Department of the headquarters of All China Women's Federation. Many projects and workshops organized by the Network would not have been possible without the contribution of officials working in different branches of the All China Women's Federation, often in the Rights and Interests Department (ibid.).

The All China Women's Federation is a massive, influential administrative state apparatus that can exert unrivaled impact on other state institutions and reach government leaders in ways that NGOs are never able to. It enjoys "the legitimacy of the Party-state ... is regularly consulted at national and local levels on policy and legislative changes" (Howell 2005: 61). The All China Women's Federation was founded in March 1949 as a country-wide women's organization in the People's Republic of China. Its founding mission was to represent and safeguard the rights and interests of women and children. The organization runs two publications, the *Chinese Women's Newspaper* and the *Chinese Women's Magazine*, as well as the Chinese Women's University in Beijing. It has ten departments, including the

Rights and Interests Department. It manages fourteen institutions, including the Legal Aid Center and Women's Research Institute. The headquarters runs a session every five years to elect its executive committee, who, in turn, convene at annual meetings. The All China Women's Federation has almost a million branches and subsidiary offices in almost every province, city, county, township, village, and street (Ministry of Finance 2019).

The mutual concern about the issue of domestic violence facilitated the collaboration of the Network and the All China Women's Federation. Since the Network's main goal is policy change and legal reform, rather than social service, partnership with the All China Women's Federation was strategic and instrumental in accessing the crucial state institutions that could bring those goals to fruition. While the Network relied on the Federation for its political capital, the Federation's subsidiary branches, with a declining state-provided budget, benefited from the Network's financial resources from foreign funding by international foundations (Zhang 2008).

It was this mutual-assistance partnership that helped disseminate information about domestic violence to nooks and crannies of communities across the country, a task that the Network would never have been able to accomplish on its own. Because the Network, as an NGO, was not legally authorized to submit its legislative proposals to the state, it was the national general secretary of the All China Women's Federation who called for a meeting with thirty representatives of the National People's Congress to discuss the proposal prepared by the Network (Zhang 2008). With the endorsement of these representatives in the meeting, the Network submitted the proposal to the Legislative Planning Committee of the 10th National People's Congress Standing Committee (ibid.). As mentioned above, in 2015, the Anti-Domestic Violence Law was successfully passed.

While the Network's affiliation with government agencies helped reach its goal, it also caused drawbacks and limitations that eventually led to its closedown in 2014. Because its co-founders and most of its members were scholars, government officials, and teachers who worked in the state apparatus, the Anti-Domestic Violence Network, to them, was a mere pastime activity, rather than a lifetime career (Dong 2014). The life and death of the Network was not their top concern. Due to the lack of their commitment to the Network, as the activists in the group told me, the Network had a huge turnover rate of staff members, making the organization unstable and unsustainable in the long term. Moreover, the reliance on government agencies compelled the Network to incorporate the state discourse of "family harmony" and "social stability," which eroded its original discourse concerning women's rights and interests (Zhang 2008).

However, since the implementation of the newly instituted 2014 law that prohibits NGOs from conducting political activities, this symbiotic relationship between NGOs and the state has changed into a hierarchical one. As discussed in previous sections, in tandem with the law, the Public Security Bureau has set up a separate office dedicated to managing, regulating, and supervising all NGOs in China. The Public Security Bureau and state apparatus are held responsible for designing the areas of activities and lists of projects for NGOs. These activities must be conducted in alliance with Chinese state authority departments, state-owned organizations, and state-owned institutions. These state-owned organizations and institutions must seek state approval of these activities fifteen days prior to the start of the activities. This new 2014 law and the new supervising office at the Public Security Bureau not only forced NGOs such as the Anti-Domestic Violence Network to close down, but also turned the relationship from a symbiotic one into a supervising-supervised one.

Connecting Women's Status with China's Status

Activists in NGOs related to me the importance of connecting women's status with the superior status and reputation of the state on the global stage. Activists in the Beijing Qianqian Law Firm, for instance, declared the following in their proposal to revise certain stipulations in the Anti-Domestic Violence law:

> China is one of the first group of countries that have signed the United Nations Convention on the Elimination of All Forms of Discrimination against Women and the Declaration to Eliminate All Violent Actions against Women, forbidding all forms of violence against women. It is an international recognition of the need to protect women and children from violence. In our country, it is reflected in public power's intervention and control of all violence … It can enhance our country's reputation and status in the international community. (Lv 2017: 208)

As shown, activists connected protection of women from violence and China's superior status and reputation on the global stage. In Chinese history, during the May Fourth and New Culture Movements at the turn of the nineteenth century, women's social status was regarded as the symbol of the progress and modernity of the Chinese nation (Chow 1960). This perception continued during the Communist era, when women's liberation was upheld as the symbol of the liberation and modernity of the nation (Zheng 2009a). During post-socialist China, as my research demonstrates, activists have strategically perpetuated this rhetoric and argued that the Chinese state will be able to prove its superior status and reputation on the global stage through enhancing its women's status and tackling the social issue of domestic violence. In so doing, they appealed to the government to take actions to protect women and intervene in domestic violence.

This appeal to the state to take the initiative to crack down on domestic violence and protect women's interests is crucial. In order to battle against domestic violence, all state institutions are required to collaborate and coordinate in joint efforts, without which this cause would be impossible. These multiple agencies include, but are not limited to, hospitals, the Public Security Bureau, the court, the All China Women's Federation, and residential committees. These are state institutions with state leadership, with a hierarchical power structure from the headquarters to subsidiary branches at the province, city, county, township, village, and street level. As mentioned in the previous sections, the Anti-Domestic Network, for instance, embraced the support of the All China Women's Federation, which coordinated with state institutions to establish a "multi-agency cooperation to recognize and intervene in domestic violence" in Hunan Province (Lv 2017: 143). This collaboration was instrumental in reaching the preset goals, as it would have been impossible for NGOs to carry out the intervention task without state support.

Appropriating the State Discourse

Activists, in general, avoid politically sensitive discourse such as human rights and democracy. In congruence with the state discourse of harmony and stability, they framed domestic violence and gender inequality not as a violation of human rights but as a social issue that can cause social harm, disrupt social harmony and stability, and damage the image of China on the global stage. In appropriating the state discourse of family harmony and social stability in their activist rhetoric, they legitimized their activism and continued to carry out their mission (see Chapter 3 on the state discourse of harmony and stability).

As discussed at length in Chapter 3, President Xi Jinping gave numerous nationwide political addresses on the importance of family harmony and social stability. To ensure family-state harmony, in his multiple public addresses, Xi specifically called upon women to play their primary role in maintaining family harmony as "dutiful wives and virtuous mothers" (xianqi liangmu) who "not only take care of their husbands in daily life, but also educate and raise kids (xiangfu jiaozi), manage the household industriously and diligently, and assist their husbands in their careers (qinjian chijia)" (Chen, Zhenkai 2020).

This harmony discourse reveals the state's anxiety and concern about social polarization and class conflict as a result of the unevenly developing market economy. Utilizing the harmony discourse is a way to reassert the state's legitimacy and appease potential social uprisings. The emphasis on women's responsibility to ensure family harmony and resolve political stability encourages women to endure domestic violence and stay with abusers in order to maintain family harmony and preserve family unity. As shown in Chapter 3, the harmony discourse prompts various state institutions such as the police and the All China Women's Federation to prioritize mediation as the paramount strategy to resolve domestic violence.

For activists in NGOs, appropriating the harmony discourse provided political legitimacy for their cause to fight against domestic violence. Domestic violence was couched by activists as a threat to social harmony and social stability, calling for the state's intervention in this issue and responsibility to support activists in combating it. In this way, activists strategically advocated to the state that domestic violence is a social conflict that needs to be resolved and repressed to "maintain social harmony" and social stability (Lv 2021).

For instance, Jianmei Guo, the founder of the Beijing Qianqian Law Firm, asserted that their gender activism helped resolve social conflict and safeguard social harmony. As mentioned earlier, pro bono lawyers at the Beijing Qianqian Law Firm have provided over seventy thousand free legal consultations and handled around three thousand legal cases for vulnerable women in gender-related issues such as domestic violence. Jianmei Guo said:

China is an unevenly developed and unbalanced society. With the reform during the past thirty years, China has gained economic development and progress, but at the same time, experienced a great deal of social conflict. Issues and conflicts abound everywhere. The tremendous gap between the rich and poor and the huge rift between different regions have revealed that the fruit of the reform is not enjoyed by everyone. Distribution is not even. Only few have received more benefits. As a result, social conflicts are salient in society. As pro bono lawyers, on the one hand, we safeguard the rights of the vulnerable group and protect justice. On the other hand, we are dissolving social conflict and maintaining social harmony.

The government advocated "building a harmonious society." Our pro bono lawyers are indispensable in this regard. The social conflicts will grow sharper and more salient without our pro bono lawyers who can serve as a bridge, a lubricant, and a soothing force. So I appeal to the government to see our positive impact, not just our critical attitude toward the criminal justice departments and the government in an individual legal case.

What is the objective of our pro bono lawyers' criticisms? Our objective is to have the law implemented on the ground and get the rights of the vulnerable group protected. There is no individual intention in it. There is no political intention in it. The only thing we do is to ensure the justice of laws, which should be a lawyer's proper function. Nothing else. So I specially appeal to the government that they should be aware of that. The premise of real social harmony is fairness and justice, and the true implementation of the law.

That is real harmony. What is harmony? It is not "everything is great." Just because conflicts are not exposed, it does not mean there is no conflict. To help the government resolve these conflicts, we need to aid the government, cooperate with the government and pick up the missing parts. So I appeal to the society and government to understand the responsibility, spirit, dedication, and contribution of pro bono lawyers. (Wang 2010)

Jianmei Guo also discussed the time when she was called to the central government for a talk (Lv 2021). She said:

I talked to them [central government officials] sincerely, with tears in my eyes. I said: "You government officials—how come you don't understand that what we do is actually pick up the missing areas and supplement the deficiencies [shiyi buque] for the government? We have been trying our best to appease many conflicts in many legal cases. What we have been doing is to help the government pick up the missing areas and supplement the deficiencies, appease people's hearts, and build harmony." (ibid.)

The state's discourse on harmony, as shown in Chapter 3, subsumes women's interests into the state's interest, perpetuates violence, and reinforces victimization of women, unlike the human rights discourse that prioritizes and centers on women's human rights as first and foremost. However, as shown above, activists like Jianmei Guo evoked the state discourse of harmony and stability to legitimize their activism and underscore the indispensable function of their activism in appeasing social conflicts and preserving social stability and social harmony. As such, activists refrained from politically sensitive discourse on human rights and democracy and portrayed domestic violence as a social conflict to be resolved and appeased in order to maintain social order, build social harmony, and enhance China's image on the global stage. As many of them declared, their activism should be celebrated and embraced by the state as it works to legitimize state power by dissolving social dissent that could jeopardize the state.

Conclusion

The NGOs in China have successfully avoided a series of dangers in their efforts. One of the difficulties facing human rights discourse in China is the issue of nationalism. There are two pillars of Communist power in China, economic prosperity and nationalism. The issue of nationalism is particularly fraught. Like many nations, nationalism is used by the Chinese Communist Party to rally the populace behind them. It is dangerous for reformers to be seen as attacking China in the process of bringing about reform. However, the women activists have been very successful in avoiding this issue, defining anti-domestic violence reform as something that China is at the forefront of. Reformers have turned what might have been a liability into a positive force for progressive change.

As demonstrated in this chapter, since the United Nations 4th World Conference on Women that was held in Beijing in 1995, the term "domestic violence" has officially entered the state language in its policy discussions and public recognition of this issue. Incorporating this term in the state discourse marked a historical turning point in opening up social space and political legitimacy for women to engage in activism on domestic violence issues after the conference. This conference ushered in a new era of the Chinese women's movement to establish a myriad of NGOs to protect women's rights and interests, including the Beijing Maple Women's Counselling Center, the Media Monitor for Women Network/Feminist Voice, the Anti-Domestic Violence Network, and the Beijing University Law School Women's Legal Research and Service Center.

Since 2015, legislation requiring surveillance and control of NGOs has prohibited foreign funding. As a result, this forced many NGOs to close down. This 2015 law prohibits NGOs from conducting political activities in China, stipulating that the Public Security Bureau and relevant state-owned departments are responsible for designing the areas of activities and lists of projects for NGOs. The year 2020 delivered the heaviest blow to these NGOs, whose work has come to a halt. According to the activists, in 2021, nationwide, less than five social work organizations continue to provide service for victims of intimate partner violence, due to the limited funding. According to the activists that I have interviewed, intimate partner violence, gender issues, and feminism have never been supported by state authorities. As a result, activists from NGOs that focus on these issues have been struggling to survive.

Since 1995, activists at these NGOs have exercised a collective agency in promoting legal reform, providing free legal aid, and advocating public awareness of intimate partner violence in society. Their collective activism has produced many positive legal reforms and social changes that individuals could never have been able to achieve on their own. Their collective agency has demonstrated their shared drive and steadfast commitment toward fighting against gender-based violence and building a society that ensures gender equality and social justice for the vulnerable population in the society.

Since these feminist NGOs were founded in 1995, activists have been carrying out their agenda of fighting domestic violence and advancing gender equality through working within the state apparatus. However, since the implementation of the newly instituted 2015 law that prohibits NGOs from conducting political activities, this symbiotic relationship between NGOs and the state has changed into a hierarchical one. In tandem with the law, the Public Security Bureau has set up a separate office dedicated to managing, regulating, and supervising all NGOs in China. This new 2015 law and the new supervising office at the Public Security Bureau not only forced NGOs such as the Anti-Domestic Violence Network to close down, but also turned the relationship from a symbiotic one into a supervising-supervised one.

Activists depoliticized their activism and avoided challenging or opposing the state in order to survive the political environment. Through this strategic depoliticizing, non-oppositional relationship, activists sought to bring about policy changes and legal reforms through engaging with state institutions, accessing state mechanisms, and confining their strategies within the state framework. This pragmatic, strategic alliance with different government agencies was successful in accomplishing one of their paramount goals. In 2015, the Anti-Domestic Violence Law that the Anti-Domestic Violence Network drafted and proposed was finally passed, marking a historical milestone of being the first law against domestic violence in Chinese history.

As illustrated, activists in NGOs actively collaborated with the state and appropriated the state discourse in order to legitimize their activism and implement their agenda to fight domestic violence and gender inequality. To do so, in addition to cooperating with the state discourse on "family harmony" and "social stability," they continued the rationale of the linkage between women's social status and the global reputation and status of China as a nation. For activists in NGOs, appropriating the state's discourse on harmony provided a political legitimacy for their cause to fight against domestic violence. Domestic violence was couched by activists as a threat to social harmony and social stability, calling for the state's intervention in this issue and responsibility to support activists in combating it. In this way, activists strategically advocated to the state that domestic violence is a social conflict that needs to be resolved and repressed to "maintain social harmony" and social stability.

As demonstrated, activists avoided politically sensitive discourse such as human rights and democracy. In appropriating the state discourse of family harmony and social stability in their activist rhetoric, they legitimized their activism as well as state power. Through strategically advocating to the state that their activism sought to maintain social harmony and social stability through dissolving and repressing domestic violence as a social conflict, they proclaimed themselves as an indispensable part and parcel of the state apparatus to maintain state order. In so doing, they risk losing their independent status, identity, and voice, while at the same time legitimizing and reinforcing state power.

AFTERWORD

During the Covid-19 pandemic in 2020, throughout China, many cities, towns, and counties were under lockdown. Xiao Qin's story below offers one example of intimate partner violence that took place during the Covid-19 pandemic.[1]

Xiao Qin had been divorced two years before, but her ex-husband, who used to physically abuse her when they were married, knelt in front of her with their two children, begging her to spend the Chinese New Year with them in his hometown. She agreed. In February 2020, she went to her ex-husband's home. A couple of days later, he beat her once again.

Xiao Qin took her two children, a suitcase in hand, and walked toward her natal family's hometown, which was over 20 kilometers away. She called the police and reported the intimate partner violence inflicted by her ex-husband, but the police refused to come out and offer any help.

She called relatives from her natal family, requesting their help to have the entrance unblocked so that she and her children could be allowed to enter the village upon arrival. When her relatives went to the village committee for help, they were told that they had to get a stamp of permission from the upper-division township committee. A village cadre told them:

> There's simply no way that the township committee will provide you a stamp of permission. It's been extremely strict everywhere. No one's allowed to leave where you are. No cars are allowed on the road except for emergencies. Now in your case, you want to bring people into the village from the outside, which makes it even more impossible. Even if someone did give you a stamp of permission, that person would be held responsible for violating the regulations.

During the Covid-19 pandemic, cities, counties, and townships had all the entrances and exits blocked. No one was allowed to leave or get in without a stamp of permission from the authorities. Xiao Qin and her two children walked for five hours in the freezing winter weather, with nothing to eat. On the journey, they saw only one truck passing by. They waved their hands at the truck, but it did not stop.

One of Xiao Qin's relatives finally used his network and contacted a close classmate who worked in the township police station. This policeman managed to provide a stamp of permission for their entry into town. By the end of the day, when Xiao Qin and her two children reached the entrance, her relatives were waiting for them there. Xiao Qin presented their IDs, which showed that their house registration was in this town. Her relatives showed the stamp of permission for entry. They were finally allowed in, putting an end to all their worries and anxieties, and the continuous efforts of her natal relatives.

Xiao Qin's ex-husband took advantage of the extreme situation of the Covid-19 pandemic and inflicted violence on her. He knew that, given the circumstance where all the entrances and roads were blocked, she would have nowhere else to go but to return home and submit to him. Despite Xiao Qin's call to the police for help against the intimate partner violence, the police refused to come out to help. Her neighbors and street committees believed that it was a family affair and no one offered help either. The extreme circumstance of Covid-19 exacerbated the police inaction and remiss of the neighbors and street committees, which encouraged, fueled, and perpetuated intimate partner violence.

During the same time, in February 2020, a woman named Zhang in Shandong Province was severely beaten by her husband, after which she committed suicide. In 2021, the Chinese Supreme Court publicized this legal case as a "typical domestic-violence legal case" (Gao 2021). During the sixteen-year marriage, Zhang suffered long-term physical abuse by her husband. On the morning of February 24, 2020, during the Covid-19 pandemic, he beat her face, chest, and back severely. After taking their son to her parents, who saw her swollen face and ruptured lips, she committed suicide by throwing herself into the river. Her husband was sentenced to six years in prison, which suggests that some progress has been made (ibid.).

As shown in the above two cases, the Covid-19 pandemic has aggravated the issue of intimate partner violence. While abusers took advantage of the lockdown to inflict more violence on their victims, the police refused to respond when called for help. In the dearth of legal and social aid, while Xiao Qin was fortunate enough to have a well-connected natal family who provided a refuge, Zhang found no alternative but to take her own life. As shown in this book, it was reported by the All China's Women Federation that, every year in China, 60 percent of around 157,000 women who committed suicide did so as a result of intimate partner violence (Ma 2019).

As this book demonstrates, guided by the state discourse on family harmony that deems it women's responsibility and women's virtue to sacrifice themselves for family harmony and political stability, light sentences between six months and six years were given to abusers who had brutally beaten their wives to death, but much heavier sentences between more than ten years in prison and a death sentence were given to wives who had killed their abusers in self-defense. Once again, as shown throughout this book, in spite of what the law says, how it is interpreted is highly prejudicial against women. Chinese criminal law recognizes the right of self-defense and, yet, women who killed their husbands in self-defense are given long sentences and, in some cases, even the death penalty. It seems to me that this can only be interpreted as a continuation of the historic failure of the Chinese culture to recognize women as full human beings. The gender inequity implicit in this legal structure fails to provide victims with the necessary legal recourse to rectify the violence and seek justice. It also violates the Chinese Constitution that guarantees equal protection under the law. This dearth of support by the criminal justice system often forced women to return to their abusers after divorce because the divorce often robbed them of not only their child custody rights, but also visitation rights, with no compensation or support from the criminal justice system. The dearth of legal support also fueled suicides among female victims.

This book makes several contributions to the existing literature. First, this book opposes the individual-factor approach and argues for a sociocultural and political economic framework to study intimate partner violence. Linking cultural ideologies with structural factors in China, this book connects the personal with the structural to explore the broader cultural context that informs intimate partner violence and structures women's lived experiences. It demonstrates the ways in which violence is supported and bolstered by cultural discourses and broader social structures in China that hold women responsible for maintaining family harmony and political stability at the expense of their health and well-being. This cultural discourse defines women's primary role as "dutiful wives and virtuous mothers" and defines women's virtue in terms of their sacrifice for family harmony and state legitimacy. This cultural discourse also defines violence as only those activities causing severe physical injuries such as broken bones. Rather than holding men responsible for their violence, men's violence is defined in this cultural discourse as instinctual, biological, and uncontrollable. For instance, it portrays men's sexual urges that result in violence toward women as natural and something that must be accepted in the marriage contract. This cultural discourse also distinguishes worthy victims of sexual violence versus unworthy victims, and blurs the boundary between sexual coercion and consensual sex between intimate partners. These gender-based discourses represent a biologically determined, unequal gender approach to governance in post-socialist China.

A further point might be made that once we open the door to biological interpretation of human nature that suggests that men are naturally violent and cannot help themselves, one has to question whether this might not be the same case for women with regard to the mother-child relationships. In other societies, it is generally assumed that the mother-child bond is primary. Women give birth to children. Women nurse their children. Women are early shapers of their children. It seems inconsistent that when the Chinese cultural discourse uses biology to defend the rights of men, biology is ignored when it comes to the rights of women. While the Chinese law recognizes the mother-child bond for the first two years of the child's life, as illustrated in Chapter 2, it does not recognize the continuing bond above the child's age of two. One might speculate about the trauma caused to the child as well as the mother by the sudden burst of this bond at the age of three or even later.

Second, in post-socialist China, the mechanism of neoliberal governance places the responsibility for change on the marginalized population of victims of violence, thus shedding the state's responsibility (see also Zheng 2015). Informed by the neoliberal governing ideology, individuals are expected to be self-regulating, self-monitoring, self-disciplining, prudent, and responsible "entrepreneurs of themselves," capable of changing themselves and avoiding behaviors that could potentially subject them to physical and sexual violence.

As Chapter 2 shows, sexual coercion is redefined as women's responsibility, and women are advised to transform themselves in order to end physical and sexual violence against them. Such neoliberal governance and disciplinary mechanisms conceal and mask structural violence that shapes and maintains violence against women.

Third, this book unearths invisible structural violence in China through a multilayered historical, political, and economic approach. It provides a chronological narrative of a history of intimate partner violence, women's experiences of and responses to violence, men's perceptions about and rationalizations of their violence against women, the history of the legal framework of violence against women, limitations and strengths of activism, and cultural discourses that inform women's experiences of and reactions to sexual violence in their daily lives. Each approach adds an indispensable piece to the puzzle in order to allow us to fully grasp the complexity of the issue, weaving the micro-level individual experiences into the macro-level historical, cultural, and political economic structure in China. As the book shows, in post-socialist China, women in general are disadvantaged because they lack economic opportunities, suffer salary gaps, and face job and education discrimination. In addition, the deeply seated patriarchal history of China that viewed women as instruments persists and underlies the issue of intimate partner violence. Women are expected to fulfil their traditional gendered roles, which are illustrated in state discourses on family harmony and men's rationalization of their violence against women. Women's unequal access to legal, social, and economic resources exacerbates the violence against them.

As the book shows, government officials, local officials, and law enforcement officials in the judicial system often hold deeply embedded patriarchal ideas of male dominance and favor men. Women's futile attempts to seek help from state institutions such as police stations, the courts, community committees, and the All-China's Women's Federation contribute to the perpetuation of violence against women. The institutional inaction and male-biased deliberations lead to the glaring discrepancy between the law and practice, curtailing women's ability to leave the violent relationships and prolonging and reinforcing the violence against them. A critical issue to be remembered is the powerful influence of Confucianism in allowing judges to disregard the law and favor their own judgment, which was heavily influenced by traditional patriarchal culture. This powerful cultural influence continues today even in contemporary Chinese culture, much to the detriment of justice to women.

We live in a patriarchal world. This has been so since the transition from hunting-gathering societies to agricultural societies. The practice of patriarchy may vary around the world, but there are some constants. Society is male-dominated and organized according to male myths. We are hierarchical and a high value is placed upon power and competition. The ability to inflict violence is seen as necessary to maintain society and is an important part of male identity. Young boys are trained to be tough and brave; young girls to be nurturing and more passive. The external world of commerce and military affairs is seen as an exclusively male domain and the household is seen as the domain of women.

Looking beyond China, for the origins of Western Civilization, we look to first Greece and then Rome. In Greece we find no women among the great comedians and tragedians. We see no women among the great philosophers, although Plato, uncharacteristically, does grant women a role as potential philosopher kings (queens?). As became common following the decline of the ancient world, women's place was in the home, tending to children and creating a comfortable environment for men. Remarkably, as we will see throughout history, some women do triumph against the odds, for example, the great poetess, Sapho, in Greece. Similar is the case in Rome. Men had life-and-death control over their wives who were relegated to the home and to women's work. We see no famous artists or poets and no great rulers.[2]

The social history of the Middle Ages is scant, in spite of the French Annales school's emphasis upon social history. We do know of a few extraordinary women who achieved greatness against the odds, Joan of Arc, for instance, or Hildegard Von Bingham. Primogeniture was the rule in Europe, meaning that the oldest son inherited the estate or the kingdom. The one attempt, during the Middle Ages, to leave the crown to a woman ended in failure, as Empress Matilda failed to gain the crown, even though it was willed to her by her father. One hint about the plight of ordinary women is expressed in an English law that limits the width of a stick with which a man may beat his wife to the size of his thumb. Perhaps for the time this may be seen as progressive legislation. At the beginning of the early modern period, we have the phenomena of burning witches, nearly all of whom were women, but we also see two very competent women ascending the English throne, Mary and Elizabeth. Elizabeth's long reign saw Britain rise to become one of the great European and even world powers.

In spite of the eighteenth-century Enlightenment which extolled the rights of men, women did not immediately benefit; however, undoubtedly the values of the Enlightenment influenced women to snap out of their torpor and begin pursuing their own rights, supported by a few progressive men such as John Stuart Mill and William Godwinson. During the nineteenth century we have a flurry of great women writers: Jane Austin, the Bronte sisters, and George Eliot (although it is noteworthy that the latter chose to use a male pseudonym). This is also the century when women began to organize and demand rights, especially the right to vote.

On the dark side, this is also the century when women began a practice emblematic of male dominance, corseting. Like other practices around the world, this phenomenon is characterized by a metaphor of control. The woman is tightly bound and covered from neck to toe. For sexual titillation, the corset squeezes the waist to a tiny circle, ideally small enough that a husband can encircle it with two hands, and consequently puts an emphasis upon the breasts and hips which appear exaggerated in comparison to the tiny waist. This was seriously damaging to the woman's health, squeezing her organs in an unnatural way. The woman became an emblem of her husband's status, exuding sexuality, but off limits to other men, who could be titillated but could not touch. This is what we call today a trophy wife, a woman important as an adornment but not having any intrinsic worth.

This practice has a twentieth- and twenty-first-century equivalent sans corsets. Young women are presented with an ideal image of what a woman should be. This is presented in advertising, beauty contests, and even comic books. Like its nineteenth-century predecessor, it includes a tiny waist and exaggerated breasts, but it is achieved through starvation diets and/or diet pills and breast implants, which can be very dangerous to the health. This has resulted in anorexia, a psychological state in which young girls starve themselves in the belief that they are overweight when in fact they are seriously underweight. This also includes something perhaps analogous to foot-binding, the high-heeled shoe, which distorts the shape of the foot and suggests longer legs. One of the bizarre images growing out of the high-heeled culture is women in beauty contests, wearing bathing suits and high-heeled shoes that do not seem to go together, except that they both are seen as sexually suggestive. Like the other practices listed above, high heels are damaging to women's bodies. Often in later life, women experience knee problems and foot problems as a result of wearing high heels. Of course, there is no law requiring women to wear high-heeled shoes but, in the male-dominated patriarchal world, women tend to do so to secure their professional careers. This suggests the power of patriarchal culture whose influence makes women willing accomplices in conforming to a patriarchal ideal for women.

Turning from Western Civilization back to China, this power of patriarchal culture was symbolized by foot-binding for thousands of years, where mothers were the accomplices helping their daughters conform to a male ideal (see the introduction). Even though various forms of violence against women such as foot-binding and arranged exogamy were abolished, as we have seen in the book, deeply seated patriarchal ideas of male dominance and the superiority of men are still held by government officials, local officials, and law enforcement officials in the judicial system, which encourages, reinforces, and perpetuates violence against women.

Understanding Chinese culture today requires understanding how the Chinese understand themselves and their own past. This begins with the geography that Chinese culture must respond to. One important factor is the relative isolation of China from other major and contrasting cultures. The vast area of China is cut off from the great Indus culture to the southwest by the world's tallest mountains. To the North is the Siberian tundra with its scattered tribal societies. Also to the North are fierce steppe peoples such as the Mongols and the woodland dwellers, the Manchus. Both have threatened the political autonomy of China but have never threatened their cultural supremacy. To the East and immediate South are Korea, Japan, and Vietnam. All three of these peoples have developed their own cultures with heavy borrowings from China, especially the Confucian influence. When China looks in their direction, it sees a mirror and not a challenge. Finally, to the West, vast distances, desert, and mountains isolate the Chinese from European and Islamic cultures, with a trickle of trade along the Silk Road winding through this region.

As a result, the Confucian culture, affirmed during the Han Dynasty, was not challenged until the twentieth century. It is misleading to see Confucius as the founder of Chinese culture. Confucius regarded himself not as a creator, but as one who rediscovered the old culture. As one might expect of an agrarian peasant culture, Confucius and China are profoundly conservative. To solve the troubles of his time (the Warring States period 475–221 BC), Confucius found solutions in returning to the past, a time of stability and relative peace. He also found stability in a rigid structure of authority where age and gender were central. Confucius believed that a harmonious family supported a peaceful and harmonious state. He spelled out lines of authority very clearly. The father was head of the family and required obedience of his wife, sons, and daughters. Further down the line, elder brothers held authority over younger brothers and sisters and, after the death of a father, even their mother. Of course the head of the entire Chinese family was the emperor, who required obedience from all. There are at least two interesting features of this system, the first of which is problematic, and second of which is hopeful.

Confucius's notion of the role of education is problematic. You might imagine that the system described above might lend itself to tyranny. In the West, following Lord Acton (in the nineteenth century), it is generally believed that power corrupts and absolute power corrupts absolutely. Confucius, like his rough contemporary in the West, Plato (fourth century BC), believed that properly educated people would always do the right thing. The emperor advised by Confucian educated scholars would be selfless and do what was just and right for his people, just as the wise father and elder brother would administer justice for the benefit of his family. In the West it was not the Platonic notion that prevailed, but the Christian view of man as flawed and sinful, leading in the long run to limitations on governing power. Chinese history is full of wise mandarin advisors who did their duty, sometimes at the cost of their lives, but it is also fraught with injustice and cruelty.

Another aspect of this system, which long precedes Confucius, is the "Mandate of Heaven." The mandate affirms the power of the emperor's authority to rule, but it also makes clear that the mandate can be lost if the emperor is incompetent or a tyrant. This is a potential escape valve from tyranny, but does not necessarily correlate with the justice of the system. The mandate is also unique to China. Only the Chinese emperor can have the mandate, which has the effect of subordinating all other societies to China, at least in the eyes of the Chinese. After suffering the conquest and brief rule of Mongol foreigners in the thirteenth century, China became even more insular, ignoring the world outside its own sphere. Even China's name for itself is the middle kingdom (zhong guo), implying the importance and centrality of China in the universe and making clear that only China had the mandate of heaven. This was the stagnant insular culture that must face the West and its growing commercial and military aggression. In the first Opium War, British steam-powered boats with artillery destroyed the Chinese navy and bombarded their coastal cities. During this time, China also lost a second Opium war to Britain and France, underwent the most devastating rebellion in history, and later lost the area of Manchuria to their "little brother," Japan.

Along with the abdication of the last emperor, Pu Yi, China finally experienced a radical cultural challenge from within. Amidst the breakdown of the entire system, the "New Culture Movement," led by intellectuals and the youth they inspired, began demanding change. This is a complex and powerful movement, but I will focus on what is relevant to the subject. A younger generation of Chinese, educated by Western missionaries and sometimes even educated in the West or Japan, finally began to see the depth of the problem in China. They saw that authority had crushed change and innovation and that a great symbol of this tyrannous authority was the oppression of women. Women became part of this movement, rejecting foot-binding along with the authority of fathers. The liberation of women was taken up by the new Communist Party, which was organized in 1921. Later Mao would proclaim that women "hold up half the sky." Mao gained the enthusiastic labor of women in rebuilding China, and also their political allegiance. How much this changed the lived lives of Chinese women in a culture with such deep roots in the past is another question but, at least for a time, the ideological current was on the side of women.

Below is a brief recollection of what the most patriarchal cultures meant to women in day-to-day terms. First, every young Han Chinese girl could expect her feet to be bound beginning at the age of four up till seven. For several years this process would cause excruciating pain as the bones were broken and the foot misshapen to a "golden Lilly" four inches long. During this period, it is estimated that about 10 percent of these children would die of gangrene (Stewart 2014: 423). The survivors would hobble and live in pain for the rest of their lives. What was the purpose of this excruciatingly painful and deadly practice? The major purpose was to enhance the sexual pleasure of men, give men power and control, and thwart women's mobility and possible adultery. Other patriarchal cultures in the world also had inflicted pain and suffering on women, ranging from clitorectomy to honor killings to sati. All these traditions involved controlling the sexuality of women and limiting a woman to one man.

Another aspect of the daily life of Chinese women was represented by arranged exogamy. Until very recently, China was an overwhelmingly rural society. The common tradition was that young girls would be engaged, usually through a go-between, to a boy from another village. She would then be transported to this village where she would marry a boy she had never met and be under the control of him and a mother-in-law who usually saw her as a domestic slave. Typically, she would never see her family again. It was also the case that the woman would not always be given the human dignity of a name or, as it happened during the one-child era, be given a name such as "hope for a brother."

While the New Culture Movement and Communism gave hope to Chinese women, for the last several years, we have seen the growing dominance of the traditional culture. This return to the traditional Chinese paradigm has been particularly notable under the rule of President Xi Jinping. As President Xi has asserted more totalitarian rule, the power of women and the safety of women has declined. Women, caught between an empowering feminist activist ideology and traditional Chinese values, are struggling to achieve a degree of autonomy and safety.

The difficulties for Chinese feminist, activist reformers are made more problematic by Xi's return to totalitarian rule. It is very difficult to achieve reform in a system that uses nationalism in order to bolster its claim to power. Any attempt to reform involves implicit criticism of the government, which is generally not tolerated by totalitarian systems. It would behoove Chinese reformers to take this into account and to carefully position the rhetoric of their reform in line with the state discourse of family harmony and state stability.

NOTES

1 It was often said that girls are useless to a family, because their labor would go to someone else. In many areas, it was the overwhelming *norm* to wish for a son. Young daughters were often given names such as "hope for a brother" to signify this. During the period of the one-child policy, abortion of female fetuses was common and even female infanticide was not unknown. The result was an estimated imbalance in sex ratio at birth: 118.08 males to 100 females (UPI 2011). In 2015, this sex ratio in the countryside was 122.8 males to 100 females (Cheng 2019). Since the implementation of the three-child policy in 2021, the sex ratio of the third baby has been 148.5 males to 100 females (Duo 2021).
2 It was reported that gender discrimination in the college acceptance process took place in 66 percent of universities offering engineering degrees (Huang 2020).
3 The All China Women's Federation was founded in March 1949 in the People's Republic of China as a countrywide women's organization. Its founding mission was to represent and safeguard the rights and interests of women and children. The organization runs two publications, the *Chinese Women's Newspaper* and the *Chinese Women's Magazine*, as well as the Chinese Women's University in Beijing. It has ten departments, including the Rights and Interests Department. It manages fourteen institutions, including the Legal Aid Center and Women's Research Institute. The headquarters run a session every five years to elect its executive committee, who, in turn, convene at annual meetings. The All China Women's Federation has almost a million branches and subsidiary offices in almost every province, city, county, township, village, and street (Ministry of Finance 2019).
4 It is likely that these factors are not equal causes of intimate partner violence. Around the world, it has been observed that one of the correlating factors of intimate partner violence is whether or not the abuser experiences abuse within the family where s/he grows up (Moffitt 2013).
5 Examples of these institutions are "the family and the army, schools and the police, individual medicine and the administration of collective bodies" (Foucault 1978: 141).

Chapter 1

1 It was recorded that, in Guangzhou (77.2 percent), Tianjin (85.7 percent), Beijing (89 percent), and Chengdu (82.9 percent), more women proposed divorce than men (Wang 2008).
2 In Shandong Province, officials refused to process a woman's divorce request, causing her to be brutally abused to death by her husband (Li 2008).
3 For details on safe houses in China, see Chapter 5.
4 For more details about NGOs and activism in the area of intimate partner violence, see Chapter 6.

Chapter 2

1 For more information on #me too movement in China, see Chapter 6.

Chapter 3

1 Hong posted her story on Weibo—see Fan (2020).
2 Hong posted the audio online. See Fan (2020).
3 The All China Women's Federation was founded in March 1949 in the People's Republic of China as a country-wide women's organization. Its founding mission was to represent and safeguard the rights and interests of women and children. The organization runs two publications, the *Chinese Women's Newspaper* and the *Chinese Women's Magazine*, as well as the Chinese Women's University in Beijing. It has ten departments, including the Rights and Interests Department. It manages fourteen institutions, including the Legal Aid Center and Women's Research Institute. The headquarters run a session every five years to elect its executive committee, who, in turn, convene at annual meetings. The Federation has almost a million branches and subsidiary offices in almost every province, city, county, township, village, and street (Ministry of Finance 2019).
4 Although the Anti-Domestic Violence Law stipulates that local governments should provide funding to support training, research has shown that no funding was ever provided. Nor was any statistics or information released on domestic violence cases (Li 2016).
5 For more information about safe houses, see Chapter 5.
6 In one case, Yuan Zhang's husband, a son of the CEO of a chemical company in Hebei Province, gambled every night and used his wife Zhang as a gambling chip to pay off his debts (Zhao, Ming 2019). Every time when Zhang's husband lost in a gamble in the middle of the night, he would give his house key to his creditor to enter his house and rape his wife as a way to offset his debt. Zhang later realized what was going on, and then one night decided to hide a scissors beneath her pillow. The following night, her husband came to bed and admitted what he had done. He attempted to rape her in bed, and she resisted. He started inflicting violence on her, and so she took the scissors from underneath her pillow and stabbed him; he died later. Despite the fact that Zhang resisted her abuser's violence in self-defense, she was sentenced to death and was executed a couple of months later (Zhao, Ming 2019).
7 A Chongqing female doctor, Zhang Xiaoyan, owned her own clinic, with an annual income of millions of RMB. For years, she suffered heavy physical beatings from her ex-husband Huang Xuetong. She escaped home four times but had to return home each time. She sustained heavy injuries such as bone fractures in her legs to the extent that she had to use a cane to walk. In her private clinic, people saw him beating her with a club, but no one intervened. Huang used threats and exerted control over her social contacts to prevent her from escaping, telling her and her kids that he would kill all of them if she continued to escape. In 2016 she was beaten severely and poisoned to death by her husband, for which he was sentenced to six months in prison (Yong 2016).
8 In 2019, 28-year-old Yu Ya, a famous Weibo blogger, posted a live video of herself being physically beaten by her boyfriend Guang Weizheng, a photographer, inside an elevator

in Chongqing, Sichuan. Her video was subsequently viewed and supported by tens of thousands of netizens. She reported that Guang physically abused her for more than half a year, and that her forgiveness only made it worse. Guang strangled her neck, hit her head onto the wall, thrashed her onto the cement floor, used his feet to tread on her face and her body, causing her to immediately lose feeling in both her legs. After each episode, it took her between a week and one month to recover. One time she was not able to walk for an entire month. She also posted two more videos where his two ex-wives narrated their experiences of his domestic violence. Guang is a 44-year-old photographer, divorced three times. With the help of the video recording of the entire physical abuse in the elevator, witnesses' testimonies, medical reports of injuries sustained by her, and an enormous amount of media pressure, Guang was detained by the Chongqing Public Security Bureau for twenty days on November 25, 2019 (Wang, Ning 2019).

9 As discussed above, light injuries, according to the Chinese Criteria for Assessing the Extent of Bodily Injuries (2014), include scalp laceration of more than 40 cm, skull fracture, broken ribs, facial laceration of more than 6 cm, hearing impediment, burning over 20 percent of the body, spine fracture, rupture of stomach, or gallbladder, or spleen, hip fracture, penetrating injuries to the eyeballs.

Chapter 5

1 Xiao Jie posted her story online (Jiang 2018).
2 As we have seen, the All China Women's Federation from which she sought help also called her hometown to send her back to the place of violence and her abuser.
3 In Xiamen, only four victims utilized the service of safe houses in 2014 (Zhang, Zheng 2015).
4 This is reminiscent of the arranged exogamy discussed in the introduction of this book.
5 Research (Chen et al. 2013; see also Morrissey 1998) has shown that children who are exposed to domestic violence are up to 3.8 times more likely to become either perpetrators or victims when they grow up.

Chapter 6

1 For more about #me too movement, see Chapter 2.
2 See Chapter 3 for the illustration of this point.
3 See similar stories of Chinese women killing their abusers in Chapters 1, 3, and 5. The Battered Woman's Syndrome, in the West, has been utilized to comprehend victims' understanding of their relationships with the abusers, their perceptions of themselves, and their perceptions of the abusers. One example is that victims tend to perceive their abusers as "omnipotent and omniscient" (Walker and Conte 2017: 53). In one legal case, for instance, a forty-year-old woman Catherine shot her abuser dead. In court, Catherine described to the jury how her abuser, after a great deal of drinking, ordered her to lie next to him on the bed, with a loaded gun on the night table. Threatening to shoot her, he put the gun to her head. She was sure that he was going to kill her, so she took the gun and shot him. She was not convinced that the shot really killed him, so she took a knife and continuously stabbed his dead body. The Battered Woman's

Syndrome was employed to explain why Catherine, even though she had shot her abuser dead, continued to believe that he could still harm her (Walker and Conte 2017: 53). She was exonerated.
4   See the discussion of this case in Chapter 3.

Afterword

1   Xiao Qin had her experience recorded online (see Qiao 2020).
2   This is from a discussion with my mentor Jack Wortman.

REFERENCES

Abraham, Margaret. 2000. *Speaking the Unspeakable: Marital Violence among South Asian Immigrants in the United States*. New Brunswick, NJ: Rutgers University Press.

Acton, John. 1907. "Letter to Bishop Mandell Creighton." In *Historical Essays and Studies*. Edited by John Neville Figgis and Reginald Vere Laurence, p. 504. London: Macmillan.

Adelman, Madelaine. 2004. "Domestic Violence and Difference." *American Ethnologist* 31 (1): 131–41.

Ai, Jing. 2006. "The Power to Divorce and the Difficult Situation of Divorce: An Investigation of Female Divorce Situation in the Republic Era" (Lihun de Quanli Yu Lihun de Nanju: Minguo Nvxing Lihun Zhuangkuang de Tanjiu). *Xinjiang Social Sciences* (Xinjiang Shehui Kexue) 6 (May): 109–15.

Alcalde, M. Cristina. 2006. "Migration and Class as Constraints in Battered Women's Attempts to Escape Violence in Lima, Peru." *Latin American Perspective* 33 (6): 147–64.

Alcalde, M. Cristina. 2010. *The Women in the Violence: Gender, Poverty, and Resistance in Peru*. Nashville, TN: Vanderbilt University Press.

Aldarondo, Sugarman. 1996. "Risk Marker Analysis of the Cessation and Persistence of Wife Assault." *Journal of Consult Clinical Psychology* 64 (October): 1010–19.

An, Kang. 1952. "Zhuanqu Tudigaige Zhong de Funvgongzuo Zongjie" (Summary of Women's Work in An Kang during Land Reform). *Shaanxi Dang An* (Shaanxi Archive) 6 (1): 4.

An, Ti. 2005. "Xingsaorao Lifa Weihe Jie Funv Baohu Zhike" (Why the Law of Sexual Harassment Is Placed under Women's Protection). *Nanfang Dushi Bao* (South Metropolitan Newspaper). June 29: 11.

Andrews, Penny. 2001. "Democracy, Intersectionality, and Violence." In *Race, Ethnicity, Gender, and Human Rights in the Americas: A New Paradigm for Activism*. Edited by Celina Romany, pp. 102–4. Washington, DC: American University Press.

Anglin, Mary K. 1998. "Feminist Perspectives on Structural Violence." *Identities: Global Studies in Culture and Power* 5 (2): 145–51.

Anonymous. 2003. "Bei Qianhui de Sun Zhigang Zhi Si" (The Death of Repatriated Sun Zhigang(*Nanfang Dushibao* (South Municipal Newspaper). http://www.sina.com.cn. April 25. http://news.sina.com.cn/s/2003-04-25/11111016223.html (accessed March 20, 2019).

Anti-Domestic Violence Law. 2015. The 12th National People's Congress Standing Committee. People's Republic of China.

Babu, Bontha, and Shantanu K. Kar. 2010. "Domestic Violence in Eastern India: Factors Associated with Victimization and Perpetration." *Public Health* 124 (3): 136–48.

Bancroft, Lundy. 2003. *Why Does He Do That?: Inside the Minds of Angry and Controlling Men*. New York: Berkeley Books.

Bei, Bao. 2020. "24Nian, 4000Qi Anjian, 12Wan Ming Funv, Shawei Wushuge Li Xingxing Er Zhan!" (She Has Fought for 120,000 Women and Countless Li Xingxing in 4,000 Legal Cases in the Past 24 Years!). *Zhongguo Baogao Wenxue* (Chinese Report Literature). April 17.

Bei, Qing. 2019. "16 Sui Nvhai Zhongkaoqian Bei Fuqin Shahai" (Sixteen-Year-Old Girl Was Murdered by Her Father). *Shanguan Xinwen* (Shangguan News). June 25: 9.

Beijing Declaration and Platform for Action. 1995. United Nations 4th World Conference on Women in Beijing. United Nations Women.

Ben, Baoxun. 1953. "Quanguo Henduo Diqu de Shishibiaoming Hunyinfa Zhixingqingkuang Jibupingheng" (Nationwide Facts Show Unbalanced Implementation of the Marriage Law). *Renmin Ribao* (People's Daily). February 1: 1.

Beske, Melissa. 2016. *Intimate Partner Violence and Advocate Response: Redefining Love in Western Belize*. Lanham, MD: Lexington Books.

Bieju, An. 1937. Bieju An (The Bieju Case). *Chengdu Dang An Guan* (Chengdu Archive Bureau) 94: 5849.

Block, Sharon. 2006. *Rape and Sexual Power in Early America*. Chapel Hill: University of North Carolina Press.

Bourgois, Philippe. 2004. "The Everyday Violence of Gang Rape." In *Violence in War and Peace: An Anthology*. Edited by Nancy Scheper-Hughes and Philippe I. Bourgois, pp. 343–47. Oxford: Blackwell.

Brownell, Susan. 1999. "Strong Women and Impotent Men: Sports, Gender, and Nationalism in Chinese Public Culture." In *Spaces of Their Own: Women's Public Sphere in Transnational China*. Edited by Mayfair Mei-hui Yang, pp. 207–31. Minneapolis: University of Minnesota Press.

Brownell, Susan, and Jeffrey N. Wasserstrom. 2002. "Introduction." In *Chinese Femininities, Chinese Masculinities*. Edited by Susan Brownell and Jeffrey Wasserstrom, pp. 1–89. Berkeley: University of California Press.

Bryant-Davis, Thema. 2010. "Cultural Considerations of Trauma: Physical, Mental and Social Correlates of Intimate Partner Violence Exposure." *Psychological Trauma: Theory, Research, Practice, and Policy* 2 (4): 263–5.

Burazeri, Genc, Enver Roshi, and Nertila Tavanxhi. 2006. "Intimate Partner Violence in the Balkans: The Example of Albania." *Journal of Public Health* 14 (4): 233–6.

Burgess, Robert L., and Patricia Draper. 1989. "The Explanation of Family Violence: The Role of Biological, Behavioral, and Cultural Selection." *Crime and Justice* 11: 59–116.

Cai, Jue. 2020. "Wang Xiaoyang Jiang Nver Dusi, Bei Pan 3 Nian Lao" (Wang Xiaoyang Is Sentenced to 3 Years in Prison for Poisoning His Daughter to Death) *Zhongguo Caipanwenshu Wang* (Chinese Court Verdict Net). January 22.

Cai, Yiping, Feng Yuan, and Guo Yanqiu. 2001. "The Women's Media Watch Network." In *Chinese Women Organizing: Cadres, Feminists, Muslims, Queers*. Edited by Ping-Chun Hsiung, Maria Jaschok, and Cecilia Milwertz with Red Chan, pp. 209–26. Oxford: Berg.

Campbell, Jacquelyn C. 1999. "Sanctions and Sanctuary: Wife-Battering: Cultural Contexts versus Social Sciences." In *To Have and to Hit: Cultural Perspectives on Wife Beating*, 2nd ed. Edited by Dorothy A. Counts, Judith K. Brown, and Jacquelyn C. Campbell, pp. 261–85. Urbana: University of Illinois Press.

Chai, Jing. 2019. "Chai Jing: Naxie Bei Jiabao Hou Yibao Zhibao De Zhongguo Nvren" (Chai Jing: Those Chinese Women Who Fought Their Abusers with Violence). *Teng Xun Wang* (Teng Xun Net). November 28.

Chang, Libing. 2013. "Suzao Hunyin Yu Nongmin Guojia Guannian de Xingcheng—Yi Guanche 1950nian Hunyinfa Wei Kaocha Duixiang" (Shaping Marriage Laws and Formulating Peasants' Perceptions about the State—on the 1950s Marriage Law). *Jinyan Xuekan* (Jinyang Academic Journal) 000 (003): 85–94.

Chen, Duxiu. 1920. "Nanxizhi Yu Yichanzhi" (Patrilineality and Inheritance) . *Xin Qing Nian* (New Youth) 7 (2): 21.

Chen, Liping. 2013. "2012 Niandu Xingbie Pingdeng Shida Xinwen Shijian Pingxuan Jieguo Jiexiao" (The Evaluation Result of The Top 10 News Reports of Gender Equality in 2012). *Fazhi Ribao* (Law Daily). January 14.

Chen, Liyan. 2020. "Lihun Lengjingqi Laile" (Here Comes Divorce Cooling Period). *Qilu Wanbao* (Qilu Evening Newspaper). December 2: 10.

Chen, Ping-Hsin, Abbie Jacobs, Susan L. D. Rovi. 2013. "Intimate Partner Violence: Childhood Exposure to Domestic Violence." FP Essent. 412 (September): 24–7.

Chen, Qingyuan. 2019. "Wopasizai Nagejiali" (I am Afraid of Being Dead at That Home). *Hongxing Xinwen* (Hongxing News). October 21: 19.

Chen, Wangdao. 1979. *Chenwang Dao Wenzhang* (Chenwang Ethics Articles). Shanghai: Shanghai Renmin Chubanshe (Shanghai People's Publishing House).

Chen, Yan. 2015. "Nvda Xuesheng Jiuhou Dao Jiaoshoujiazhong Chengbei Qiangjian, Chunvmo Weiposun" (Female College Student Reports Being Raped by a Professor, Unbroken Hymen). *Nanfang Dushibao* (South Metropolitan Newspaper). February 12: 6.

Chen, Yaya. 2012. "Woguo Jiuye Zhong de Xingbie Qishi Wenti" (Gender Discrimination in the Job Market in China). *Shehui Chuangye Jia* (Social Entrepreneurs) 7 (51): 1–3.

Chen, Zhaoshi. 1917. "No Evidence for Abuse" (Nuedai Bingwu Zhengju). *Shen Newspaper* (Shenbao). March 5: 11.

Chen, Zhenkai. 2020. "Xi Jinping Tan Jiafeng Jianshe" (Xi Jinping Discuss Family Construction). *Renmin Ribao* (People's Daily). July 22.

Cheng, Yusan. 2020. "Women Weishenme Buxiang Chunlei Jihua Juanzhu Nanhaizi" (Why We Do Not Want the Hope Plan to Help Boys). *Chengyusan* (Orange Umbrella). December 20.

Chinese Criminal Law. 2020. The 13th National People's Congress Standing Committee. People's Republic of China.

Chinese Criteria for Assessing the Extent of Bodily Injuries. 2014. Supreme Court, People's Republic of China.

Chinese Supreme Court. 1984. *Directives of Legal Practices in Legal Cases of Rape* (Banliqiangjiananjian Zhong juzhiyingyongfalv de Ruoganwenti de Jieda). Chinese Supreme Court, Supreme People's Procuratorate, and Ministry of Public Security. April 26.

Chow, Tse-tsung. 1960. *The May Fourth Movement: Intellectual Revolution in Modern China*. Cambridge, MA: Harvard University Press.

Chu, Bailiang. 2016. "Lvshi Wang Yu Fufu Bei Zhengshi Pibu, Beikong Dianfu Guojiang Zhengquan" (Lawyer Wang Yu and Her Spouse Were Arrested on the Charge of Overthrowing State Power). *Niuyue Shibao Zhongguo Wang* (New York Times Chinese Website). January 14.

Chu, Lun. 2016. "Renshen Anquan Baohuling Yao Shenyong Yanfa" (Safety Protection Order Should Be Strict to Issue). *Renmin Fayuan* (People's Court). August 4: 7.

Chu, Tianjin. 2016. "Wuhan Jiabao Jiuzhuzhan Wuren Wenjin" (No One Visited the Domestic Violence Aids Station in Wuhan). *Shehui* (Society). April 6.

Civil Affairs Department (Minzhengbu). 2003. *Hunyinfa* (Marriage Law). Zhonghuarenmingongheguo Zhongyangrenminzhengfu (Central People's Government of People's Republic of China). January 1.

Civil Law. 1931. The Chinese Laws and Regulations Committee (Zhongguo Fagui Kanxing Shebianshen Weiyuanhui). No. 1057.
Civil Law Deliberation. 1933a. Supreme Court Deliberation. No. 256.
Civil Law Deliberation. 1933b. Supreme Court Deliberation. No. 207.
Clinton, Hilary. 1995. "Remarks for the United Nations Fourth World Conference on Women." The United Nations Fourth World Conference on Women. Beijing, China. September 5.
Coker, Donna. 2001. "Piercing Webs of Power: Identity, Resistance, and Hope in LatCrit Theory and Praxis: Shifting Power for Battered Women." In *Race, Ethnicity, Gender, and Human Rights in the Americas: A New Paradigm for Activism*. Edited by Celina Romany, pp. 121–9. Washington, DC: American University Press.
Constable, Nicole. 2003. *Romance on a Global Stage*. Berkeley: University of California Press.
Convention on Children's Rights. 1989. General Assembly Resolution. United Nations Human Rights Office of the High Commissioner.
Convention on the Elimination of All Forms of Discrimination against Women. 1985. General Assembly Resolution. United Nations Treaty Collection.
Copelon, Rhonda. 1995. "Gendered War Crimes: Reconceptualizing Rape in Time of War." In *Women's Rights, Human Rights: International Feminist Perspectives*. Edited b Julie Peters and Andrea Wolper, pp. 197–214. New York: Routledge.
Dai, Peng. 2013. "Changsha Jizhe Ban Liulanghan Jin Jiuzhuzhan, Zao Ren Wei'ou Quancheng Chumu Jingxin" (Changsha Journalist Entered Aid Station as a Vagrant, Was Ambushed and Attacked from All Sides). *Sanxiang Dushi Bao* (Sanxiang Metropolitan Newspaper). January 9.
Dasgupta, Shamita Das. 2013. "Women's Realities: Defining Violence against Women by Immigration, Race, and Class." In *Domestic Violence at the Margins: Readings on Race, Class, Gender, and Culture*. Edited by Natalie J. Sokoloff and Christina Pratt, pp. 56–70. New Brunswick, NJ: Rutgers University Press.
Declaration of the Elimination of Violence against Women. 1993. General Assembly Resolution. United Nations Human Rights Office of the High Commissioner.
Deng, Xiaohong. 2002. "Mei Xiangnan Nengbuneng Jiu Ziji?" (Can Mei Xiangnan Save Herself?). *Zhongguo Funv* (Women of China) 1: 41–3.
Di, Di. 2019. "Li Yang Qianqi Yuanliang Jiabao, Qita Shouhai Zhe Zenme Ban" (Li Yang's Ex Wife Has Forgiven His Domestic Violence, What Should Other Victims Do). *Bai Ke* (Bai Ke). December 16.
Di, Yufei. 2016. "Beijing Zhuming Funv Falv Yuanzhu Zhongxin Beipo Guanbi" (The Famous Beijing Women's Legal Aid Center Was Forced to Close Down). *Niuyue Shibao Zhongwen Ban* (New York Times Chinese Version). February 1.
Di, Yufei. 2017. "Zhongguo Nvquan Zuzhi 'Nvquan Zhisheng' Weibo Zhanghao Bei Jinyan." (Chinese Feminist Group's Social Media Account Suspended). *Niuyue Shibao Zhongguo Wang* (New York Times Chinese Version). February 23.
Diao, Chazu. 1952. "Yan'an Zhuanshu Yan'an Xian Siqu Sixiang Liuge Cunzi Hunyin Diaocha Cailiao" (Survey Materials of Four Districts and Four Townships and Six Villages in Yan'an). *Shaanxi Dang An* (Shaanxi Archives) 178 (2): 25.
Dibble, Ursula, and Murray A. Straus. 1980. "Some Social Structure Determinants of Inconsistency between Attitudes and Behavior: The Case of Family Violence." *Journal of Marriage and Family* 42 (1): 71–80.
Ding, Guofeng. 2016. "Mintiaozhanxia Yizhihua" (A Flower of Mediation). *Fazhi Ribao* (Law Daily). September 25.

Ding, Mu. 2019. "Beida Funv Falv Zhongxin Beiche Shimo" (The Beginning and End of Beijing University's Revoking Women's Legal Center). *Shidai Zaixian* (Times Online). August 14.

Ding, Yi. 1953. "Shangxian Yiqu Ganbu Yong Guanliaozhuyi Taidu Duidai Qunzhong Hunyin Wenti" (Officials Treat Marriage Issue with Red Tapes in Shang County). *Qunzhong Ribao* (Qunzhong Daily). April 30: 3.

Dobash, R. Emerson. 1979. *Violence against Wives: A Case Study against the Patriarchy*. New York: Free Press.

Dong, Yige. 2014. "The Rise and Fall of the Anti-Domestic Violence Network." *China Development Brief*. November 24.

Du, Shuo. 2020. "Qizigongkai Jiabao 16nian, Zhangfu beichuxingzhengjuliu 7tian" (Wife Publicized Husband's 16 Years of Domestic Violence, Husband Detained 7 Days). *Pengpai Xinwen* (Pengpai News). April 3.

Duan, Jiling. 2012. "Yan Li, Killer of the Husband" (Shafuzhe Liyan). *Wanyi Women* (Wangyi Nuren). December 13: 1.

Duke, Michael, and Carol Cunradi. 2011. "Measuring Intimate Partner Violence among Male and Female Farmworkers in San Diego Country, CA." *Cultural Diversity and Ethnic Minority Psychology* 17 (1): 59–67.

Duo, Shu. 2021. "Santai Zhengce Xia, Women Dui Laogong, Nvxing Quanli he Yanglao de Jige Youlv" (After The Third-Child Policy, We Have Concerns about Labor, Women's Rights, and The Aging Population). *Duo Shu Pai* (The Majority Party). June 3.

Ebrey, Patricia. 1990. "Women, Marriage, and the Family in Chinese History." In *Heritage of China—Contemporary Perspectives on Chinese Civilization*. Edited by Paul Ropp, pp. 197–223. Berkeley: University of California Press.

Edwards, Louise. 2000. "Policing the Modern Woman in Republican China." *Modern China* 26 (2): 115–47.

Edwards, Louise. 2009. "Diversity and Evolution in the State-in-Society: International Influences in Combating Violence against Women." In *The Chinese State in Transition: Processes and Contests in Local China*. Edited by Linda Chelan Li, pp. 108–26. London: Routledge.

Eidenmuller, Michael. 2009. "Top 100 Speeches of the 20th Century by Rank." *American Rhetoric*. https://www.americanrhetoric.com/top100speechesall.html. Retrieved May 25, 2021.

Fa, Niu. 2020. "Jiatingbaoli Qizi zenme Zhengqu Fuyangquan" (How Can the Domestic Violence Victim Fight for Custody Rights). *Souhu Xinwen* (Souhu News). September 18.

Fan, Bao. 2011. "Zoujin Jiabao, Jiejin Zhenxiang: Kim Xiegei Minjian Funv Zuzhi de Xin" (Walk Close to Domestic Violence, Close to the Truth: Kim's Letter to Grassroots Women's Organization). *Zhongguo Fazhan Jianbao* (China Development Brief). October 20.

Fan, Changjiang. 1950. "Jige Zhide Zhuyi de Hunyin Shijian" (Several Marriage Incidents Worthy of Attention). *Renmin Ribao* (People's Daily). September 17: 2.

Fan, Debiao. 2020. "Beiqiannanyou Oudabaoanhou" (After Calling the Police for Being Beaten by Boyfriend). *Zhongguo Shuzi Shidai* (China Digital Times). March 4.

Fan, Jing. 1990. *Zhongguo Hunyin de Lishi Yu Xianzhuang* (The History and Reality of Chinese Marriage). Bejing: Zhongguo Guoji Guangbo Chubanshe (Chinese International Broadcasting Publishing House).

Fan, Zimei. 1902. "Funv Shifang" (Liberation of Women). *Wanguo Gongbao* (Wanguo Public Newspaper) 165 (34): 21322.

Fan, Zimei. 1905a. "Zhongguo Zhenxing Nvxue Zhie" (Promoting Women's Education in China). *Wanguo Gongbao* (Wanguo Public Newspaper) 200 (38): 23656.

Fan, Zimei. 1905b. "Riben Mingshi Fuzeyuji Shilue" (Discussions by Japanese Celebrities Fukuzawa). *Wanguo Gongbao* (Wanguo Public Newspaper) 138 (31): 19413.

Fan, Zimei. 1906. "Ruidian Nvzi de Diwei" (Women's Status in Sweden). *Wanguo Gongbao* (Wanguo Public Newspaper) 206 (39): 24103.

Farmer, Paul. 1992. *AIDS and Accusation: Haiti and the Geography of Blame*. Berkeley: University of California Press.

Farmer, Paul. 1996. "On Suffering and Structural Violence: A View from Below." *Daedalus* 125 (1): 261–83.

Farmer, Paul. 2004a. "Sidney W. Mintz Lecture for 2001: An Anthropology of Structural Violence." *Current Anthropology* 45 (3): 305–25.

Farmer, Paul. 2004b. "On Suffering and Structural Violence: A View from Below." In *Violence in War and Peace: An Anthology*. Edited by Nancy Scheper-Hughes and Philippe I. Bourgois, pp. 281–9. Oxford: Blackwell.

Feng, Yuan. 2013. "Lijin He Liyan, Fanjiabao de Liangge Butongjieju" (Two Different Results of Li Jin and Li Yan in Anti-Domestic Violence Cases). *Niuyue Shibao Zhongwenwang* (New York Times Chinese Net). February 23.

Feng, Yuan. 2018. "Different Sectors Need to Work Together to Fight Domestic Violence." *UN Women*. May 22.

Feng, Yuan. 2019. "Manman Daxiao 'Kongtong' De Xiguan" (Slowly Eliminating the Habit of Fear of Same-Sex Attracted People). *Zhongguo Tongzhi Falv Quanyi Changdao* (Advocating for Chinese Tongzhi's Legal Rights and Interests). April 27.

Feng, Yuan. 2020a. "Fanjiabaofa Shishi Jiance Baogao Xilie (Anti-Domestic Violence Law Implementation Report and Investigations). *Beijingshi Weiping Funv Quanyi Jigou* (Beijing Weiping Women's Rights Organization). March 8.

Feng, Yuan. 2020b. "Zhongguo Xinwenjie Chengli Funv Chuanmei Jiance Wangluo" (Chinese News Arena Formed Media Monitor for Women Network). *Xinwen Sanwei* (News Sanwei). May 30.

Fineman, Martha, ed. 1994. *The Public Nature of Private Violence: The Discovery of Domestic Abuse*. New York: Routledge.

Foucault, Michel. 1978. *History of Sexuality*. Vol. I. New York: Random House.

Fu, Lian. 1950. "Shangluo Fenqu Hunin Wenti Baogao" (A Report of the Marriage Issue in Shangluo District). *Shaanxi Shangluo Dang An* (Shaanxi Shangluo Archive) 17 (1): 3.

Fu, Ping. 1952. "Fuping Xian Fulian Xuanchuan Gongzuo Jianbao" (Work by Fuping Women's Federation). *Shaanxi Dang An* (Shaanxi Archive) 2 (19): 15.

Galtung, Johan. 1969. "Violence, Peace, and Peace Research." *Journal of Peace Research* 6 (3): 167–91.

Gan, Nectar. 2021. "Chinese Feminists Are Being Silenced by Nationalist Trolls: Some Are Fighting Back." *CNN*. April 19.

Gao, Pingshu. 1984. *Complete Works by Cai Yuanpei* (Cai Yuanpei Quanji). Beijing: Chinese Book Store (Zhonghua Shuju).

Gao, Shan. 1914. "Lihun Ziyou Yu Zhongguo Nvzi" (Freedom of Divorce and Chinese Women). *Dongfang Zazhi* (Eastern Magazine) 10 (9): 12.

Gao, Xin. 2021. "Zuigaojian Fabu Jiabao Dianxing Anlei" (The Supreme Court Publicizes Typical Domestic Violence Legal Cases). *Hongxing Xinwen* (Red Star News). May 7.

Gao, Zhonghua. 2009. "Cong Shourong Qiansong Dao Jiuzhu Guanli" (From Custody and Repatriation to Aid Management). *Dangdai Zhongguo Shi Yanjiu* (Modern Chinese History Study) 6: 86–93.

Gelles, Richard J. 1979. *Family Violence*. Beverly Hills, CA: Sage.
Gelles, Richard J. 1985. "Family Violence." *Annual Review of Sociology* 11 (August): 347–67.
Gilmartin, Christina. 1990. "Violence against Women in Contemporary China." In *Violence in China: Essays in Culture and Counterculture*. Edited by Jonathan Lipman and Steven Harrel, pp. 203–25. New York: State University of New York Press.
Gilsenan, Michael. 2002. "On Conflict and Violence." In *Exotic No More: Anthropology on the Front Lines*. Edited by Philippe Bourgois, Nancy Scheper-Hughes, Jane Schneider, Chris Hann, Michael Gilsenan, Richard Jenkins, and William O. Beeman, pp. 99–113. Chicago: University of Chicago Press.
Glosser, Susan L. 2002. "'The Truths I Have Learned': Nationalism, Family Reform, and Male Identity in China's New Culture Movement, 1915–1923." In *Chinese Femininities, Chinese Masculinities*. Edited by Susan Brownell and Jeffrey N. Wasserstrom, pp. 120–44. Berkeley: University of California Press.
Goldstein, Daniel. 2004. *The Spectacular City: Violence and Performance in Urban Bolivia*. Durham, NC: Duke University Press.
Goldstein, Diane, and Alan Rosenbaum. 1985. "An Evaluation of the Self-Esteem of Maritally Violent Men." *Family Relations* 34 (3): 425–28.
Gong, Min. 2020. "Zhongguo Nvgongmin Benqi Timing: Guo Jianmei" (Nominee of a Chinese Female Citizen: Guo Jianmei). *Wangyi Nvren* (Wangyi Women). November 3.
Gordon, Jennifer. 2017. *Race and the Brazilian Body: Blackness, Whiteness, and Everyday Language in Rio de Janeiro*. Oakland: University of California Press.
Gordon, Linda, ed. 1979. *The Struggle for Reproductive Freedom: Three Stages of Feminism*. New York: Monthly Review Press.
Green, Linda. 1994. "Fear as a Way of Life." *Cultural Anthropology* 9 (2): 227–56.
Gremillion, Helen. 2005. "The Cultural Politics of Body Size." *Annual Review of Anthropology* 34 (October): 13–32.
Grieder, Jerome. 1970. *Hu Shih and the Chinese Renaissance*. Cambridge, MA: Harvard University Press.
Gu, Su. 2015. "Puyangshizhuchiren Chaimou Jiabao" (CCTV Anchor Chai Domestic Violence). *Gushu Wanbao* (Gusu Evening Newspaper). July 7.
Guan, Hao. 2019. "Hefei Yinvzicheng Zaojiabao Zhibilianggguzhe, Qujianchangyuan Buyulianhefa" (A Woman Declared Domestic Violence That Caused Her Nasal Bone Fracture, District Court Would Not Establish a Legal Case). *Pengpai Xinwen* (Pengpai News). December 27.
Guan, Wei. 2005. "Xinwenhua Yundong Shiqi Guanyu Lihun Ziyou Wenti de Taolun" (A Discussion of the Freedom of Divorce during the New Culture Movement). *Guizhou Shifan Daxue Xuebao* (Journal of Guizhou Normal University Social Science) 134 (3): 83–6.
Guo, Ji. 2011. "Zhengxie Weiyuan Zhang Xiaomei: Guli Gengduo Funv Neng Huigui Jiating" (Xiaomei Zhang, National Committee Member of the Chinese People's Political Consultative Conference, Encourages More Women to Return Home). *Guoji Zaixian* (International Online). March 9.
Guo, Jian. 2000. *Shanghai Funv Zhi* (A History of Shanghai Women). Shanghai: Shanghai Social Science Council Publishing House (Shanghai Shehui Kexueyuan Chubanshe).
Guo, Jianmei. 2012. "The Case of the Death of Dong Shanshan due to Domestic Violence" (Dong Shanshan Jiabao Zhisi An). *Beijing Zhongze Women's Law Consultation Center* (Beijing Zhongze Funv Falu Zixun Zongxin). August 27.

Guo, Jianmei. 2014. "Bufen Jiating Baoli Anjian Jieshao" (Introduction to Some Domestic Violence Legal Cases). Beijing Zhongze Funv Falu Zixun Zongxin (Beijing Zhongze Women's Law Consultation Center). January 20.

Guo, Jianmei, ed. 2003. *Domestic Violence and Legal Aid* (Jiating Baoli Yu Falv Yuanzhu). Beijing: China Social Science Press (Zhongguo Shehui Kexue Chubanshe).

Guo, Rui. 2019. "Nuquan Zhisheng Bei Xiaoyin de 100 Tian" (100 Days after Feminist Voice Was Silenced). *Zhongguo Nvquan Hezuo* (Chinese Feminist Collective). March 5.

Guo, Yi. 1951. "Duiyu Zhongzui Qingpan de Nuesha Funv An Ying Chongxin Panli" (We Should Prosecute Those Who Torture Women to Death). *Renmin Ribao* (People's Daily). November 3: 2.

Guo, Yanqiu, and Cai Yiping. 2000. "Xiaochu Jiating Baoli, Xingwen Meijie Ruhe Jingzhong Changming" (How Should News Media Ring the Alarm Bell in Order to Eradicate Domestic Violence). In *Shuishi Baowang Shuishi Ji: Yong Nvxing De Yanjing Kan Chuanmei* (Who Is the King and Who Is the Concubine: Investigating the Media through Women's Eyes). Edited by Guo Yanqiu and Feng Yuan, pp. 168–74. Beijing: China Women's Press.

Hamby, Sherry. 2000. "The Importance of Community in Feminist Analysis of Domestic Violence among American Indians." *American Journal of Community Psychology* 28 (5): 649–69.

Hammer, Jalna, and Mary Maynard, eds. 1987. *Women, Violence, and Social Control*. Atlantic Highlands, NJ: Humanities Press International.

Hautzinger, Sarah. 2007. *Violence in the City of Women: Police and Batterers in Bahia, Brazil*. Berkeley: University of California Press.

He, Shuhong. 2001. "A Study of Law Transformation of Marriage Cases from Late Qing to the Republic Era." Department of History. PhD Dissertation. People's University (Zhongguo Renmin Daxue).

He, Xin, and Kwai Hang Ng. 2013a. "In the Name of Harmony: The Erasure of Intimate Partner Violence in China's Judicial Mediation." *International Journal of Law, Policy and the Family* 27 (1): 97–115.

He, Xin, and Kwai Hang Ng. 2013b. "Pragmatic Discourse and Gender Inequality in China." *Law & Society Review* 47 (2): 279–310.

He, Zuo. 2018. "Nvzizaojiabaoshicong Beipanbuyulihun" (Divorce Is Rejected despite Loss of Hearing as a Result of Domestic Violence). *Souhu Xinwen* (Souhu News). November 28.

Hester, Marianne. 2012. "Globalization, Activism, and Local Contexts: Development of Policy on Domestic Violence in China and England." *Advances in Gender Research* 16 (July): 273–94.

Hinton, Alexander Laban. 2002. *Annihilating Difference: The Anthropology of Genocide*. Berkeley: University of California Press.

Hoff, Lee Ann. 1990. *Battered Women as Survivors*. New York: Routledge.

Honig, Emily, and Gail Hershatter. 1988. *Personal Voices: Chinese Women in the 1980s*. Stanford, CA: Stanford University Press.

Hou, Changlin. 2019. "Shexian Qiangjianfanzui Youxiao Bianhu Tujing" (Defense Methods for Rape Charge). *Jinan Xingshi Lvshi Wangzhai* (Jinan Criminal Law Lawyer). March 3: 2.

Hou, Juan, Li Yu, Siu-Man Raymond Ting, Yee Tak Sze, and Xiaoyi Fang. 2011. "The Status and Characteristics of Couple Violence in China." *Journal of Family Violence* 26 (2): 81–92.

Howell, Jude. 2005. "Women's Organizations and Civil Society in China: Making a Difference." In *Gender and Civil Society: Transcending Boundaries*. Edited by Jude Howell and Diane Mulligan, pp. 54–77. London: Routledge.

Howell, Jude, Gordon White, and Shang Xiaoyuan. 1996. *In Search of Civil Society: Market Reform and Social Change in Contemporary China*. Oxford: Clarendon Press.

Hu, Lian. 2016. "Sichuan Sheng Shouci Zai Jiabao Xingan Zhong Changshi Zhuanjia Zhengren Chuting Zuozheng" (Sichuan Province Has the First Expert Witness in Domestic Violence Crime Cases in Court). *Jiabao Weiji Ganyu Zhongxin* (Domestic Violence Crisis Center). April 15.

Hu, Sheng. 1950. "Quwo Xian Gequnzhong Tuanti Xiang Baoxianzhang Tichu Piping Yijian" (Groups of People from Quwo County Criticized County Head Bao). *Xinhua Yuebao* (Xinhua Monthly Newspaper). November 11: 1247–8.

Hu, Yongping. 2018. "Shishifanjiatingbaolifa Fachurenshenanquanbaohuling 2154fen" (2154 Personal Safety Protection Orders Were Issued). *Zhongguowang* (China Net). March 9: 17.

Huang, Chuanhui. 2009. *Tianxia Hunyin* (Marriage on the Earth). Beijing: Zuojia Chubanshe (Writer's Publishing House).

Huang, Fangni. 2015. "Jiabaoheshi Zouchu Jiawushi Wuqu" (When Domestic Violence Is Not Considered Family Affairs). *Zhongguo Qingnianbao* (Chinese Youth Newspaper). July 25.

Huang, Haitao. 2019. "Fanjiatingbaolifa Zuowei Caipanguizezhi Shixiaoxingfenxi" (An Analysis of Anti-Domestic Violence Law in Justice Sentence). *Beida Fabao* (Beida Law Newspaper). May 7: 4–6.

Huang, Jian. 2019. "Guo Jianmei: Cong Shouqinhai Zhe Shenshang Kandao Le Liliang, Renxing Zhiguang" (Guo Jianmei Saw Strength and the Light of Human Nature in Victims of Abuse). *Nanfang Renwu Zhoukan* (Southern People Weekly). November 23.

Huang, Qingchang. 2008. "Zhongguo Jiating Baoli Fashenglv Da 35.7%" (35.7 Percent Occurrences of Intimate Partner Violence in China). *Renmin Ribao* (China Daily). October 7: 9.

Huang, Ye Yunzi. 2020. "Nvren Xie Shiping" (Women Write Comments). *Wangyi Nvren* (Wangyi Women). Vol. 124.

Huang, Youkai. 2019. "Jiabaonan Beixingzhengjuliu 5ri" (The Abuser Was Detained 5 Days). *Guangzhou Shenbaolvshi Shiwusuo* (Guangzhou Shenbao Lawyer Office). December 12.

Jeganathan, Pradeep. 1995. "A Space for Violence: Anthropology, Politics, and the Location of a Sinhala Practice of Masculinity." In *Subaltern Studies XI: Community, Gender, and Violence*. Edited by Partha Chatterjee and Pradeep Jeganathan, pp. 37–65. New York: Columbia University Press.

Jeyaseelan, Lakshmanan, Laura S. Sadowski, Shuba Kumar, Fatma Hassan, Laurie Ramiro, and Beatriz Vizcarra 2004. "World Studies of Abuse in the Family Environment—Risk Factors for Physical Intimate Partner Violence." *Injury Control and Safety Promotion* 11 (2): 117–24.

Ji, Jin. 2019. "Fan Jiabao Fa Shishi 3 Nian, Yudao Jiabao Haibu Zhidao Zenme Ban" (Three Years into the Implementation of the Anti-Domestic Violence Law, What If You Still Don't Know What to Do upon Domestic Violence). *Nandu Guancha* (Nandu Observation). February 28.

Jia, Ning. 2018. "Cong Hunnei Qiangjian de Fanzuihua Kan, Shouhaizhe Jingyan Dui Falv Zhi Biyao" (Criminalization of Marital Rape: Necessary Law from Victims' Experiences). *Wu Zhi* (Matters). August 2.

Jia, Xiutang. 2008. "Minguo Shiqi Lihun Xianxiang Zai Tantao" (A Discussion of Divorce in the Republican Era). *Shilin* (History Forest) 1 (13): 127–39.

Jiang, Bei. 1929. "Shaofu Ningsi Bufan Fujia" (Young Woman Would Rather Die than Returning to the Husband). *Shenbao* (Shen Newspaper). October 6: 15.

Jiang, Pengcheng. 2016. "Fanjiabaofa Shishizhong de Kunhuo" (Problems in Implementation of Anti-Domestic Violence Law). *Jiabaoweiji Ganyuzhongxin* (Center of Interfering Domestic Violence). August 5.

Jiang, Yi. 2018. "Wo Zai Pihusuo De Yiye" (The One Night I Stayed in a Safety House). *Nvquan Zhisheng* (Feminist Voice). March 6.

Jiang, Yixiao. 1930. "Jinshi Zhiye de Funv Shenghuo" (Life of Tianjin Professional Women). *Dagong Bao* (Dagong Newspaper). October 4: 4–8.

Jiang, Yixiao. 1936. "Shanghai Zhiye Funv Fangwen Ji" (Interviews with Shanghai Professional Women). *Dagong Bao* (Dagong Newspaper). October 1: 2–6.

Jiang, Zhi'an. 1934. "Lujiacun" (Lujia Village). *Shehuixue Jie* (The Sociology Field) 8 (June): 12–15.

Jie, Li. 2016. "Erhai Quanmian Fangkai ¾ Guzhu Dui Zhaopin Nvxing Zeng Gulv" (75% Companies Hesitate Hiring Women after Two-Child Policy). *Beijing Qingnian Bao* (Beijing Youth Newspaper). March 8.

Jie, Mian. 2015. "Zai Fanjiaobao Zhong Yongren Danwei Ying Jinze" (Employers Should Be Responsible for Anti-Domestic Violence). *Jiabao Weiji Ganyu Zhongxin* (Domestic Violence Crisis Center). November 25.

Jin, Mancheng. 1928. "Modern Woman Keeps Life-Long Celibacy" (Shimao Nvzi Ze Bao Dushenzhuyi). *Central Newspaper* (Zhongyang Ribao). February 27: 12.

Jing, Ru. 1933. "A Look at Marriage Customs in Beiping" (Beiping Hunjia Xisu Zhi Yiban). *Dagong Newspaper* (Dagong Bao) 11: 19–20.

Jones, Ann. 1994. *Next Time She'll Be Dead*. Boston: Beacon Press.

Ju, Jiao. 2020. "Zhigei Qiongren Da Guansi, Wo Zhen Mei Jianguo Zheme Chun De Lvshi" (Only Helping the Poor with Their Lawsuits, I Have Never Seen So Stupid Lawyers). *Wang Yi* (Wang Yi Website). August 13.

Jukes, Adam. 1999. *Men Who Batter Women*. New York: Routledge.

Kai, Yongli. 2014. "Most Abusers Are Not Held Accountable by Law" (Duoshu Shibao Zhe Buhui Chengdan Houguo). *Sichuan Legal Newspaper* (Sichuan Fazhi Bao). March 6: B01.

Karmen, Andrew. 2003. "Women Victims of Crime." In *The Criminal Justice System and Women: Offenders, Prisoners, Victims, and Workers*, 3rd ed. Edited by Barbara Raffel Price and Natalie Sokoloff, pp. 289–301. New York: McGraw-Hill.

Kerns, Virginia. 1992. "Preventing Violence against Women: A Central American Case." In *Sanctions and Sanctuary: Cultural Perspectives on the Beating of Wives*. Edited by Dorothy Counts, Judith Brown, and Jacquelyn C. Campbell, pp. 125–38. London: Routledge.

Kleinman, Arthur. 2000. "The Violences of Everyday Life: The Multiple Forms and Dynamics of Social Violence." In *Violence and Subjectivity*. Edited by Veena Das, Arthur Kleinman, Mamphela Ramphele, and Pamela Reynolds, pp. 226–41. Berkeley: University of California press.

Ko, Dorothy. 1992. "The Complicity of Women in the Qing Good Woman Cult." In *Jinshi Jiazu Yu Zhengzhi Bijiao Lishi Lunwen Ji* (Collection of Theses on Comparative History of Contemporary Lineage and Politics). Edited by Zhongyang Yanjiu Yuan Jindaishi Yanjiusuo (Institute of Contemporary History of Central Institute). Taipei: Yongyu Yinshua Chang (Yongyu Publishing House).

Ko, Dorothy. 1994. *Teachers of the Inner Chambers: Women and Culture in Seventeenth-Century China*. Stanford, CA: Stanford University Press.

Koepping, Elizabeth. 2003. "A Game of Three Monkeys: KadazanDusun Villagers and Violence against Women." *Sojourn: Journal of Social Issues in Southeast Asia* 18 (2): 279–98.

Ku, Benjamin. 2011. "Gendered Suffering: Married Miao Women's Narratives on Intimate Partner Violence in Southwest China." *China Journal of Social Work* 4 (1): 23–39.

Lan, Huaisi. 2006. "Directing a Perfect Sex (daoyan yichang wanmei xingai)." *Hers* 2 (20): 182–4.

Larson, Wendy. 1998. *Women and Writing in Modern China*. Stanford, CA: Stanford University Press.

Larson, Wendy. 2002. "The Self Loving the Self: Men and Connoisseurship in Modern Chinese Literature." In *Chinese Femininities, Chinese Masculinities*. Edited by Susan Brownell and Jeffrey Wasserstrom, pp. 175–94. Berkeley: University of California Press.

The Law of the People's Republic of China on the Protection of Women's Rights and Interests. 1992. The 7th National People's Congress Standing Committee. People's Republic of China.

Law of the People's Republic of China on the Administration of Activities of Overseas Non-Governmental Organizations within the Territory of China. 2016. No. 12 of the Standing Committee of the 12th National People's Congress. April 28.

Lee, Kim. 2014. "Abuse, Fear and Shame in China." *New York Times*. January 29.

Lei, Jiaqiong. 2005. "Women's Escape of Marriage and Struggle for Decisions in Marriage during the Ten Years after the May Fourth Movement." Modern Chinese Society and Folk Culture—the First Collection of Papers at the International Symposium of Modern Chinese Social History. Beijing, China.

Levinson, David. 1989. *Family Violence in Cross-Cultural Perspective*. Newbury Park, CA: Sage.

Li, Changyong. 2018. "Qiangjianan Wuzuibianhu De Zhengju Shencha" (Investigation into Rape Charge). *Jinya Dazhuang Lvshi Wang* (Jinya Dazhuang Lawyer Net). April 22.

Li, Dong. 2011. "Nvxing Yanjiu Zhuanjia Zhang Xiaomei Jianyi Guli Bufen Nvxing Huigui Jiating" (Zhang Xiaomei, National Committee Member of the Chinese People's Political Consultative Conference, Encourages Some Women to Return Home). *Guangzhou Ribao* (Guangzhou Daily). March 8.

Li, Dun. 1998. "Geti Quanli Yu Zhengti Liyi Guanxi" (The Relationship between Individual Rights and Group Interests). In *Falv Shehuixue* (Legal Sociology). Edited by Dun Li. Zhongguo Zhengfa Daxue Chubanshe (Beijing, China: Chinese University of Politics and Law Publishing House), pp. 533–4.

Li, Gang. 1936. "Woguo Funv de Xinjiu Guan" (*The View on Chinese Old and New Women*). Shenbao (Shen Newspaper). September 5: 3–4.

Li, Hongbao. 1932. "Lihongbao Suqing Lihun An" (Li Hongbao Files for Divorce). *Jiangsu Dang'an Guan* (Jiangsu Archive Bureau). 1042 (2): 2432.

Li, Honghe. 2008. "Jianguo Chuqi Yu Hunyin Jiating Xiangguan de Funu Siwang Wenti Tanxi" (An Analysis of Death of Women Associated with Marriage and Family at the Beginning of the PRC). *Funu Yanjiu Luncong* (Collection of Women's Studies) 86 (3): 24–30.

Li, Li. 2007. *Xinhun Nannv Bixiuke* (Mandatory Courses for Newly Weds). Renmin Junyi Chubanshe (People's Medicine Publisher).

Li, Qun. 2016. "Pouxi Zhongguo Fanjiabao Fa de Lifa Yu Shijian" (An Analysis of the Implementation of the Anti-Domestic Violence Law). *Nandou Guancha* (Nandou Observation). December 17: 14.

Li, Wenhai. 2005. Minguo Shiqi Shehui Diaocha Congbian Hunyin Jiating Juan (Marriage and Family in the Social Survey during the Republican Era). Fuzhou: Fujian Education Publishing House (Fujian Jiaoyu Chubanshe).

Li, Xiaolin. 1994. "Chinese Women Soldiers: A History of 5,000 Years." *Social Education* 58 (2): 67–71.

Li, Xiaozhou. 2009. "Lao Gong Weishenme Zongshi Da Laopo" (Why Does the Husband Always Beat the Wife)? *Doushi Nvbao* (Metropolitan Female Newspaper). November 6.

Li, Xujia. 2020. "Jiabao Conglaibushi Jiawushi" (Domestic Violence Is Never Family Affairs). *Shaanxi Ribao* (Shaanxi Daily). December 3: 8.

Li, Zhao. 2003. "Shilun Wusi Yundong Hou Zhongguo de Nvxing Yu Hunyinjiating" (A Discussion of Chinese Women, Marriage, and Family after the May Fourth Movement). *Mudanjiang Shifan Xueyuan Xuebao* (Mudanjiang Normal University Journal) 5 (3): 62–4.

Lian, Qingqing. 2012. "Diaochabaogaocheng Quanguo Meinianyou 10wan Jiating Yinjiabao Jieti" (Survey Showed 100,000 Families Dissolved due to Domestic Violence Every Year). *Guangzhou Ribao* (Guangzhou Daily). June 29.

Liao, Lili. 2012. "Nvda Xuesheng Guangzhou Shangyan Zhanling Nan Cesuo Xingwei Yishu" (Female University Students Staged a Performance Art of Occupying Men's Restroom). *Zhongguo Xinwen Wang* (Chinese News Website). February 19.

Lin, Jian. 2012. *Falv Shouyeren* (Law Vigilant). Beijing: Beijing Lianhe Chubanshe (Beijing Alliance Publishing House).

Lin, Jianhua. 2018. "Beida Gongbu 20nian Qian Chufen Wenjian" (Beijing University Publicized the Disciplinary Action Document from Twenty Years Ago) *Jinri Toutiao* (Today's Headline). April 9.

Lin, Lezhi. 1899. "Meinu Keguishuo" (Beauties Are Distinguished). *Wanguo Gongbao* (Wanguo Public Newspaper) 118 (29): 18534–6.

Lin, Lezhi. 1905. "Ji Tianzuhui Yanshuoshi" (A Report of Tianzu Conference). *Wanguo Gongbao* (Wanguo Public Newspaper) 193 (2): 23185.

Lin, Wei. 1953. "Jiuzheng Chuli Hunyin Jiufenzhong de Qiangzhi Tiaojie Xianxiang" (Correcting the Phenomenon of Forcing Reconciliation in Marriage Disputes). *Renmin Ribao* (People's Daily). May 30: 3.

Lin, Xiao. 2021. "Nashenme Jieshu Zheyiduan Nieyuan" (What Can End the Abusive Marriage?). *Xinlang Xinwen* (Xinlang News). January 25.

Lina, Hua. 2020. "Lina Hua de Mom" (Mom of Lina Hua). *Weibo* (Weibo). November 28 (21).

Ling, Yun. 2003. "Gaozhi fuqi tongshuo hunwaiqing" (Speaking of Extramarital Affairs). *Zhongguo Funu* (Women of China) 1 (2): 34.

Liu, Dalin. 1993. *Zhongguo Gudai Xing Wenhua* (The Sex Culture of Ancient China). Yinchuan: Ningxia Renmin Chubanshe (Ningxia People's Publishing House).

Liu, Huan. 2020. "Renshenanquanbaohulingzhidu Cunduochongkunjing" (Multiple Difficulties of the Personal Safety Protection Order). *Fazhi Ribao* (Legal Daily). January 8.

Liu, Jianfei. 1984. "Survey of Zhouping Customs" (Zhouping Xian Fengsu Diaocha Gangyao). *Construction of Countryside* (*Xiangcun Jianshe*) 3 (7): 36–40.

Liu, Lushi. 1927. "Shaofu Qingqiu Lihunan Houxiangcha Zaixun" (Young Woman Requested for Divorce). *Shenbao* (Shen Newspaper). October 24: 15.

Liu, Ruhua. 2019. "Guo Jianmei: 2019 Nuobeier Tidaijiang Dezhu, Zhongguo Shouwei Zhuanzhi Gongyi Lvshi" (Guo Jianmei: Winner of the Alternative Nobel Prize). *Falv Chuban* (Law Publication). October 13.

Liu, Weiming. 2018. *ShiXiang Fazhi Zhongguo* (Driving Toward Legal China). Beijing: Zhongguo Wenshi Chubanshe (China Literature and History Publishing House).

Liu, Xiaodong. 2019. "Zhuhai Yiweifan Renshen Anquanbaohuling de Jiabaoshibaozhe Bei Juliu" (A Domestic Abuser Who Violated Safety Protection Order Was Detained). *Xinhuawang* (Xinhua Net). June 19: 8.

Liu, Xingyu, and Jiang Xu. 2005. "Hunyin: Nurende quanli he zeren" (Marriage: Women's Rights and Responsibilities). *Zhongguo Funu* (*Women of Women*) April 2 (647): 32–3.

Liu, Yan. 2019. "Nvxing Qiuzhi Jiuye Zong Beiwen Shengmei Shengwa, Shengyu Qishi Jishi Xiu" (Women Are Always Asked Whether They Have Given Birth Or Not, When the Pregnancy Discrimination Can End). *Zhongguo Qingnian Bao* (Chinese Youth Newspaper). July 4.

Liu, Yao. 2021. "Beinuesi De Shandongnvren de Yisheng" (A Shandong Woman Abused to Death). *Wangyi* (Wang Yi). January 31.

Liu, Yongting. 2019. "Zhiding Fanjiatingbaolifa Shishixize" (Stipulate Details in Implementation of Anti-Domestic Violence Law). *Guangmingwang* (Guangming Net). December 5: 18.

Lodhia, Sharmila. 2010. "Constructing an Imperfect Citizen-Subject: Globalization, National 'Security,' and Violence against South Asian Women." *Women's Studies Quarterly* 38 (1/2): 161–77.

Long, Xuan. 2016. "Weifanjinling Saoraoqizi Nanzibeifakuan 500yuan" (A Man Was Fined 500RMB for Violation of Personal Safety Protection Order). *Wenzhou Ribao* (Wenzhou Daily). March 11.

Lou, Yinsheng. 2013. "Liyang Lihun An Tuxian Renshen Baoquan" (Yang Li's Divorce Case Demonstrates Physical Safety Issue). *Renmin Fayuan Bao* (People's Court Newspaper). March 3: 3.

Lu, Cuiying. 1930. "Young Woman Begs for Divorce the Second Time" (Shaofu Erci Qi). *Shen Newspaper* (Shenbao). March 5: 15.

Lu, Pin. 2018. "Two Years On: Is China's Domestic Violence Law Working?" *Amnesty International*. March 7.

Lu, Yijie. 2018. "Beida Jiaoshi Huiyi Gaoyan Zisha Shijian" (Beijing University Professors Recall the Incident of Gao Yan's Suicide). *Zhongqing Zaixian* (Chinese Youth Online). April 8: 9.

Luo, Jieqi. 2019. "Jiabao, Siqiu he Yibu Falv de Dansheng" (Domestic Violence, Death Sentence, and the Birth of a Law). *Jiemian Xinwen* (Jiemian News). May 9.

Luo, Mei. 2021. "2021 Nian Zhichang Mama Shengcun Zhuangkuang Diaocha Baogao Chulu" (The Arrival of the 2021 Survey of the Living Conditions of Mothers in the Job Market). *Jiangnan Shibao* (Jiangnan Times). May 10: 10.

Luo, Suwen. 1996. *Women and the Modern Chinese Society* (Nvxing Yu Jindai Zhongguo Shehui). Shanghai: Shanghai People's Publishing House (Shanghai Renmin Chubanshe).

Luttrell, Wendy. 1996. "Sex and Violence." *American Anthropologist* 98 (4): 858–60.

Lv, Congcong. 2021. "79Ji Xiaoyou Guo Jianmei: Zuo Gongyi Lvshi Wo Hen Kuaile" (79 Alumni Guo Jianmei: I Am Very Happy Being a Pro Bono Lawyer). *Xiao You Feng Cai* (Alumni Story). Beijing: Beijing Daxue Fa Xue Yuan (Beijing University Law School).

Lv, Heng. 1951. "Fujian Hui'an Xian Diniu Qu Zenyang Xuanchuan Hunyinfa" (How the Ninth District, Hui'an County, Fujian Province, Propagates the Marriage Law). *Xinhua Yuebao* (Xinhua Monthly Newspaper). October 10 (3).

Lv, Pin. 2018. "Nvquan Busi" (Feminism Is Not Dead). *Los Angeles Review of Books: China Channel* 2 (1): 12.

Lv, Shi. 2009. "Bantuibanjiu Budengyu Qiangjian" (Half Pushing and Half Acquiescing Is Not Rape). *Nanjing Bihu Lvshiwang* (Nanjing Defensive Lawyer Net). December 7.

Lv, Xiaoquan. 2017. *Yang Fazhi Zhijian Cheng Jiabao Zuilin* (Using the Sword of Law to Punish Domestic Violence Perpetrators). Beijing: Zhongguo Renmin Gongan Daxue Chubanshe (Chinese People's Public Security Publishing House).

Ma, Kui. 2020. "Shinian Jiabaoyizhao Gai, Renmin Tiaojie Xingfulai" (One Day Correction of Domestic Violence, Mediation Brought Happiness). *Yumen City Sifaju* (Yumen City Justice Bureau). January 20.

Ma, Lan. 2015. "Yan Li Yin Jiabao Shafu Fenshi An Xuanpan: Sixing Gaipan Sihuan" (The Sentence of Yan Li for Killing the Husband due to Intimate Partner Violence: Death Penalty Changed to Death Penalty with Delay). *Chengdu Xinwen* (Chengdu News). April 24: 2.

Ma, Mingyue. 2019. "Weihe Zhuanzhi Fa Jiabao" (Why Should He Focus on Anti-Domestic Violence). Fenghuang Wang (Fenghuang Net). June 14: 10.

Marriage Law. 2001. The Ninth National People's Congress Standing Committee. People's Republic of China.

Martin, Tsui. 1999. "Domestic Violence in Northern India." *American Journal of Epidemiology* 150 (4): 417–26.

McCall, George J., and N. M. Sheilds. 1986. "Social and Structural Factors in Family Violence." In *Violence in the Home: Interdisciplinary Perspectives*. Edited by Mary Lystad, pp. 98–123. New York: Brunner/Mazel.

McCauley, Kern. 1995. "The 'Battering Syndrome': Prevalence and Clinical Symptoms of Domestic Violence in Primary Care Internal Medicine Practices." *Annual Internal Medicine* 123 (10): 737–46.

McClusky, Laura J. 2001. *Here, Our Culture Is Hard: Stores of Domestic Violence from a Mayan Community in Belize*. Austin: University of Texas Press.

McGillivray, Anne, and Brenda Comaskey. 1999. *Black Eyes All of the Time: Intimate Partner Violence, Aboriginal Women, and the Justice System*. Toronto: University of Toronto Press.

Measures for the Administration of Government Procurement of Services. 2020. "Instrumentalities of the State Council and Ministry of Finance." March 1, 2020.

Mei, Mu. 2020. "Nvzi Liangci Yin Jiabao Qisu Lihun, Fayuan Weipizhun, Zuihou Zaozhangfu Chidao Shahai" (A Woman Sued for Divorce Twice due to Domestic Violence, Denied by Court, in the End Killed by the Husband). *Meiri Toutiao* (Daily Headline). June 14.

Merry, Sally Eagle. 2006a. *Human Rights and Gender Violence: Translating International Law into Local Justice*. Chicago: University of Chicago Press.

Merry, Sally Eagle. 2006b. "Transnational Human Rights and Local Activism: Mapping the Middle." *American Anthropologist* 108 (1): 38–51.

Merry, Sally Eagle. 2009. *Gender Violence: A Cultural Perspective*. Malden, MA: Wiley-Blackwell.

Mi, Na. 2021. "Zhongguo Qingnian Nvquan Yundong Jianshi" (A Concise History of Chinese Youth Feminists' Campaigns). *Nvquan Xuelun* (Feminism Forum). April 5: 1–5.

Ministry of Finance of the People's Republic of China. 2019. *Report of the Situation of Reform and Development of Chinese Communist Central Cultural Enterprises: Appendix 2*. Ministry of Finance of the People's Republic of China. May 15.

Mo, Chi. 2021. "Jiaoyubu Jinzhi Xingbie Qishi, Weihe Haiyou Gaoxiao Shezhi Nan Nv Sheng Luqu Bili" (The Ministry of Education Bans Gender Discrimination, Why Colleges Continues to Require a Gender-Based Quota). *Wang Yi* (Wangyi). April 3.

Moffitt, Terrie. 2013. "Childhood Exposure to Violence and Lifelong Health: Clinical Intervention Science and Stress Biology Research Joint Forces." *Development Psychopathology* 25 (4): 1619–34.

Morrissey, Marietta. 1998. "Explaining the Caribbean Family: Gender Ideologies and Gender Relations." In *Caribbean Portraits: Essays on Gender Ideologies and Identities*. Edited by Christine Barrow, pp. 78–90. Kingston, Jamaica: Ian Randle.

Nan, Du. 2019. "Yudaojiabao Zenmeban" (What You Should Do When You Encounter Domestic Violence). *Nandu Guancha* (Nandu Observer). November 27.

Nanjing Law Administration. 2000. *A Survey of Civil Affairs*. Beijing: The Chinese University of Politics and Law Publishing House (Zhongguo Zhengfa Daxue Chubanshe).

National People's Congress Standing Committee. 2016. *Zhonghua Renmin Gongheguo Fajiating Baolifa* (PRC Anti-Domestic Violence Law). March 1.

National People's Congress Standing Committee. 2017. *Zhonghua Renmin Gongheguo Xingfa* (PRC Criminal Law). November 4.

Naved, Ruchira Tabassum, and Lars Ake Persson. 2005. "Factors Associated with Spousal Physical Violence against Women in Bangladesh." *Studies in Family Planning* 36 (4): 289–300.

News. 1933. "Nuedai Lihun An De Zhongcai" (Court Proceedings of Abuse-Related Divorce Cases). *Faling Zhoukan* (Law Weekly). 161: 22.

Ni, Wei. 2019. "Beinanyou Dacheng Zhiwuren Zhihoude 5nian" (5 Years after Being Beaten to a Vegetative State). *Kandian Kuaibao* (Kandian Express). November 29.

Nicarthy, Ginny. 1989. "From the Sounds of Silence to the Roar of a Global Movement: Notes on the Movement against Violence against Women." *Response to the Victimization of Women and Children* 12 (2): 3–10.

Nordstrom, Carolyn, and Antonius C. G. M. Robben. 1995. *Fieldwork under Fire: Contemporary Studies of Violence and Survival*. Berkeley: University of California Press.

Palmer, Alex. 2017. "Flee at Once: China's Besieged Human Rights Lawyers." *New York Times*. June 25.

Pan. Yongyi. 2018. "Chen Min: Zhuan Zhu Yu Jianjiu Fan Jiabao Falv" (Chen Min: Focused on Studying Anti-Domestic Violence Law). *Wenzhou Wang* (Wenzhou Net). November 28.

Parish, William, Tianfu Wang, Edward Laumann, Suiming Pan, and Ye Luo. 2004. "Intimate Partner Violence in China: National Prevalence, Risk Factors and Associated Health Problems." *International Family Planning Perspectives* 30 (4): 174–81.

Peng, Hsiao-yen. 1995. "The New Woman: May Fourth Women's Struggle for Self-Liberation." *Zhongguo Wenzhe Yanjiu Jikan* (Chinese Journal of Philosophy and Literature) 6 (March): 259–338.

Peng, Yi. 2020. "Hunan Yiyang Yiminjing Beiqianqi jubaochangqi Jiabao" (A Policeman Was Reported by His Ex for Long-Term Domestic Violence). *Hongxing Xinwen* (Hongxing News). April 10: 19.

Pi, Xiaoming. 1991. "Jiating Baoli Baipi Shu" (White Paper on Domestic Violence). *Zhongguo Funvbao* (Chinese Women Newspaper). July (2): 9–11.

Plesset, Sonja. 2006. *Sheltering Women: Negotiating Gender and Violence in Northern Italy*. Stanford, CA: Stanford University Press.

Pournaghash-Tehrani, Said. 2011. "Domestic Violence in Iran: A Literature Review." *Aggression and Violent Behavior* 16 (1): 1–5.

Public Security Ministry. 2015. "Nabalei Nvxing Zuirongyi Zaoshou Xingqin" (Eight Types of Women that Are the Easiest Targets of Sexual Assault). *Henan Sheng Pingan Zhongyuan* (Henan Province Safe Advices). October: 2.

Qi, Yi. 1936. "Yanjiu Ji Xiyi" (A Study and Investigation). *Faling Zhoukan* (Law Weekly). 295: 1088.

Qian, Fan. 2015. "Diaochaxianshi Zhongguoren Pingjun Zaoshao 35ci Jiabao Cai Baojing" (Survey Showed that People Called the Police after 35 Times of Domestic Violence on Average). *Jiefang Ribao* (Jiefang Daily Newspaper). September 10.

Qiao, Feng. 1922. "Zhongguo de Lihun Fa" (Divorce Law in China). *Funv Zazhi* (Women's Journal) 8 (4): 12.

Qiao, Meili. 2020. "Yiqi Fenglu, Yujiabao Wucheketao" (Roads Are Blocked during Covid-19, Nowhere to Escape upon Domestic Violence). *Yuan Xiao Gu* (Original Tinybone). February 29.

Qin, Liwen. 2014. "'Violence against Women' Combating Domestic Violence: Embassy of the United States of America." *Global Women's Issues* 4 (September): 1–5.

Qing, Gan. 2019. "Zenme Jujue Hunqian Xingxingwei" (How to Refuse Premarital Sex). *Susu Wang* (Susu Net). July 20.

Qing, Geletu. 2000. "Jianguo Chuqi Suiyuan Diqu Guanche Huninfa Yundong" (The Campaign of the Marriage Law in Suiyuan Area at the Beginning of the PRC). *Neimenggu Shehui Kexue* (Inner Mongolia Social Science) 2 (May): 12–34.

Qu, Hongrui. 2016. "Liushou Funv Bei Qiangjian Baojing Zaoju Zisha" (Stay-at-Home Wife Was Raped, Reported It to the Police but Rejected, Committed Suicide). *Shangyou Xinwen* (Shangyou News). January 14.

Qu, Ya. 2020. "Xuexi Xi Jinping Guanyu Lingdaoganbu Jiafengjianshe de Zhongyaolunshu" (Studying Xi Jinping's Important Sayings about Family Construction of Cardres). *Dangzheng Luntan* (Party Forum). December 28.

Ren, Jianxin. 1953. "Dali Zhunbei Kaizhan Guanche Hunyinfa de Qunzhong Yundong" (Mass Campaigns to Implement the Marriage Law). *Renmin Ribao* (People's Daily). February 1: 1.

Richardson, Sophie. 2018. "China's Victims of Sexual Harassment Denied Justice." *Human Rights Watch*. July 31.

Rivera, Jenny. 2001. "Women, Race, Ethnicity, and Violence." In *Race, Ethnicity, Gender, and Human Rights in the Americas: A New Paradigm for Activism*. Edited by Celina Romany, pp. 105–7. Washington, DC: American University Press.

Robben, Antonius, and Marcelo Suarez-Orozco. 2000. *Cultures under Siege: Collective Violence and Trauma*. Cambridge: Cambridge University Press.

Roberts, Lawrence. 1998. "The Impact of Domestic Violence on Women's Mental Health." *Australian and New Zealand Journal Public Health* 22 (7): 796–801.

Rong, Weiyi. 2003. "Zhongguo Fanjiabao Shiye Xiang Zongsheng Fazhan" (The Chinese Anti-Domestic Violence Campaign Further Develops). *Funv Yanjiu Luntan* (Women's Studies Forum) 1: 66–71.

Rong, Weiyi. 2006. "Fandui Zhendui Funv de Baoli" (Fighting against Violence against Women). In *Zhongguo Funv Fazhan Baogao* (A Report on Women Development in

China). Edited by Jinling Wang. Beijing: Beijing Sheke Wenxue Chubanshe (Beijing Social Science Literature Press of China).
Rosaldo, Renato. 2004. "Grief and a Headhunter's Rage." In *Violence in War and Peace*. Edited by *Nancy Scheper-Hughes and Philippe I. Bourgois*, pp. 150–6. Oxford: Wiley-Blackwell.
Roy, Maria, ed. 1977. *Battered Women: A Psychosociological Study of Domestic Violence*. New York: Van Nostraind Reinhold .
Ru, Cha. 2016. "Hunyindengjichu Zuai Bieren Lihun Hai Yangyang Deyi de Naxie 'Youxiu Yuangong'" (Those "Outstanding Staff Members" Who Obstruct Others' Divorce). *Huanqiuwang* (Around the Globe). March 2.
Rui, Di. 2013. "Guo Jianmei: Jiabao Shouhai Zhe Huo Jixing Shi Fazhide Beiai" (Guo Jianmei: Death Sentence to Victims of Domestic Violence Is the Sadness of a Legal System). *RFI*. January 27.
Rui, Yin. 2020. "Lihunzhende Xuyao Lengjingqi ma" (Does Divorce Really Need a Cooling Period?). *Ruiyin Lvshi Shiwusuo* (Ruiyin Lawyer Office). August 10.
Ruo, Feiwen. 2020. "25 Zai Gongyi Lvshi Guo Jianmei" (25-Year Pro Bono Lawyer Jianmei Guo). *Shishang Cosmo* (Cosmopolitan). April 17.
Schecher, Susan. 1982. *Women and Male Violence: The Visions and Struggles of the Battered Women's Movement*. Boston: South End Press.
Scheper-Hughes, Nancy. 2004a. "Two Feet under and a Cardboard Coffin: The Social Production of Indifference to Child Death." In *Violence in War and Peace: An Anthology*. Edited by Nancy Scheper-Hughes and Philippe I. Bourgois, pp. 275–80. Oxford: Blackwell.
Scheper-Hughes, Nancy. 2004b. "Ishi's Brain, Ishi's Ashes: Anthropology and Genocide." In *Violence in War and Peace: An Anthology*. Edited by Nancy Scheper-Hughes and Philippe I. Bourgois, pp. 61–8. Oxford: Blackwell.
Scheper-Hughes, Nancy, and Philippe I. Bourgois. 2004. *Violence in War and Peace: An Anthology*. Oxford: Blackwell.
Schmidt, Bettina, and Ingo Schroeder, eds. 2001. *Anthropology of Violence and Conflict*. New York: Routledge.
Scott, Joan. 1986. "Gender: A Useful Category of Historical Analysis." *American Historical Review* 91 (5): 1053–75.
Severdia, Sandra. 2017. "Zhang Leilei—Tamen Shuo 'Ni Bixu Jiaoting Ni Faqi de Fanxingsaorao Xingdong'" ("Zhang Leilei—They Said, 'You Must Terminate Your Anti-Sexual Harassment Activities'). *Zhongguo Shuzi Shidai* (China Digital Times). May 18.
Shen, Renshi. 1928. "Furen Kongqing Lihun An Hou Xuanpan" (Young Woman Filed for Divorce). *Shenbao* (Shen Newspaper). March 10: 15.
Shi, Jiao. 2016. "Xiangbaituo Jiatingbaoli Meiname Rongyi" (It Is Not Easy to Rid Domestic Violence). *Zhonghuanvzi Xueyuan* (Chinese Women's College). December 16.
Shi, Yafang. 2019. "Mitu Zai Zhongguo: he Zhonguo Nvquan Yundong" (Me Too in China and Feminist Movement in China). *Tiexin Jiemei Wang* (Loving Sister Net). October 27.
Shou, Xia. 2021. "Nianqing Mama Daizhe Liang Youzi 24lou Zhuixia" (A Young Mother Jumps Off a 24-Floor Building with Two Babies). *Pengpai Xinwen* (Pengpai News). April 8: 9.

Siu, Helen. 1990. "Recycling Tradition: Culture, History and Political Economy in the Chrysanthemum Festivals of South China." *Comparative Studies in Society and History* 32 (4): 765–94.

Sluka, Jeffrey, ed. 1999. *Death Squad: The Anthropology of State Terror*. Philadelphia: University of Pennsylvania Press.

Sokoloff, Natalie with Christina Pratt, eds. 2005. *Domestic Violence at the Margins: Readings on Race, Class, Gender, and Culture*. New Brunswick, NJ: Rutgers University Press.

Sokoloff, Natalie J., and Ida Dupont. 2005. "Domestic Violence: Examining the Intersections of Race, Class, and Gender—an Introduction." In *Domestic Violence at the Margins: Readings on Race, Class, Gender and Culture*. Edited by Natalie J. Sokoloff and Christina Pratt, pp. 1–14. New Brunswick, NJ: Rutgers University Press.

Song, Jindong. 1918. *Song Jindong Case* (Song Jindong Anjian). Beijing: Beijing Archive Bureau (Beijing Shi Dang An Guan Dang An). 181: 21022.

Song, Licai. 2019. "Fan Jiabao Kecheng Cheng Hubei Minjing Ruzhi 'Bixiu Ke'" (Anti-Domestic Violence Classes Have Become 'Required Courses' of New Recruits of Hubei Police). *Zhongguo Funv Bao* (Chinese Women's Newspaper). March 21.

Song, Meiya, and Xue, Ninlan, eds. 2003. "A True, Oral Record of Women under Domestic Violence" (Funu Shoubao Koushu Shilu). Beijing: China Social Science Press (Zhongguo Shehui Kexue Chubanshe).

Song, Peipei. 2016. "Wanquan Zhongli De Zhuanjia Zhengren" (Neutral-Positioned Expert Witnesses). *Sichuan Fazhi Bao* (Sichuan Legal Newspaper). April 12.

Spires, Anthony. 2011. "Contingent Symbiosis and Civil Society in an Authoritarian State: Understanding the Survival of China's Grassroots NGOs." *American Journal of Sociology* 117 (1): 1–45.

The State Department of the People's Republic of China. 2003. "Aid Management Methods of Vagrant Beggars in the City." No. 381 Order of the State Department of the People's Republic of China. June 20.

Stauffer, Brian. 2021. "Zhongguo Erhai Zhengce Zaocheng Pubian Qishi" (China: The Two-Child Policy Has Caused General Prejudice). *Human Rights Watch*. June 1.

Stephen, Lynn. 2005. *Zapotec Women: Gender, Class, and Ethnicity in Globalized Oaxaca*. Durham, NC: Duke University Press.

Stewart, Mary White. 2014. *Ordinary Violence: Everyday Assaults against Women Worldwide*. Santa Barbara, CA: Praeger.

Straus, Murray, Richard Gelles, and Suzanne Steinmetz. 1980. *Behind Closed Doors: Violence in the American Family*. Garden City, NY: Anchor Books.

Sun, Maoning. 2017. "Jiabao beiyaodiao Bizi Zuorixuanpan" (Yesterday the Domestic Abuser Who Bit Off His Wife's Nose Was Sentenced). *Yangshi Xinwen* (CCTV News). April 18.

Sun, Pu. 2013. "Cong 'Shoubao Ren' Dao 'Shibao Ren' de Tuibian" (The Transformation from the 'Abused' to the 'Abuser'"). *Zhongguo Funu Bao* (Chinese Women's Newspaper). August 20: B02.

Sun, Qian. 2012. "Guangzhou Siming Nvsheng Dangjie Ti Guangtou, Kangyi Xinyi Gaoxiao 'Xingbie Qishi'" (Guangzhou Four Female Students Shaved Their Heads, Resisting Their Desired Universities' "Gender Prejudice"). Long Hu Wang (Long Hu Web). September 2.

Supreme Court Document on Child Custody of Divorce Cases. 1993. Supreme Court.

Supreme Court Document to Improve Verdicts on Civil Affairs and Reform Work Mechanism. 2018. Supreme Court.

Tan, Zhiyun. 2007. "Minguo Nanjing Zhengfu Shiqi de Funv Lihun Wenti—Yi Jiangsusheng Gaodeng Fayuan 1927–1936 Nian Minshi Anli Wei Lei" (Women's Divorce in the Republican Era during the Nanjing Nationalist Government: Civil Litigation Cases at the Jiangsu Supreme Court from 1927 to 1936). *Funv Yanjiu Luncong* (Collection of Women's Studies) 81 (4): 35–43.

Tang, Gaojie. 2021. "Zhongguode Lihunlvgao" (High Divorce Rate in China). *Pengpaixinwen* (Pengpai News). January 22.

Tang, Mu'an. 1931. "Tang Mu'an Suqing Lihun An." (Tang Mu'an File for Divorce). *Jiangsu Dang'an Guan* (Jiangsu Archive Bureau). 1042-2: 2409.

Tang, Shuiqing. 2010. "20 Shiji 50 Niandai Chuqi Zhongguo Xiangcun Guanche Hunyinfa Guochengzhong de Siwang Xianxiang Tanxi" (An Analysis of the Death Phenomenon in Implementing the Marriage Law in the Early 1950s). *Shehui Kexue* (Social Science) 2 (May): 138–47.

Tao, Liheng. 2004. "Education Picture Book for Perpetrators of Violence" (Shibaozhe Jiaoyu Huace). Beijing: China Social Science Press (Zhongguo Shehui Kexue Chubanshe).

Tatlow, Didi Kirsten. 2013. "Chinese Courts Turn a Blind Eye to Abuse." *New York Times*. January 30.

Tellez, Michelle. 2008. "Community of Struggle: Gender, Violence, and Resistance on the U.S./Mexico Border." *Gender and Society* 22 (5): 545–67.

Tian, Xia, and Yue'an Tian. 1999. "Ershi Shiji Shangbanqi Nongcun Jiating Fuqi Guanxi Tanxi" (An Analysis of Rural Couple Relationship at the Beginning of the Twentieth Century). *Renwen Zazhi* (Humanities Journal) 4 (14): 53–6.

Tishkov, Valery. 2004. "Chechnya: Life in a War-Torn Society." Berkeley: University of California Press.

Todhunter, Robbin, and John Deaton. 2010. "The Relationship between Religious and Spiritual Factors and the Perpetration of Intimate Personal Violence." *Journal of Family Violence* 25 (8): 745–53.

United Nations. 2006. "In-Depth Study on All Forms of Violence against Women." Report of the Secretary-General. New York: General Assembly.

UPI. 2011. China Reports Latest Sex Ratio Figures. http://www.upi.com/Top_News/World-News/2011/08/16/China-reports-latest-sex-ratio-figures/UPI-94121313495480/ 2011, August 16.

Ventura, Lois A., and Gabrielle Davis. 2005. "Domestic Violence." *Violence against Women* 11 (2): 255–77.

Verdict. 1930. "The Verdict of the Case between Cunfu and Gaoshi and Their Children" (Jingshi Cunfu Yu Cungaoshi Yin Shenfen Guanxi Ji Zinv Jianhu Shengming Shangsu Yi'an de Shenpan Jieguo). *Daliyuan Civil Affairs Archives* (Daliyuan Minshi Dang An). 131: 1051.

Vest, Joshua, Tegan Catlin, John Chen, and Ross Brownson. 2002. "Multistate Analysis of Factors Associated with Intimate Partner Violence." *American Journal of Preventative Medicine* 22 (3): 156–64.

Volpp, Leti. 2013. "Feminism versus Multiculturalism." In *Domestic Violence at the Margins: Readings on Race, Class, Gender, and Culture*. Edited by Natalie J. Sokoloff and Christina Pratt, pp. 39–49. New Jersey: Rutgers University Press.

Walker, Lenore A. 1984. "Battered Women, Psychology, and Public Policy." *American Psychologist* 39 (10): 1178–82.

Walker, Lenore. 2006. "Battered Woman Syndrome: Empirical Findings." In *Annals of the New York Academy of Sciences: Vol. 1087. Violence and Exploitation against Women and Girls*. Edited by Florence Denmark, Herbert H.Krauss, Esther Halpern, and Jeri A. Sechzer, pp. 142–57. New Jersey: Blackwell.

Walker, Lenore, and Carlye Conte. 2017. "Women, Domestic Violence, and the Criminal Justice System: Traumatic Pathways." In *Gender, Psychology, and Justice: The Mental Health of Women and Girls in the Legal System*. Edited by Corinne Datchi and Julie Ancis, pp. 48–74. New York: New York University Press.

Wang, Chunxia. 2020. "Zaoyujiabaoqisulihun Fayuanzenmepan?" (How the Court Handles Domestic Violence Cases). *Zhongguo Funvbao* (Chinese Women's Newspaper). August 10: 13.

Wang, Gao. 2008. "20shiji 20–30niandai Nvzi Lihun Zhudongquan Zhuanbian Tanwei" (A Survey of Women Filing for Divorce from the 1920s to the 1930s). *Funv Yundongshi Yanjiu* (A Study of Women's Movement History) 1 (78): 50–3.

Wang, Jingzhu. 2018. "Jiashishenpanzhong Fanjiabao Chengxujizhi Yanjiu" (Study of Anti-Domestic Violence Mechanism in Family Affairs Cases). *Beijing Fayuan* (Beijing Court). June 25: 10.

Wang, Jun. 2001. "Zhengxie Weiyuan Changyi Yihun Nv Zhigong Tuigang Xiangfu Jiaozi" (National Committee Member of the Chinese People's Political Consultative Conference Advocates Married Female Workers to Give Up Their Posts and Return Home to Take Care of Their Husbands and Raise and Educate The Next Generation). *Nan Fang Wang* (South Web). March 7.

Wang, Jun. 2019. "Fanjiabaofa Shishi 3nian" (Three Years after the Implementation of Anti-Domestic Violence Law). *Xinjingbao* (Xinjing Newspaper). December 6: 15.

Wang, Jun. 2020. "Duodi Fan Jiabao Pihusuo Xianzhuang Diaocha" (Investigation into Anti-Domestic Violence Safe Houses in Multiple Places). *Xin Jing Bao* (Xin Jing Newspaper). November 25.

Wang, Kai. 2014. "Nuedaiqizi Zhisi, Anqing Yinanzi Huoxing Sinian" (A Man Was Sentenced to Four Years in Prison for Abusing His Wife until She Was Dead. *Zhongan Zaixian* (Zhongan Online). July 3.

Wang, Ning. 2019. "Wanghongbozhu Yuya Beijiabao" (Weibo Blogger Yuya Encountered Domestic Violence). *Zhong Xin Wang* (Zhong Xin Net). November 26: 21.

Wang, Ping. 2000. *Aching for Beauty: Footbinding in China*. Minneapolis: University of Minnesota Press.

Wang, Ping. 2015. "Zuo Funv De Tonghang Ren: Wang Xingjuan" (Be Women's Companion: Wang Xingjuan). *Wiko Heping Funv* (Wiko Peace Women). November 3.

Wang, Qiumeng. 2016. "Domestic Violence Law of China and the Institutional Design of Counter-DV Mechanism." MA Thesis in International Studies: China. University of Washington.

Wang, Shifu.1998. *Xi Xiang Ji* (Romance of the Western Chamber). Renmin Wenxue Chubanshe (People's Literature Publisher).

Wang, Si. 2017. "Nanning Fayuan Kaichu 'Hunyinxingfuchufang' Gei Fufu Chongqi Xingfujihui" (Nanning Court Wrote a "Marriage Happiness Prescription" to Start a Couple's Happiness). *Renmenwang* (People Net). August 15: 10.

Wang, Xiaoyi. 2010. "Guo Jianmei: Zuo Gongyi Lvshi, Shi Wo Yongyuan Bubian de Xuanze" (Guo Jianmei: It Is My Unchanging Choice to Be a Pro Bono Lawyer). *Wangyi Nvren* (Wangyi Women). November 2.

Wang, Xiaoyi. 2013. "Li Yan Yin Shou Jiabao Shafu An Shimo" (The Beginning and End of Li Yan's Killing of Her Husband due to Domestic Violence). *Wangyi Nvren* (Wangyi Women). February 5.

Wang, Xiaoyi. 2020. "Shenzhen Jingfang Huiying Tiaojieyuan Dui Zao Jiabao Baojing Nvzi Yongyu Bu Guifan: Jiang Jiaqiang Jiaoyu" (Shenzhen Public Security Bureau Responded that the Mediator Used Non-standard Language toward the Woman Who Reported Domestic Violence: Will Strengthen Education). *Huan Qiu Wang* (Around the World Net). February 27.

Wang, Xingjuan. 2012. "Wang Xingjuan: Minjian Funv Yanjiu Yu Fuquan Zhi Lu" (Wang Xingjuan: Her Path to Women's Studies on the Ground and Feminism). *Zhongguo Fazhan Jianbao* (Chinese Development Newsletter). December 14.

Wang, Yizhi. 1979. *A Female School during the May Fourth Movement: Memoir of the May Fourth Movement*. Beijing: The Chinese Social Sciences Publishing House (Zhongguo Shehui Kexue Chubanshe).

Wang, Yongqin. 2016. "Nvjizhe Hongmei Zhisi" (The Death of Hong Mei—A Female Journalist). *Zhongguo Funvbao* (Chinese Women's Newspaper). April 28.

Wang, Yubo. 1984. *A History of the Head of Family* (Lishi Shang de Jiazhang Zhi). Beijing: People's Publishing House (Renmin Chuban She).

Wang, Zhang. 1944. "The Divorce Case of Wang Zhang Shi" (Wang Zhang Shi Lihun An). Chengdu City Archive Bureau (Chengdushi Dang An Guan). 94: 2367.

Wang, Zheng. 2003. "Gender, Employment and Women's Resistance." In *Chinese Society: Change, Conflict and Resistance*. Edited by Elizabeth J. Perry and Mark Selden, pp. 162–90. London: Routledge.

Wang, Zheng. 2015. "Detention of the Feminist Five in China." *Feminist Studies* 41 (2): 476–82.

Wang, Zheng, and Ying Zhang. 2010. "Global Concepts, Local Practices: Chinese Feminism since the Fourth UN Conference on Women." *Feminist Studies* 36 (1): 40–70.

Wang, Zuxin. 2018. "Shou Shanghai Hou, Zheli You Yichu Bifeng Ganwan" (A Quiet Bay after Being Hurt). *Beijing Wanbao* (Beijing Evening Newspaper). March 14.

Watson, Rubie. 1991. "Marriage and Gender Inequality." In *Marriage and Inequality in Chinese Society*. Edited by Rubie S. Watson and Patricia B. Ebrey, pp. 231–55. Berkeley: University of California Press.

Wei, Fu. 1928. "Wei Fushi Suqing Lihun An" (Wei Fushi File for Divorce). *Jiangsu Dang'an Guan* (Jiangsu Archive Bureau). 1042–2: 2328.

Wei, Furong. 2019. "Yimingjingcha de Fanjiabaoguancha" (A Policeman's Observation of Anti-Domestic Violence). *Xin Jing Bao* (Xin Jing Newspaper). July 31: 23.

Wei, Lina. 2017. "Quanguo 10wanfen Shejiabaolihunpanjueshu" (100,000 Verdicts on Domestic Violence Related Divorce Nationwide). *Guanchanzhe* (Observer). 8: 7.

Wei, Lu. 1933. "Lihun Anjian He Qiduo" (Why So Many Divorce Cases). *Suzhou Mingbao* (Suzhou Morning Newspaper). September 11: 2.

Wei, Meng. 2019. "Zhuhai Yiweifan Renshenanquanbaohuling de Jiabao Shibaozhe Bei Juliu" (A Domestic Violence Abuser in Zhuhai Violated Protection Order and Was Detained). *Xinhua Wang* (Xinhua Net). June 19: 18.

Wei, Quan. 2019. "Bantuibanjiu Fasheng Xingguanxi" (Sexual Intercourse with Half Pushing and Half Acquiescing). *Xinlang Wang* (Xinlang Net). March 12: 6.

Wei, Shengyao. 2019. "Zhuanjia: Yilingrongren Qiaduan Jiatingaizheng Mengya" (Experts: Nip the Bud of Family Cancer). *Xinhuawang* (Xinhua Net). November 25.

Wen, Ruo. 2020. "Gongyi Lvshi Guo Jianmei: Jianchi Caiyou Xiwang" (Pro Bono Lawyer Guo Jianmei: Perseverance Can Lead to Hope). *Nanfang Zhoumo* (South Weekend). December 29.

Wen, Shi. 1913. "Wen Shi Case" (Wen Shi Anjian). Beijing: Beijing Archive Bureau (Beijing Shi Dang An Guan Dang An). J 181: 2129.

White, Evelyn. 1985. "The Psychology of Abuse." In *Chain, Chain Change: For Black Women Dealing with Physical and Emotional Abuse*. Seattle: South End Press.

Wies, Jennifer, and Hillary J. Haldane. 2015. *Applying Anthropology to Gender-Based Violence: Global Responses, Local Practices*. Lanham, MD: Lexington Books.

Williams, Alison. 2021. "Closure of Online Feminist Groups in China Sparks Call for Women to 'Stick Together.'" *Reuters*. April 14.

Wolf, Margery. 1972. *Women and the Family in Rural Taiwan*. Stanford, CA: Stanford University Press.

World Health Organization. 2002. *World Report on Violence and Health*. Geneva: World Health Organization. Chapter 6, p. 149.

WHO (World Health Organization). 2017. "Violence against Women." *World Health Organization*. November 29.

Wu, Gumin. 1936. "Zhouping Diyinian Shengming Tongji zhi Fenxi" (The First Annual Analysis of the Statistics of Life in Zhouping). *Xiangcun Jianshe* (Construction of Countryside) 6 (1): 123–6.

Wu, Jiezhen. 2017. "Shiwanfen She Jiabao Panjueshu" (Ten Thousand Domestic Violence Court Cases). *Guangzhou Ribao* (Guangzhou Daily). May 5: 16.

Wu, Mei. 2020. "Fanjiabaofa Shishi 4 Zhounian" (4 Years after the Anti-Domestic Law Implementation). *Guangzhou Wumei Lvshishiwusuo* (Guangzhou Wumei Legal Affairs Office). March 9.

Wu, Shi. 1926. "We Shi Case" (We Shi Anjian). Beijing: Beijing Archive Bureau (Beijing Shi Dang An Guan Dang An). 181: 50902.

Wu, Xiaolei. 2010. "Beida Rongbuxia Guojianmei" (Beijing University Cannot Hold Guo Jianmei). *Shidai Zhoubao* (Times Weekly). April 15.

Wu, Zhixin. 2005. "Zuijing Shiliu Nian Zhi Beiping Lihun An" (The Divorce Cases in Beijing in Recent Sixteen Years). In *Minguo Shiqi Shehui Diaocha Congbian Hunyin Jiating Juan* (Marriage and Family in the Social Survey during the Republican Era). Edited by Wenhai Li, p. 400. Fuzhou: Fujian Jiaoyu Chubanshe (Fujian Education Publishing House).

Wu, Zhushi. 1927. "Young Woman Awaits Verdict in Her Divorce Case" (Shaofu Kongqing Lihun An Hou Xuanpan). *Shen Newspaper* (Shenbao). September 22: 15.

Wu, Ziyin. 1921. "Benjing Xinwen" (Benjing News). *Jinghua Ribao* (Jinghua Daily). No. 2506: 3.

Xi, Bei. 1953. "Xibeiqu Guanche Hunyinfa Zhongdian Shiban Gongzuo de Jingyan" (Experiences from Implementation of the Marriage Law in Northwest, China). *Renmin Ribao* (People's Daily). March 31 (3): 9.

Xi, Guofang. 2017. "Zhangfu danghaizimian Daojialaopobozishang, Fayuanrengpan Buzhunlihun" (The Court Still Rejected Divorce for Cases Where the Husband Put a Knife on His Wife's Neck). *Nanmuxuan* (Nanmuxuan). August 19.

Xia, Dan. 2019. "Peiwaxiezuoye, Zhangfuba Qizi Dachengzhongshang" (Husband Beat the Wife with Heavy Injuries). *Zuigaorenmin Jianchayuan* (The Supreme People's Court). July 8.

Xia, Tian. 2020. "Zhongguorenmingongheguo Fanjiatingbaolifa Shishisizhounian JIancebaogao" (A Survey Report of Four-Year Anniversary of the PRC Anti-Domestic Violence Law). *Weiping Funv Quanyijigou* (Weiping Female Rights Organization). April.

Xia, Xian. 1952. "Niu Shengqing Shasi Qizi Fu Cuilian Yi Bei Daibu Faban" (Niu Shengqing Murdered Wife Fu Cuilian, Arrested). *Qunzhong Ribao* (Qunzhong Daily). August 19: 2.

Xiao, Du. 2021. "Zhanan Suanshenme" (What Does It Mean to Be "Zhanan"?). *Xinlang Xinwen* (Xinlang News). March 16.

Xiao, Feng. 2020. "Panxing, Shifou Yingxiang Zinv Qiancheng" (Can Criminal Charges Affect the Future of Kids?). *Xinlang Caijing* (Xinlang Finance). October 12.

Xiao, He. 2019. "Dagai Shi Wo Juede Zui Ku De Lvshi le" (Maybe the Coolest Lawyer I Know). *Zhi Hu* (Zhi Hu Website). October 14.

Xiao, Jie. 2018. "Ta Ceng Yin Zaoshou Jiabao Huode Nvquan Zuzhi Bangzhu, Rujin Ta Yaowei Nvquan Fasheng" (She Used to Receive Help from the Feminist Voice NGO due to Domestic Violence, Now She Wants to Speak Out for Feminist Voice). *Nvquan Zhisheng* (Feminist Voice). May 9.

Xin, Jia. 2012. "Li Yang Gei Qizi Duanxin Baoguang: Zai Meiguo Ni Hui Bei Zhangfu Qiangsha" (Li Yang Exposed His Wife's Texts: In the US, You Will Be Killed by Your Husband with a Gun). *Zhongguo Jiangsu Wang* (China Jiangsu Website). April 12.

Xin, Taijia, Jie Hou, and Xiaomin Xi. 2008. "Dagongbao Yu Minguo Shiqi Zhonguo Nvxing Yanjiu" (A Study of Chinese Women during the Republican Era in Dagong Newspaper). *Nanfang Luntan* (Southern Forum) 9 (3): 66–77.

Xing, Dongwei. 2013. "Abusers Are Not Punished, Pushing Intimate Partner Violence to Escalate." *Legal Daily Newspaper* (Fazhi Ribao). December 18: 004.

Xing, Hongmei. 2011. "Jiating Baoli Shounue Shafu Funv de Xinli: Dui Sichuan Sheng Mou Nvzi Jianyu de Diaocha Baogao" (Psychology of Women Abused by Domestic Violence and Committing Murder of Husbands—an Investigation Report of a Woman Prison in Sichuan Province). *Zhonghua Nvzi Xueyuan Xuebao* (Journal of China Women's University) 3 (6): 13–18.

Xu, Hengyan. 1951. "Zhengque Zhixing Hunyinfa, Xiaomian Fengjian de Hunyin Zhidu" (Correctly Implementing the Marriage Law, Eliminating Feudal Marriage System). *Xinhua Yuebao* (Xinhua Monthly Newspaper). May: 5.

Xu, Xiao, Fengchuan Zhu, Patricia O'Campo, Michael Koenig, Victoria Mock, and Jacquelyn Campbell. 2005. "Prevalence of and Risk Factors for Intimate Partner Violence in China." *Research and Practice* 95 (1): 78–85.

Xue, Ninglan. 2016. "Gaojie Zhidu" (Warning System). *Funvyanjiu Luncong* (Women's Studies) 1 (August): 5–9.

Ya, Zhou. 2020. "Zhong Guo: Zhaopin Xingbie Qishi Chixu Cunzai" (China: Gender Discrimination in Job Posts Continue to Exist). *Human Rights Watch*. April 29.

Yang, Debin. 2017. "Guangxi Faguan Zao Chidao Baofu Shahai" (Guangxi Provincial Judge Was Killed Out of Reprisal." *Xinlang Xinwen* (Xinlang News). February 6: 28.

Yang, Feng. 2015. "MinzhengJu Gua Qishi Nvxing Haibao Yin Zhengyi" (The Civil Affairs Bureau Hung Posters That Despise Women). *Xin Jing Bao* (Xin Jing Newspaper). April 21.

Yang, Jie. 2007. "Zuiqian 'Deficient Mouth': Discourse, Gender and Domestic Violence in Urban China." *Gender and Language* 1 (1): 107–18.

Yang, Ming. 2018. "Xi Jinping: Jiafengshi JIatingde Jingshenneihe, Yeshi Shehuide Jiazhisuoying" (Xi Jinping: Family Harmony Is the Spiritual Core of Family and Microcosm of Social Values). *Gongchandangyuan Wang* (CCP Net). May 8.

Yang, Tongtong. 2021. "Yingpin Bei Yaoqiu Shumian Baozheng Huaiyun Zhudong Cizhi" (The Appointment Requires a Written Promise to Resign upon Pregnancy). *Da Zhong Wang* (Da Zhong Web). March 16.

Yang, Yukun. 1952. "Hualaixian Yangzhuangzi Cun Ganbu Baobanhunyin Nuedai Funv Yingshou Chufen" (Village Officials in Yangzhuangzi Village, Huailai County Should Be Punished for Abusing Women and Forcing Marriage). *Renmin Ribao* (People's Daily). May 21 (2): 12–13.

Yang, Zhihui. 2016. "Nvzi Zaoshou Jiabao Shafu Huoxing 8 Nian" (A Victim of Domestic Violence Was Sentenced to 8 Years in Prison for Killing Her Abusive Husband). *Yunnan Wang* (Yunnan Website). May 13.

Yang, Zhushi. 1931. "Mamian Fu Qing Lihun" (Freckled-Faced Woman Filed for Divorce). *Shenbao* (Shen Newspaper). May 29: 11.

Ye, Jinfu. 2020. "Xiaoer Nvxing Jiuye Xingbie Qishi Xu Duofang Geili" (Multiple Agencies Should Work Together to Eliminate Gender Discrimination in Work). *Dong Fang Wang* (East Net). June 22.

Yi, Ming. 2016. "Jiabao bushi Jiashi" (Domestic Violence Is Not Family Affairs). *Renmin Wang* (People Net). April 29.

Yi, Xin. 2018. "Nvxing Ziwo Baohu de 6ge Fangfa" (Six Ways for Women to Protect Themselves). *Xinli Zhubituan* (Psychology League). September 4: 3.

Yong, Hu. 2016. "Chongqing Nvyisheng Zhangxiaoyan Jiabao Shenwang" (Chongqing Female Doctor Zhang Xiaoyan Died due to Domestic Violence). *Zhihu* (Zhihu). October 24.

Yong, Jiaxiang. 1898. "Jie Chanzu Lun" (Aborting Footbinding). *Wanguo Gongbao* (Wanguo Public Newspaper) 118 (29): 18086.

Yoshihama, Mieko. 2002. "Battered Women's Coping Strategies and Psychological Distress: Differences by Immigration Status." *American Journal of Community Psychology* 30 (3): 429–52.

You, Tong. 1957. "Duiyu Dangqian Lihun Wenti de Fenxi he Yijian" (An Analysis and Opinion about the Current Divorce Issue). *Renmin Ribao* (People's Daily). April 13: 2.

Yount, Kathryn M., and Li Li. 2009. "Women's 'Justification' of Domestic Violence in Egypt." *Journal of Marriage and Family* 71: 1125–40.

Yu, Cherrie. 2015. "Working with Women's Rights Activists in Beijing." *Women's Institute for Freedom of the Press*. June 10: 12–20.

Yu, Jimmy. 2012. "Self-Inflicted Violence." In *The Wiley-Blackwell Companion to Chinese Religions*. Edited by Randall L. Nadeau, pp. 461–80. New Jersey: Blackwell.

Yu, Xiaoling. 2019. "Quanguo 2.7 Yi Ge Jiatingzhong 30% Yihun Funv Ceng Zao Jiabao" (30% of Married Women Encountered Domestic Violence in 270 million Families across the Country). *Yangshi Wang* (Chinese Central Net). January 25.

Yuan, Chuang. 2020. "Beiqianfu Shaoside Lamu" (Lamu Was Burned Dead by Her Husband). *Pengpai Xinwen* (Pengpai News). October 2.

Yuan, Lin. 2015. "Fayuan Shizhong Jianchi Hemu Sixiang, Weihu Hemu Jiating" (Courts Insists in the Harmony Discourse and Safeguard Harmonious Family). *Renmin Fayuanbao* (People's Court Newspaper). October 9: 7.

Yue, Qingping. 1994. *Zhongguo Minguo Xisu Shi* (A History of Chinese Customs during the Republic Period). Beijing: People's Publishing House (Renmin Chuban She).

Zang, Baiting. 2018. "Fengkuang Yingyu Chuangshi Ren Li Yang Jiabao An" (The Domestic Violence Case of Crazy English Founder Li Yang). *Renmin Fayuan Bao* (People's Court Newspaper). December 16.

Zhan, Fuman. 2020. "Xi Jinping Zongshuji Gaoduzhongshi Lingdaoganbu Jiafengjianshe" (Xi Jinping Highly Emphasizes Family Construction of Cadres). *Zhongguo Jijianjiancha Zazhi* (Chinese Discipline Supervision). July 1.

Zhang, Bayi. 2018. *Yixuezhuanjia Jiedu: Nvxing* (Medical Experts Interpret Women). Beijing: Renmin Junyi Chubanshe (People's Medicine Publisher).
Zhang, Hongwei. 2014. "Domestic Violence and Its Official Reactions in China." In *The Routledge Handbook of Chinese Criminology*. Edited by Liqun Cao, Ivan Y. Sun, and Bill Hebenton, pp. 224–34. Oxon: Routledge. Zhang, Jiahua. 2001. "A Comparative Study of Two Revolutions on Chinese Social Customs" (Liangci Geming Dui Zhongguo Shehui Fengsu Yinxiang Zhi Bijiao Yanjiu). *Journal of Huaiyin Institute of Technology* 10 (2): 53–63.
Zhang, Li. 2007. "A Study of Chinese Women's Life Conditions in the 1920s and 1930s." MA Dissertation. Xiamen: Xiamen Daxue (Xiamen University).
Zhang, Liyu, and Meng Liu. 2004. *A Study of China's Domestic Violence* (Zhongguo Jiating Baoli Yanjiu). Beijing: China Social Science Press (Zhongguo Shehui Kexue Chubanshe).
Zhang, Lu. 2008. "Transnational Feminism in Translation: The Making of a Women's Anti-Domestic Violence Movement in China." MA Thesis of Women's Studies. Ohio State University.
Zhang, Lu. 2009a. "Chinese Women Protesting Intimate Partner Violence: The Beijing Conference, International Donor Agencies, and the Making of a Chinese Women's NGO." *Meridians: Feminism, Race, Transnationalism* 9 (2): 66–99.
Zhang, Lu. 2009b. "Domestic Violence Network in China: Translating the Transnational Concept of Violence against Women into Local Action." *Women's Studies International Forum* 32 (3): 227–39.
Zhang, Lulu. 2015. "An Analysis of Chinese Women's Fight for Human Rights in the Beginning of the 20th Century" (20 Shijichu Zhongguo Nvxing Renquan Douzheng Lunxi). *Journal of Beihua University (Social Sciences)* (Beihua Daxue Xuebao) 16 (3): 128–33.
Zhang, Ning, and Yinhuan Wang. 2008. "Minguo Shiqi Beijing Hunyin Jiating Zhong Funv de Diwei" (Women's Status in Marriage and Family in Beijing during the Republican Era). *Beijing Shehui Kexue* (Beijing Social Sciences) 6 (3): 47–52.
Zhang, Nianliang. 2014. "Jin 10% Guyi Sharen Anjian Sheji Jiabao" (Around 10% Intentional Murder Cases Involve Domestic Violence). Renmin Gong An Bao (People's Public Security Newspaper). February 28: 2.
Zhang, Qing. 2016. "Guo Jianmei: Zhongguo Shouwei Gongyi Lvshi De Ku Yu Le" (Jianmei Guo: The Bitterness and Happiness of China's First Pro Bono Lawyer). *Zhongguo Baogao Wenxue* (The Chinese Report Literature). May 9.
Zhang, Qingjun, and Guoxiang Meng. 1997. *Minguo Sifa Heimu* (The Dark Scene of Law in the Republican Era). Nanjing: Jiangsu Ancient Books Publishing House (Jiangsu Guji Chubanshe).
Zhang, Ran. 2004. "Fanjiating Baoli Congshu Zuori Shoufa" (Anti-Intimate Partner Violence Books Published Yesterday). *Beijing Yule Xinbao* (Beijing Entertainment Newspaper). December 6: 1.
Zhang, Wu. 2018. "Shenyang Xingqin Shijian Jubaoren Li Youyou: Yilianxi Dao Shouqinhai de Qita Jiwei Nvsheng" (Li Youyou Reported Shenyang's Sexual Assault: There Are Other Female Student Victims Too). *Xiandai Nvbao* (Modern Female Newspaper). April 8: 6.
Zhang, Xiaoya. 2016. "Wushuzhidaojiabao bei fa Renshenbaohuling" (Personal Protection Order Was Issued due to Domestic Violence). *Xinlang Xinwen* (Sina News). July 21.
Zhang, Xitan. 1922. "Fakan Zhiqu" (Fun Writing). *Funv Zazhi* (Women's Journal) 8 (4): 12.

Zhang, Zheng. 2015. "Jiabao Pihusuo Weihe Xianzhi" (Why Safe Houses for Victims Are Idle). *Zhongguo Qingnian Bao* (Chinese Youth Newspaper). October 16.

Zhao, Fang. 2017. "Quanzhi Zhufu Yeshi Yifen You Jiazhi de Gongzuo" (Full-Time Housewife Is a Valuable Job). *Zhongguo Qingnian Bao* (Chinese Youth Newspaper). August 3.

Zhao, Jiandong. 2019. "Muguangzong: Gaolihunlv Beihoude Judafengxian" (Massive Risks behind the High Divorce Rate). *Huanqiuwang* (Globe Net). March 30.

Zhao, Ming. 2019. "Zhangfudubo Shuqian, Geiduifangyaoshi Xingqinzijilaopo Dizhai Beisha" (The Husband Lost Money in Gambling, Gave Creditors the Key to His House to Rape His Wife to Pay for the Debt, but Was Killed by His Wife). *Xinlang Xinwen* (Sina News). May 9.

Zhao, Shi. 1925. "Zhao Shi Case" (Zhao Shi Anjian). *The Second Chinese Archive Bureau* (Zhongguo Di Er Lishi Dang An Guan). 1051: 8996.

Zhao, Wen. 2014. "Shoubao Ren Zaoyu Weiquan Nan" (The Abused Find It Difficult to Preserve Their Rights). *Sichuan Fazhi Bao* (Sichuan Legal Newspaper). March 6: B02.

Zhen, Jiang. 2018. "Zuigaorenmin Fayuan Jintiangongbu Sifadashuju Zhuanti Baogaozhi Lihunjiufen" (The Supreme Court Published Data on Divorce Conflicts). *Caihong Wang* (Caihong Net). October 29: 18.

Zheng, Tiantian. 2006. "Cool Masculinity: Male Clients' Sex Consumption and Business Alliance in Urban China's Sex Industry." *Journal of Contemporary China* 15 (46): 161–82.

Zheng, Tiantian. 2009a. *Red Lights: The Lives of Sex Workers in Postsocialist China*. Minneapolis: University of Minnesota Press.

Zheng, Tiantian. 2009b. *Ethnographies of Prostitution in Contemporary China: Gender Relations, HIV/AIDS, and Nationalism*. New York: Palgrave Macmillan.

Zheng, Tiantian. 2012. "Female Subjugation and Political Resistance." *Gender, Place and Culture* 19 (5): 652–69.

Zheng, Tiantian. 2015. *Tongzhi Living: Men Attracted to Men in Postsocialist China*. Minneapolis: University of Minnesota Press.

Zhi, Chang. 2021. "Sanhai Zhengce Chutai, Zhichang Xingbie Qishi Danyou Jiaju" (After the Third-Child Policy, Gender Discrimination in the Job Market Gets Intensified). *Zhongguo Laogong Tongxun* (Chinese Labor Bulletin). June 10.

Zhong, Guo, ed. 1991. *Beijing Zhongmei Funv Wenti Yantao Hui Lunwen Ji* (Beijing China-US Women's Issues Conference Papers). Hubei: Hubei Renmin Chubanshe (Hubei People's Publishing House).

Zhong, Yang. 1953. "Zhongyang Guanche Hunyinfa Yundong Weiyuanhui" (Implementation of the Marriage Law). *Renmin Ribao* (People's Daily). February 25: 17.

Zhuo, Dongqing. 2017. "1000 Fen Shejiabao Panjueshu Gaosu Women de Naxieshi" (What 1000 Domestic Violence Verdicts Told Us). *Jiashi Falv Quan* (Family Affairs Law Circle). March 30.

Zhou, Jing. 2012. "Wu Chengshi Nv Qingnian Yi Ranxue de Hunsha Xingwei Yishu Fandui Jiating Baoli" (Five Female Youth Used Performance Art of Wedding Gowns with Blood against Domestic Violence). *Zhejiang Xinwen* (Zhejiang News). December 3.

Zhou, Jing. 2016. "Erhai Zhengce Rang Zhongguo Gengduo Zhiye Nvxing Huigui Jiating" (The Open Two-Child Policy Has Made More Professional Women to Return Home). *Xin Hua She* (Xinhua Agency). February 24.

Zhou, Jingjing. 2020. "Nanzi Liantong Qiannvyou 20duodao Huoxing 14geyue" (A Man Was Sentenced to 14 Months for Knifing His Girlfriend 20 Times). *Zhonghuawang Xinwen* (Zhonghuawang News). December 20.

Zhou, Nan. 2015. "Nvzi Zaoyu Jiabao Shafu Fenshi Gaipan Sihuan, Duoming Lvshi Ceng Huyu Daoxia Liuren" (Numerous Lawyers Call for Lenience, the Verdict of a Female Victim Killing Her Abuser Is Revised as a Death Sentence with Reprieve). *Xinhua Xinwen* (Xinhua News). April 26.

Zhou, Yun. 2018. "Nvquan Zhisheng Bei Xiaoyin de 100 Tian: Meiyou Shenme Bi Zuo Activist Geng Lingren Zhenfen" (The 100 Days after Feminist Voice Was Silenced: Nothing Is as Exciting as Being an Activist." *Duan Chuanmei* (Duan Media). June 23.

Zhu, Shi. 1927. "Youyi Furen Kongqing Lihun An" (Another Young Woman Filed for Divorce). *Wanguo Public Newspaper* (Wanguo Gongbao). September 13: 15.

Zhuxianzhi. 1936. *Zhu Xiang Shi* (A History of Zhu County). Zhuxian: Hebei Municipal Government.

INDEX

abandonment 28
abuse
  accept 117
  ad hoc 28
  alcohol 13
  avoid 111
  case of 68
  domestic 27, 35
  drug 40
  evidence of 99
  of foot-binding 124
  freedom from 22, 34, 40
  habitual 28
  history of 13, 91
  at home 12,
  by the husband 27–30, 32–4, 37, 55, 70, 73, 76, 86, 101–2, 109, 111–23, 139, 147, 161–2, 173
  by the husband and parents 22, 38
  intent to 112
  intimate partner 24, 29, 31, 35
  of the judicial system 18, 29
  and law 37, 38, 57, 61, 66, 106, 114, 123
  mental 143
  of the officials 33
  physical 5, 27, 30, 55, 101, 103, 109–10, 162, 173
  rate of, 34
  reasons for 112
  reduce 110
  resist 112, 145
  sexual 41, 142
  spousal 146
  stop 112
  substance 13
  tolerance of 123
  trigger 113
  victims of 144
  within the family 171
  of women 124
  see also domestic violence; intimate partner violence
abuser *see* abuse
activism
  appropriation of the state discourse 152–60
  collective 139, 159
  contribution of 139–52
  history of 122–39
  and intimate partner violence 24, 121–2
  and NGO 126–56
  strength of 17
activist *see* activism
administrative detainment 58, 62–3
agency
  collective 159
  of women 5, 18, 24, 26, 100, 105, 108, 117
aggression
  military 167
  physical 24, 43–4, 94
  sexual 24, 44
All China Women's Federation 5, 9, 11–12, 18, 32, 36–7, 57, 61, 65–70, 72, 77–9, 88, 95, 102–7, 113, 115–17, 119, 121–4, 129–31, 147, 149, 150–1, 153–6, 171–3
almshouse 30
Amnesty International 148
Anorexia 166
Anti-Domestic Violence Law 5, 22, 25, 35, 36–9, 47, 53, 57, 58–62, 64–7, 69, 71, 72, 75, 81, 87–8, 99–100, 104–5, 108, 113, 117, 121, 129, 131–3, 140–2, 146–51, 153–5, 159, 172
Anti-Domestic Violence Network 121–2, 127–8, 131, 133, 140, 145, 146, 148, 149, 152–5, 158–9
arranged marriage 6, 27, 31

Battered Woman's Syndrome 118, 144, 173–4
beggars 104, 106, 107, 118
behavioral correction 142
Beijing Declaration and Platform for Action 125, 141
Beijing Fanbao organization 69
Beijing Maple Women's Counselling Center 127–8, 139–40, 158
Beijing Qianqian Law Firm 100, 139, 143, 147–51, 155–6
Beijing University Law School Women's Legal Research and Service Center 38, 127, 129, 139, 140–2, 158
Beijing Zhongze Women's Legal Aid Organization 38
betrothal gifts 26
bride price 26, 34–5

Capital Normal University 129
chain of evidence 77
chastity
  of widow 26
  of women 48
child custody 2, 3, 18, 23, 30, 83, 84–6, 88, 104, 114, 143, 146, 163
child support 35, 84–5, 87, 104, 142, 146
China Law Society 121, 129, 152–3
China University of Political Science and Law 10, 128
China Women's University 128
China's Pro Bono Lawyer Network 131, 143
China's State Council 121, 129, 134
China's Two Sessions 141
Chinese Academy of Management Science 123, 128, 152
Chinese Criminal Law of Abuse 57
Chinese Criminal Law of Intentional Harm for Strangers 57
Chinese Criteria for Assessing the Extent of Bodily Injuries 58, 87, 173
Chinese Cyber Security and Leading Information Office 138
Chinese Supreme Court 28, 48, 62, 64, 70, 80, 83, 87, 121, 129, 147, 148, 149, 162
Chinese Women's News 122, 126, 128, 144, 153, 171, 172

Civil Affairs and Reform Work Mechanism 80
Civil Affairs Bureau 9, 42, 47, 56, 59, 80, 83, 86–7, 153
Civil Court 36
Civil Law 28–31, 38, 56–8, 87
clan 3, 54
class
  conflict 5, 7, 57, 156
  and intimate partner violence 99
  mandarin 89
  upper 6
  violence 13
coerced sex 47
  see also sexual coercion
collective agency 159
Communist Party 7, 9, 31–2, 34, 46–7, 54–5, 124, 127, 158, 168
compensation 35, 84, 143, 146, 148–9, 163
compulsory reporting 59, 67–8
conflict
  class 5, 7, 34, 57, 156–9, 160
  couple 81
  family 18, 23–4, 55, 66, 72, 79, 80, 82, 87, 103, 123
  with father 79
  marital 91, 92
  in marriage 3, 13, 51, 55
  physical 64–5
  resolving mechanism 65
  social 24, 156
  and violence 13
Confucianism 9, 26, 39, 55, 89, 164
Confucius 89, 166–7
consensual sex 14, 23, 43, 50, 163
Constitution 59, 86, 115, 117, 162
Convention on Children's Rights 141
Convention on the Elimination of All Forms of Discrimination against Women 155
cooperatives 34
corruption 53–4, 90
corset 165–6
counselling 24, 99, 122, 127–8, 139–40, 143, 149, 152, 158
COVID 7, 24, 161–2
  see also pandemic
Crazy English 146

credit card 86
Criminal Code 26, 38
Criminal Justice System 5, 18, 23, 38, 51, 53, 84–8, 100, 105, 109, 113, 115–16, 140, 144, 162–3
criminal record 85–6
criminalized minefield 134
criticism 44, 60–2, 99, 124, 134, 150, 157, 169
Custody and Repatriation Center/System 105–6
Cyber Management Office 138

damage 23, 40, 45, 50, 54, 58, 77, 82, 84, 87, 103, 142, 156
Declaration of the Elimination of Violence against Women 141
Department of Justice 72, 81
depression 40, 130, 144
discourse
  cultural 5, 14, 17–19, 23–4, 42–3, 91–3, 95–8, 163–4
  of gender equality 138
  of harmony
  of human rights 127, 157–9
  legal 42, 49
  media 94, 96, 151
  medical 5, 49, 97
  official 45, 94, 97, 124
  popular 42–5, 49–50, 94, 97
  state 4–5, 7–8, 16–18, 21, 24, 53, 57, 83, 88, 106, 117, 122, 125, 152, 154, 156–9, 162, 164, 169
  of women's rights and interests 154
divorce 2, 3, 5, 14, 18, 23, 27–39, 47, 55–7, 62, 66, 71–2, 75–85, 87–8, 92, 96, 99–101, 104, 111–12, 114–15, 117, 123, 146, 161–2, 171, 173
divorce law *see* law
domestic violence
  activist *see* activism
  and All China Women's Federation 95, 103, 117
  in China 21
  ethnography of 12
  and judge 55, 65, 67, 71–2, 76, 80–1, 85
  law 5, 12, 22, 25, 35, 36–7, 39, 47, 53, 57–62, 64–5, 67, 69, 71–2, 75, 81, 87–8, 99–100, 104–5, 108, 113, 117, 129, 131–3, 140–2, 146–51, 153–5, 159, 172
  legal cases 71–2, 76–7, 82, 85
  media of 94
  perception of 92, 96
  prevention of 116
  protect against 39, 98
  resist against 119
  as a social conflict 24
  and technology of the self 97
  in the world 35
  and women's rights 12
  women to endure 5, 8, 57, 117
  see also abuse, intimate partner violence, NGO
dowry 26, 31
drug abuse 40
drug addicts 107, 118
dutiful wives and virtuous mothers (xianqi liangmu) 7, 14, 54, 156, 163

Embassy of Sweden 128
Enlightenment 165
entrance exam 10, 86
escape 18, 26–7, 30–1, 51, 71, 75, 78, 100–8, 112, 117, 123, 167, 172
Excellent Mediating Talent 81
Excellent Mediator of the People 81
expert
  in Confucianism 89,
  and laws 131–2, 139–41, 149
  legal 140
  psychology 93, 97
  witness 144–5, 147
expert witness *see* expert
extramarital affairs 66, 69, 94–6, 109

family harmony *see under* harmony
family integrity 127
family-state 54, 156
family values 83
female inmates 37, 116
feminism 134, 138, 144, 158
Feminist Voice 104, 127, 128, 134, 137–8, 150–2, 158
feudalism 9, 55
fight back 111
foot-binding 6, 26–7, 124, 166, 168

forced penetration 41–2
Ford Foundation 123, 128, 129
foreign aid 121, 125, 133–4
Fourth World Women's Conference *see* World Women's Conference
fracture 58, 61, 63, 75–7, 82, 87, 103, 109, 114, 142, 172–3
French Annales School 165

gender equality 7, 26, 39, 122, 124–5, 128, 138–9, 141, 145, 150, 152, 159
gender hierarchy 23, 39
Guo, Jianmei 126, 129, 139, 141–3, 147–8, 151, 156–7
  see also Jianmei Guo

half pushing and half acquiescing (bantui banjiu) 48–9
harm 9, 25, 37, 40, 58, 71, 75–6, 118, 127, 142, 147–8, 156, 174
harmony
  in Confucianism 38
  and court clerks 67
  discourse 5, 7, 8, 18, 53, 57, 106, 117, 152, 154, 156–7, 159
  family 4–9, 14–18, 22–4, 53–7, 60, 65, 72, 80–1, 83, 87–8, 106, 117, 146, 152, 154, 156, 159
  family-state 54
  social 8, 24, 53–4, 56, 156–60
hearing
  impediment 58, 63, 75, 76, 173
  loss of 55, 80, 82
high-heeled shoe 113, 166
Hillary Clinton 125–9
HIV/AIDS 17, 40, 134
household registration 103, 105, 107–8, 117–18
human rights 5, 41, 122, 125–8, 141, 148, 156–9

income 7, 36, 99, 142, 172
informal network 108–9, 117–18
informal source 100
inheritance rights 31–2, 38
injuries
  light 58, 63, 75–6, 82, 173
  minor 58–9, 75, 87
  heavy 18, 58–9, 64, 77–8, 172

institutional support 88
Institute of Law of the Chinese Academy of Social Sciences 141
International Women of Courage Award 131, 143
intimate partner violence
  and activism 121–60
  in COVID 161–2
  and criminal justice system 51–90
  fieldwork of 20–2
  history of 5–7, 25–40
  male perception of 91–8
  and political economy 16–20
  in Postsocialist China 11–13
  resistance against 99–120
  sociocultural approach to 13–16
  and women's status 7–11
  see also abuse, activism, violence, domestic violence
Introductory Certificate 107, 117

jail 36–37, 46, 71, 114, 136
Jianmei Guo *see* Guo, Jianmei
Journal on Women's News 122
judges
  and Communism 18, 29
  and Confucianism 18, 29, 39, 88–90
  and fieldwork 21
  and harmony discourse 8, 16, 55–6, 81, 83
  and intimate partner violence 17–18, 23, 29, 36, 48, 53, 65–6, 71–2, 75, 80–3, 85, 87
judicial system 17–18, 29, 31, 39, 164, 166

lao dao 91–2
law
  authority of 17, 88
  divorce 28, 34, 66, 100
  role of in traditional Chinese society 17, 29
  see also Anti-Domestic Violence Law
Law of the People's Republic of China on the Administration of Activities of Overseas Non-Governmental Organizations within the Territory of China 133, 135–6

Law of the People's Republic of China on the Protection of Women's Rights and Interests 123
Law to Protect Women's Rights 42
lawyer
  in China 48, 122–4, 126–7, 129–30, 137, 139, 145
  and NGO 66, 121, 128–9, 138, 140, 143, 147–8
  pro bono 70, 100, 125, 127, 129–31, 142–3, 148–9, 151, 156–7
  and victims of intimate partner violence 63, 67–8, 75–7, 79–80, 83, 85, 99–100, 150
legal aid 12, 38, 108, 118, 129, 139, 142, 145, 151, 154, 159, 171
legal assistance 100, 142
legal consultation 70, 131, 139, 140, 143, 156
legal justice 36, 100
legal reform 124, 127, 131, 139, 140–2, 145, 153, 154, 159
legal structure 53, 59, 86, 116, 162
legalist tradition 18, 29
LGBTQ 131–3
liberation of women 26–7, 31, 38, 168
linguistic violence 93
  see also violence
loss of vision see vision
Lv, Pin 128, 134, 137, 141, 151–2
lynching 33

Mandate of Heaven 167
marital rape see rape
Marriage Certificate 9, 107, 117
Marriage Law 31–5, 38, 56, 80, 82–3, 85, 87, 121, 129, 140
market economy 7, 8, 19, 57, 156
May Fourth Movement 26–7, 30
Measures for the Administration of Government Procurement of Services 134
Media Monitor for Women Network/ Feminist Voice 127, 158
mediation 5, 8, 18, 23, 29, 36, 39, 40, 55–7, 59–62, 65, 68, 72–5, 78–83, 87–8, 99, 105, 113, 117, 156
medical discourse 43
  see also discourse

medical report 51, 59, 67, 75, 77, 79, 82, 173
mental distress 35
#metoo movement 46, 136, 138
middle kingdom 167
miscarriage 28, 58, 78, 87, 101
modern women 27
moral character 49–50
multiagency 121, 129
murder 27, 32–5, 37, 100, 111, 113, 114, 117–19
mutilation 18, 23, 57–9, 64, 66, 82, 87, 100

natal family 33, 85, 101–2, 108–9, 118, 161–2
nation
  building 22, 40
  progress of 38, 53, 55, 155, 157
National Committee of Chinese People's Political Consultative Conference 138, 141
National People's Congress 47, 56, 121, 123, 129, 131–3, 138, 140–1, 154
National Security Departments 86
Nationalism 124, 158, 169
neoliberal governance 19, 20, 163, 164
neoliberal restructuring 98
New Culture Movement 7, 15–16, 26, 28, 155, 168
New Women 27
Nobel Peace Prize 131, 143
Non-government Organizations (NGOs) 70, 73, 78, 99–100, 102, 104, 108, 117–18, 121–2, 125–9, 131–7, 139–43, 145, 147–56, 158–9, 171
non-state network 108
Norwegian Center for Human Rights 128

occupational hazard 83
occupying men's restrooms 137, 151
Opium War 167
Overseas Non-Governmental Organizations 133, 135, 136
Oxfam Hong Kong 128
Oxfam the Netherlands 128

pandemic 7, 24, 51, 161, 162
  see also COVID
paralysis 18, 23, 57–8, 64, 66, 77, 87, 109

passion 42–4, 94, 97, 102, 126, 130
patriarchy 7, 14, 24–5, 27, 34, 124, 164
patrilineality 25–6
patrilocality 26
Personal Protection Order 55, 72, 82
petition 12, 14, 141, 147
physical disability 40
physical force 43, 49, 112
physical violence 35, 47, 79, 93 see violence
pleasing and avoiding 100, 110–12
police inaction 35–6, 73, 100, 112–13, 162
police station 17, 30, 35, 51, 61–2, 74–5, 78–9, 105, 161, 164
polygamy 26, 34
possession division 18, 23, 88
pregnancy 11, 40, 102
prison 36–7, 47, 53, 57–9, 69–71, 78, 80, 86, 109, 114–16, 136–7, 144–5, 148, 162, 172
pro bono lawyer see under lawyer
promissory note 4, 35, 71
prostitution 30–1
psychological therapy 105, 142 see therapy
public awareness 138–9, 147, 149–51, 159
public health 13, 41
Public Security Bureau 8, 37, 53, 55–6, 60–1, 67–8, 72, 75, 133, 135, 142, 154–5, 158–9, 173

rape
 by force 41
 by foreign powers 27, 4
 and law 47–8, 49
 and legal cases 47–9, 50, 116, 147, 172
 marital 42, 47, 89
 and popular discourse 44
regulatory mechanism 97
reprisal violence 36
reproductive health 41
rescue home 30
resistance
 everyday 99–100, 105, 108, 112–13, 117, 119
 by killing the abuser 39, 145
 to the Marriage Law 34
 to sex 44, 48–9
 against sexual harassment 46
 to topic of domestic violence 124

restraining orders 35, 37
rupture 58, 63, 75–6, 145, 162, 173
rural 6, 20–1, 34, 100, 105–6, 168

sacrifice
 for chastity 48, 50
 for economic reform 7, 98
 as family and state 8, 14–16, 18, 22–3, 56, 65, 81, 86–8, 162
 for the lawsuit 130
 for patriarchs 15
safe house 36, 69, 100, 102–5, 107–8, 117, 118, 171
same-sex couple 87
seduction 43
self-
 constraints 97
 defense 59, 69, 86, 114–16, 143–5, 147, 162, 172
 discipline 97
 monitor 20, 97, 163
 restraint 38
 scrutinize 97
709 Repression 137
sex drive 42–3, 49
sexual
 abuse see abuse
 advances 95, 41
 aggression see aggression
 assault 41, 44–6, 49–50
 coercion see coerced sex
 desire 42–4, 48–50, 95–7
 pursuit 43
 violence see violence
sexuality
 of men 42–3, 49
 of a person 41
 regulatory control of 19, 23, 50, 168
 of women 19, 23, 42, 49–50, 165, 168
shelter 24, 122, 127
Sick Man of East Asia 27
Simone De Beauvoir Prize 131, 143
social
 aid station 103, 105–7, 118
 chaos 34
 conflict see conflict
 control 33
 harmony see harmony

(in)stability 4, 8, 9, 18, 24, 40, 53, 55, 98, 106, 117, 127, 152, 154, 156, 158–60
media 35, 138
polarization 3, 7, 57, 156
service 18, 23, 88, 99, 128, 132, 134, 136, 154
unrest 32, 34
worker 13, 105, 128, 140, 144, 150
State Council and Ministry of Finance 134
state discourse *see* discourse
state legitimacy 4–5, 8, 14–15, 55, 57, 163
status
of activists 24
of men 47, 94
moral 23
of the nation 152, 159
of NGOs 128, 155, 160
of women 7, 9, 14, 26, 34, 38, 55, 124, 137, 152, 155, 159
socioeconomic 12, 91, 99, 130, 143
STIs 40
structural violence *see* violence
struggle session 33
suicide 27–8, 32–4, 45–8, 50, 57, 68, 78, 85–7, 100, 111, 113–15, 145, 162–3
survival 15, 23, 31, 85, 88, 124, 136

talking back 100, 111–13, 117
tax bureaus 86
technology of the self 97
technology of power 19, 97
therapy 22, 105, 142
Third World Women's Conference *see* World Women's Conference
30-day Divorce Cooling Period 56
The Right Livelihood Award 131, 143
Tongyu 132
torture 32–3, 35–6, 46, 101
totalitarian(ism) 168–9

United Nations 124–8, 131, 134, 136–7, 139–40, 155, 158

uprising 5, 8, 57, 156
urban 99, 136
uterine family 26

vagrant 106–7, 118
violence
linguistic 93
physical 35, 47, 79, 93
sexual 5–6, 14, 17–20, 23, 41–3, 47, 49–50, 70, 163–4
structural 4, 13, 16–17, 20, 22, 105, 108–9, 115–16, 164
see also intimate partner violence
virtue 8, 14, 15, 27, 54, 56, 89, 162–3
vision 51, 58
visitation rights 84, 86–7, 105, 163

Wechat 138
Weibo 35, 43, 138, 150, 172
widow chastity *see* chastity
wife beating 25–6, 71, 91–3, 96–7, 123
Women's Hotline 123, 127–8, 140
women's rights and interests 122–3, 127–8, 131, 139–44, 154, 158
World Conference on Women *see* World Women's Conference
World Health Organization 5, 41
World Women's Conference
Fourth 35, 59, 125–6, 158
Third 11, 35
wounded bride 136
Written Warning Notes 18, 23, 37, 59–62, 87–8, 99, 111, 142–3, 145, 150

you maobing 19, 91, 94–7

zui ben 93
zui jian 92
zui ying 18, 19, 91, 93, 96–7
zui zang 92